Praise for Antiquing For Dummies

"*Antiquing For Dummies* is an excellent and valuable resource for collectors. It's a must-read for those interested in antiques. Entertaining as well as informative, this book is no boring instruction manual. Even a seasoned antiquer is sure to learn something new."

—Sara L. Charniak, Editor, *Antiques & Collecting* magazine

"The last thing beginning collectors of antiques need is yet another snooty, high-brow coffee table book. What they DO need is *Antiquing For Dummies* with its practical information and insider tips. Readers learn how and where to buy antiques, and how to negotiate prices like pros."

—Mark J. Chervenka, Editor, *Antique & Collectors Reproduction News*

"This book demystifies the researching, finding, and purchasing of antiques and makes the process comprehensible. *Antiquing For Dummies* is a knowledgeable, accessible guide for both the beginner and the experienced shopper: It's great fun!"

—Lee Salem, Vice President and Editorial Director, Universal Press Syndicate

"The ultimate guide for collectors and *Antique Roadshow* groupies is here. Entertaining, packed with useful (and understandable) information, *Antiquing For Dummies* will pay for itself many times over. Do not even look at another antique before reading this book!"

—Sandra Martz, publisher of Papier-Mache Press and editor of *When I Am an Old Woman, I Shall Wear Purple*

"This book, *Antiquing For Dummies*, is great! It is a well-researched work that appeals to the novice as well as the 'seasoned' antique collector. This book is a must for all antique-lovers!"

—Lyn Fontenot, Ph.D., ASID, author of *Antique Furniture — How to Tell the Real Thing from the Fake*

"*Antiquing For Dummies* is long overdue. This book will improve the knowledge of the most experienced insider, and should be the first purchase of any beginner. I intend to buy this book for every member of our staff."

—Stephen Abt, President, Artfact.com

"*Antiquing For Dummies* provides an excellent introduction to the field of collecting. Every library needs some good books on the basics and I recommend *Antiquing For Dummies* be one of them."

—Christian A. Coleman, ISA CAPP, Executive Director, International Society of Appraisers

"This book is stimulating, fun, educational, and well-done. A 'must read' for both novices and seasoned dealers."

—Yvonne Tucker, President, Antiques & Collectibles Dealer Association

"Ron and Deborah have demystified the antiques world for the neophyte shopper, the Internet user, as well as sophisticated collectors and anyone else interested in buying or researching antiques. They provide a lot of information in an easy-to-read style."

—Susan and Al Bagdade, authors of *Warman's English and Continental Pottery and Porcelain* and *Warman's American Pottery and Porcelain*

"*Antiquing For Dummies* contains sound, helpful advice for rookies and serves as a refresher course for us veteran collectors who tend to forget past faux pas and outright errors. It's a warm welcome to the world of antiques and collectibles.

—Tom Hoepf, Editor, *AntiqueWeek Central Edition*

"More than a primer, *Antiquing For Dummies* presents the essential elements of an often complicated avocation. Whether you are a beginner or a dedicated collector, you will find chapters in this easy-to-read book that are designed to enhance your material needs."

—Milton L. Talbert, First Vice President, National Association of Dealers in Antiques

"This easy-to-read primer, written in an amusing and light-hearted fashion yet giving step-by-step pertinent facts, throws light on the multi-level and largely unregulated antiques trade and guides the new collector through this maze. A must for the novice as well as the person who thinks he knows it all but could still learn something."

—Barbara and Peter Sutton-Smith, Publisher/Editor of *Antique Showcase* magazine and *The Guide to the Antique Shops of Ontario*

"*Antiquing For Dummies* is packed with great information and will keep a smile on your face. This was a very pleasurable introduction to antiques."

—Bobanne Kalkofen, ASID

"Here is a new book that everyone who is a collector or wants to be will find entertaining and informative. Especially useful are the "Icons," snippets of information packaged for quick and easy reference. This is a fun way to give yourself a firm grounding in the wide wonderful world of antiques and collectibles."

—Kyle Husfloen, Managing Editor, *Antique Trader Weekly* and *Antique Trader's Antiques and Collectibles Price Guide*

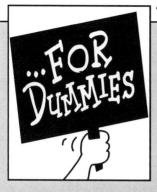

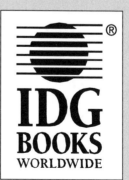

ANTIQUING FOR DUMMIES®

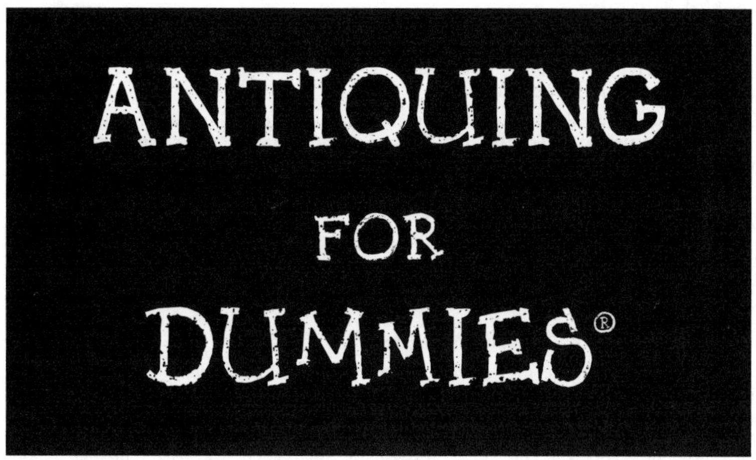

by Ron Zoglin, ASA, ISA, AAA
and
Deborah Shouse

Great to talk to you
Hope you enjoy the book.
Yours Deborah Shouse
Ron Zog

IDG Books Worldwide, Inc.
An International Data Group Company

Foster City, CA ◆ Chicago, IL ◆ Indianapolis, IN ◆ New York, NY

Antiquing For Dummies®

Published by
IDG Books Worldwide, Inc.
An International Data Group Company
919 E. Hillsdale Blvd.
Suite 400
Foster City, CA 94404
www.idgbooks.com (IDG Books Worldwide Web site)
www.dummies.com (Dummies Press Web site)

Library of Congress Catalog Card No.: 99-61894

ISBN: 0-7645-5108-6

Printed in the United States of America

10 9 8 7 6 5 4 3 2 1

1B/RT/QU/ZZ/IN

Distributed in the United States by IDG Books Worldwide, Inc.

Distributed by CDG Books Canada Inc. for Canada; by Transworld Publishers Limited in the United Kingdom; by IDG Norge Books for Norway; by IDG Sweden Books for Sweden; by Woodslane Pty. Ltd. for Australia; by Woodslane (NZ) Ltd. for New Zealand; by TransQuest Publishers Pte Ltd. for Singapore, Malaysia, Thailand, Indonesia, and Hong Kong; by ICG Muse, Inc. for Japan; by Norma Comunicaciones S.A. for Colombia; by Intersoft for South Africa; by Le Monde en Tique for France; by International Thomson Publishing for Germany, Austria and Switzerland; by Distribuidora Cuspide for Argentina; by Livraria Cultura for Brazil; by Ediciones ZETA S.C.R. Ltda. for Peru; by WS Computer Publishing Corporation, Inc., for the Philippines; by Contemporanea de Ediciones for Venezuela; by Express Computer Distributors for the Caribbean and West Indies; by Micronesia Media Distributor, Inc. for Micronesia; by Grupo Editorial Norma S.A. for Guatemala; by Chips Computadoras S.A. de C.V. for Mexico; by Editorial Norma de Panama S.A. for Panama; by American Bookshops for Finland. Authorized Sales Agent: Anthony Rudkin Associates for the Middle East and North Africa.

For general information on IDG Books Worldwide's books in the U.S., please call our Consumer Customer Service department at 800-762-2974. For reseller information, including discounts and premium sales, please call our Reseller Customer Service department at 800-434-3422.

For information on where to purchase IDG Books Worldwide's books outside the U.S., please contact our International Sales department at 317-596-5530 or fax 317-596-5692.

For consumer information on foreign language translations, please contact our Customer Service department at 1-800-434-3422, fax 317-596-5692, or e-mail rights@idgbooks.com.

For information on licensing foreign or domestic rights, please phone +1-650-655-3109.

For sales inquiries and special prices for bulk quantities, please contact our Sales department at 650-655-3200 or write to the address above.

For information on using IDG Books Worldwide's books in the classroom or for ordering examination copies, please contact our Educational Sales department at 800-434-2086 or fax 317-596-5499.

For press review copies, author interviews, or other publicity information, please contact our Public Relations department at 650-655-3000 or fax 650-655-3299.

For authorization to photocopy items for corporate, personal, or educational use, please contact Copyright Clearance Center, 222 Rosewood Drive, Danvers, MA 01923, or fax 978-750-4470.

About the Authors

Ron Zoglin: Being in the antique business is a daily blend of surprises, discoveries, interesting people, and fascinating objects. For nearly 30 years, Ron Zoglin has immersed himself in the world of antiques. He has studied them, bought them, sold them, appraised them, displayed them, and taught about them in colleges and universities. He has traveled the world searching out antiques that are beautiful and unusual and inspiring. As a senior member of the American Society of Appraisers, Ron has developed a large network of specialists with whom he consults regularly. His shop, Brookside Antiques in Kansas City, has one of the Midwest's largest collections of European antiques, Oriental furnishings, and Japanese woodblock prints.

Antiques dovetail into one of Ron's other passions: storytelling. As a professional storyteller, Ron has performed for businesses, universities, and national and international conferences. Ron feels that stories and antiques add a warmth and meaning that compliment and enhance life in this technological age. He loves to surround himself with a comfortable mixture of the latest in technology and an eclectic blend of lots of antiques. Writing *Antiquing For Dummies* is a way for Ron take his passion for antiques and share it with others.

Ron is an Accredited Senior Member of the American Society of Appraisers, a Certified Member of the Appraisers Association of America, an Accredited Member of the International Society of Appraisers, and a member of the National Association of Dealers in Antiques.

Deborah Shouse: Deborah is a writer, speaker, facilitator, and creativity coach. She loves to take dry, stilted material and make it exciting and readable. She loves to bring people together and invite in their creative skills. Her writing has appeared in periodicals such as *Reader's Digest, Newsweek, Family Circle, Woman's Day, Redbook, Family Life, Christian Science Monitor, Healthy Living,* and *MS.* She is a PEN winner and a Pushcart nominee. Her books include *Breaking The Ice, Making Your Mark* and *Name Tags Plus.* She co-authored *Working Woman's Communications Survival Guide* (Prentice Hall), which is in its fifth printing. Deborah has been included in more than a dozen anthologies, including *I Am Becoming the Woman I've Wanted, At Our Core,* and *Chicken Soup for the Mother's Soul.*

Deborah has given workshops and creative expression seminars for businesses, colleges, and organizations. She provides creativity coaching services for authors, business professionals, and other visionary souls. Deborah loves to surround herself with a mishmash of antiques and thrift store things. (The antiques are starting to take over, since she's been working on this book.)

Together, Ron and Deborah facilitate a variety of workshops that are both educational and entertaining.

ABOUT IDG BOOKS WORLDWIDE

Welcome to the world of IDG Books Worldwide.

IDG Books Worldwide, Inc., is a subsidiary of International Data Group, the world's largest publisher of computer-related information and the leading global provider of information services on information technology. IDG was founded more than 30 years ago by Patrick J. McGovern and now employs more than 9,000 people worldwide. IDG publishes more than 290 computer publications in over 75 countries. More than 90 million people read one or more IDG publications each month.

Launched in 1990, IDG Books Worldwide is today the #1 publisher of best-selling computer books in the United States. We are proud to have received eight awards from the Computer Press Association in recognition of editorial excellence and three from Computer Currents' First Annual Readers' Choice Awards. Our best-selling ...*For Dummies*® series has more than 50 million copies in print with translations in 31 languages. IDG Books Worldwide, through a joint venture with IDG's Hi-Tech Beijing, became the first U.S. publisher to publish a computer book in the People's Republic of China. In record time, IDG Books Worldwide has become the first choice for millions of readers around the world who want to learn how to better manage their businesses.

Our mission is simple: Every one of our books is designed to bring extra value and skill-building instructions to the reader. Our books are written by experts who understand and care about our readers. The knowledge base of our editorial staff comes from years of experience in publishing, education, and journalism — experience we use to produce books to carry us into the new millennium. In short, we care about books, so we attract the best people. We devote special attention to details such as audience, interior design, use of icons, and illustrations. And because we use an efficient process of authoring, editing, and desktop publishing our books electronically, we can spend more time ensuring superior content and less time on the technicalities of making books.

You can count on our commitment to deliver high-quality books at competitive prices on topics you want to read about. At IDG Books Worldwide, we continue in the IDG tradition of delivering quality for more than 30 years. You'll find no better book on a subject than one from IDG Books Worldwide.

John Kilcullen
Chairman and CEO
IDG Books Worldwide, Inc.

Steven Berkowitz
President and Publisher
IDG Books Worldwide, Inc.

Eighth Annual Computer Press Awards 1992

Ninth Annual Computer Press Awards 1993

Tenth Annual Computer Press Awards 1994

Eleventh Annual Computer Press Awards 1995

IDG is the world's leading IT media, research and exposition company. Founded in 1964, IDG had 1997 revenues of $2.05 billion and has more than 9,000 employees worldwide. IDG offers the widest range of media options that reach IT buyers in 75 countries representing 95% of worldwide IT spending. IDG's diverse product and services portfolio spans six key areas including print publishing, online publishing, expositions and conferences, market research, education and training, and global marketing services. More than 90 million people read one or more of IDG's 290 magazines and newspapers, including IDG's leading global brands — Computerworld, PC World, Network World, Macworld and the Channel World family of publications. IDG Books Worldwide is one of the fastest-growing computer book publishers in the world, with more than 700 titles in 36 languages. The "...For Dummies®" series alone has more than 50 million copies in print. IDG offers online users the largest network of technology-specific Web sites around the world through IDG.net (http://www.idg.net), which comprises more than 225 targeted Web sites in 55 countries worldwide. International Data Corporation (IDC) is the world's largest provider of information technology data, analysis and consulting, with research centers in over 41 countries and more than 400 research analysts worldwide. IDG World Expo is a leading producer of more than 168 globally branded conferences and expositions in 35 countries including E3 (Electronic Entertainment Expo), Macworld Expo, ComNet, Windows World Expo, ICE (Internet Commerce Expo), Agenda, DEMO, and Spotlight. IDG's training subsidiary, ExecuTrain, is the world's largest computer training company, with more than 230 locations worldwide and 785 training courses. IDG Marketing Services helps industry-leading IT companies build international brand recognition by developing global integrated marketing programs via IDG's print, online and exposition products worldwide. Further information about the company can be found at www.idg.com.

1/24/99

Dedication

This book is dedicated to our magnificent parents

Frank and Mollie Zoglin

Paul and Fran Barnett

who are trying their best to become legitimate antiques in their own right

And to our amazing baby brothers

Robert Zoglin

Daniel Barnett

And to two of the world's greatest daughters

Hilee and Sarah Shouse

Authors' Acknowledgments

It takes a lot of smart people to write a *...For Dummies* book.

The On and Beyond Club:

We had wonderful support and help from so many people in putting together this book.

Dennis Tesdell, antique dealer, appraiser, and writer, was a continuing source of information, ideas, and encouragement throughout the creation of the book.

Scott Bonnet, antique dealer and appraiser, shared generously of his time and expertise.

Kyle Husfloen, editor of *Antique Trader,* Tom O'Connor, editor of *Glass Collector's Digest,* and Frank Dondadee, editor of *The Collector* generously advised us and helped us with information and resources. Shirley Northern, ISA CAPP, ASA, and president of the International Society of Appraisers and our esteemed technical editor, guided us to great resources and information. Others who gave extra time and energy and helped us "get it right and get it interesting" include these knowledgeable and generous folk: Pat Saultman, ISA CAPP, Butterfield & Butterfield; Jim Messineo, Boston, MA; David Lindquist, ASA, Chapel Hill, NC; Frank Levy, New York City; Gary E. Baker, Chrysler Museum, Norfolk,. VA; Gwendolyn L. Kelso, ASA, AAA. **The staff of Brookside Antiques** helped us all the way: Mollie Zoglin, ASA, and co-owner, who nourished us in so many ways; Tom Nimmo, manager, who contributed endlessly with his time, energy, and imagination; Rose Zoglin, who never said "no" to us when we needed her, and for that matter neither did Ann Bowen, Mary Bridgens, Fern Jessee, Inez Kaufman, Marion Rosen, Jeanette Wayne, Greg Mitchell, and Jackie Henson. **The Furniture Crew and Rooms of the House crew:** These people generously furnished us with wonderful information: Pat Saultman, ISA CAPP, Butterfield & Butterfield; Frank Levy, New York City; Donald Sack and Albert Sack, New York City; Katherine Voorsinger, Metropolitan Museum of Art, New York City; Kevin Stayton, Brooklyn Museum of Art, Brooklyn, NY; Barry Harwood, Brooklyn Museum of Art, Brooklyn, NY; Donald Pierce, High Museum of Art, Atlanta, GA; Christian Carron, Public Museum of Grand Rapids, Grand Rapids, MI; Bill Turner, New York City; Dr. Kenneth L. Ames, Bard Center for Studies in the Decorative Arts, New York City; Cecily Megrue, New Canaan, CT; Patricia Patrick, Vallejo, CA; Barbara Shandley, Bethesda, MD; Mimi Findlay, New Canaan, CT; Bernard Karr, New York City; Andre Ammelounx, Palatine, IL; Art Dimsdale, Kansas City, MO; Robert Wilson, Springville, CA; Les Paul, Alameda, CA; Jan Cummings, Kansas City, MO; David Lindquist, ASA, Chapel Hill, NC; Lyman McCallum, Charleston, NC; Jim Messineo, Boston, MA; David Brouhard, Kansas City, MO; John Hays, Christie's; Mark Chervenka, Des Moines, IA; Jeannie Black, Memphis, TN; Leigh Miller, De Young Museum, San Francisco; Amy Babb, Dardanelle, AR; Carolyn Ducey, International Quilt Study Center at the University of Nebraska-Lincoln, Lincoln, NE; Brent Goodsell, Syracuse, NY; Ara Zakaryan, Kansas City, MO; Massoud Tehrani, Kansas City, MO; Val Arbab, ASA, ISA CAPP, La Jolla, CA; Tony Stone, London, England. **Buying and Selling Crew:** Thanks to the auction houses that helped us with information and resources. These include Sotheby's, Christie's, Butterfield & Butterfield, Skinner's, and Phillip's; Also thanks to Sandi Fowler, N. Billerica, MA; Judy Ratcliffe, Southlake, TX; Harry Rinker, Emmaus, PA; and Goldie Meyers, Alva, OK. Some wonderful Kansas City help came from Wendy Hoffman, Sharon Mendus, Rick Pence, Lisa R. Payne, Larry Wiebusch, Cammie Boardman, Carol Staab, and Marilyn Hu. **Glass Specialists:** Gary E. Baker, Chrysler Museum, Norfolk Va; Kyle Husfloen, Dubuque, IA; James Measell, consultant with Fenton Art Glass, Marietta, OH; Jane Spillman, Corning Glass Museum, Corning, NY; Gay LeCleire Taylor, Museum of American Glass at Wheaton Village, Millville, NJ; Kirk Nelson, Sandwich Glass Museum, Sandwich, MA; Tom O'Connor, Marietta, OH; Donald Jensen, ISA CAPP, Edmonds, Washington; Danny Gipson, Kansas City, MO; Barbara Lessig, Brookeville, MD; Wes Nedblake, Naples, FL; John Woody, Douglass, KS; Joe and Sharon Robertson, Kansas City, MO; Walter Poeth, Oakland, CA; Audrey Dickerson, Monroe, LA; Paul Nassau and staff, New York City; Ron Rosenberg and L.H. Selman, Santa Cruz, CA; Jeffrey S. Evans, Mt. Crawford, VA; Cheryl Kevish, Dillsburg, PA; Walt Nagorski, Kansas City, MO; Ellen Roberts, Butler, PA; John Shuman, Pottstown, PA; J. Alastair Duncan, New York City; Kenneth Wolf, Kansas City, MO; and Pepi Herrmann, Laconia, NH. **Ceramics People:** Susan & Al Bagdade, Chicago, IL; Beth Szescila, ISA CAPP, Spring, TX; Virginia Cannon, ISA CAPP, ASA, Decatur, IL; Chick Le Ganke, New York City; Becky Macquire, Christie's; Frances Peterson, Kansas City, MO; Shirley Swaab, ASA, Melrose Park, PA; Stuart Slavid, Skinner's; Logan Adams, ISA CAPP, Panama City, FL; Tim Allen, Richmond, VA. **Silver Folk:** Gwendolyn L. Kelso, ASA, AAA, Washington D.C.; Mary Ellen Heibel, ASA, ISA, Anapolis, MD; Kevin Stayton, Brooklyn Museum of Art, Brooklyn, NY; Rosita Kroeker, Shawnee Mission, KS; Tony Clark, McClean, VA; Sam Hough,

Gorham consultant, Cranston, RI; Carole Gliedman, New York City; Beverly Bremer, Atlanta, GA; Nannette Monmonier-Schwesitzer, Ellicott City, MD; John Harms, Butterfield & Butterfield; James Wells, Kansas City, MO; Robert Puckett, Wichita-Sedgwick County Historical Museum, Wichita, KS; and Duncan Cox, New Orleans, LA. **Decorating:** Judith Choice, Kansas City, MO.; Erin Jones, ASID, Washington, D.C.; Susan King, New York City; Bobanne Kalkofen, ASID, Kansas City, MO; Jack Harris, Kansas City, MO; Lyn Fontenot, Ph.D., ASID, Lafayette, LA; Alene Workman, Hollywood, FL; Sandra Wisot, CID, Los Angeles, CA; Jan Cummings, Kansas City, MO; Robert Todd, Memphis, TN; Joanne Baehr, Kansas City, MO; Donna Bodinson, Kansas City, MO; Patricia Moriarity, Holyoke, MA; Susan Fenner, Kansas City, MO. **Antiques by the Yard:** Barbara Israel, New York City; Michael Garden, New York City; Judy Wells, Kansas City MO; Maggie Lindquist, Chapel Hill, NC; Quinton Matson, Lawrence, KS; Christopher Hamill, Lawrence, KS; Bruce Burstert, Kansas City, MO; and Piers Mackenzie, Butterfield and Butterfield. **Orientalia**: Michael Teller, Williamsburg, VA; Geoffrey Oliver; Pittsford, NY; Gary Levine, Sotheby's; Mark Shimkus, Kansas City, MO; and Robert H. Ellsworth, New York City. **Caring for Antiques, Appraising, and other Stuff**: Penny Jones, AIC, Washington, D.C.; Craig Deller, AIC (PA), Geneva, IL; Donna Morris, La Verne, CA; Nancy Martin, ASA, Arcadia, CA; Karen Rabe, ISA CAPP, Lake Forest, IL; Laura Whitman, Christie's; Tim Ward, Kansas City, MO;. Rodney Staab, Grinter House Museum, Kansas City, KS; Betsey Garret, Christie's; Jay Kruger, National Gallery of Art, Washington D.C.; Jerry and Sue Faier, Kansas City, MO. **The Research and Tracking Section:** Paul Barnett made endless phone calls and helped us with all kinds of research issues. Thanks to Candy Schock and Robert Zoglin, who fly through the Internet with the greatest of ease. Ken Stinnett gave us endless technical help and encouragement. Thanks to the great Johnson County Kansas Library system, with special thanks to Corinth Library, Prairie Village, KS; the Kansas City, Missouri Library system; the Nelson-Atkins Museum of Art, Kansas City, MO; with special thanks to director Marc Wilson, Scott Erbes, Jeffrey Weidman, Stacey Sherman, Christina Nelson, Kathleen Garland, Paul Benson, and Robert Cohon. **Cheerleading and creative encouragement section:** We got so much help from so many creative people! Some of these amazing folks include Maril Crabtree, Sherry Schultz, Robert Brummet, and Dan Karamanski. Thanks to the wonderful people in the Kansas City Writer's Group for their creative energy and loving support: Mary Lane Kamberg, Carol Newman, Terry Hoyland, Meg Huber, Alberta Daw, Judith Bader Jones, and many more helped with ideas and encouragement. Thanks to Andrea Warren and Barbara Bartocci for their continuing guidance and support, and to Mildred's Coffeehouse for great scones and atmosphere. Thanks to Bev Cortiana, Charles Mallory, Billy Ray Boyd, Paul Anderson, Michael Friedman, Jacque Ensign, Jeffrey Marker, Geoph Kozney, Byron Nicodemus, Victoria Moran, Ruth-Ann Clurman, Anne Baber, Jackie West, Carolyn Hoppe, Susan Fenner, Guy Guber, and Jim Rzatkiewicz.

Thanks to our agent Carolyn Krupp at IMG Bach Literary Agency and to the wonderful people at IDG, including our patient and creative project editor, Colleen Totz, Holly McGuire, Maureen Kelly, Heather Prince, Jon Malysiak, and Catherine Schmitz.

Publisher's Acknowledgements

We're proud of this book; please register your comments through our IDG Books Worldwide Online Registration Form located at http://my2cents.dummies.com.

Some of the people who helped bring this book to market include the following:

Acquisitions, Editorial, and Media Development

Project Editors: Nancy Delfavero, Colleen Totz

Acquisitions Editor: Holly McGuire

Technical Editor: Shirley Northern

Editorial Manager: Mary Corder

Editorial Coordinator: Maureen Kelly

Special Help: Christine Meloy Beck, Suzanne Thomas, Jonathan Malysiak

Production

Project Coordinator: Regina Snyder

Layout and Graphics: Linda M. Boyer, Angela F. Hunckler, Anna Rohrer, Brent Savage, Mark Shirar, Jacque Schneider, Janet Seib, Michael Sullivan

Special Art: Stephen Kowalski

Proofreaders: Kelli Botta, Vickie Broyles, Jennifer Mahern, Arrielle Carole Mennelle, Nancy Price, Rebecca Senninger, Ethel Winslow

Indexer: Sherry Massey

General and Administrative

IDG Books Worldwide, Inc: John Kilcullen, CEO; Steven Berkowitz, President and Publisher

IDG Books Technology Publishing: Brenda McLaughlin, Senior Vice President and Group Pubisher

Dummies Technology Press and Dummies Editorial: Diane Graves Steele, Vice President and Associate Publisher, Mary Bednarek, Director of Acquisitions and Product Development; Kristin A. Cocks, Editorial Director

Dummies Trade Press: Kathleen A. Welton, Vice President and Publisher; Kevin Thornton, Acquisitions Manager

IDG Books Production for Dummies Press: Michael R. Britton, Vice President of Production and Creative Services; Cindy L. Phipps, Manager of Project Coordination, Production Proofreading, and Indexing, Kathie S. Schutte, Supervisor of Page Layout; Shelley Lea, Supervisor of Graphics and Design; Debbie J. Gates, Production Systems Specialist; Robert Springer, Supervisor of Proofreading, Debbie Stailey, Special Projects Coordinator; Tony Augsburger, Supervisor of Reprints and Bluelines

Dummies Packaging and Book Design: Patty Page, Manager, Promotions Marketing

◆

The publisher would like to give special thanks to Patrick J. McGovern, without whom this book would not have been possible

◆

Contents at a Glance

Cartoons at a Glance

By Rich Tennant

The 5th Wave
By Rich Tennant

"Gee, Mark– look at this pot. It's obviously quite old, but in wonderful condition..."

page 7

The 5th Wave
By Rich Tennant
ANTIQUING NIGHTMARE
We'll never get this well finished. This old pottery keeps gummin' up the drill bit.
Try this!
ANTIQUITIES DRILL BIT
Grinds through ancient artifacts in a jiffy

page 79

The 5th Wave
By Rich Tennant
AUTHENTICATING AN ANTIQUE
Refer to scholarly reference books
Ask seller to date object in writing
Toss object as high as possible and observe seller's reaction.

page 131

The 5th Wave
By Rich Tennant
Antiques

"I don't know what it is but it must be old. It was the only thing grandma didn't recognize."

page 323

The 5th Wave
By Rich Tennant

"No, I don't know how fast I was going, but would you like to know what time it is?"

page 303

The 5th Wave
By Rich Tennant
MAIN
ANTIQU

"Look at that craftsmanship. Notice the patina. It's already three years old. In the computer industry, that makes it a genuine antique."

page 213

Fax: 978-546-7747 • E-mail: `the5wave@tiac.net`

Table of Contents

Introduction

This book gives you a new way to look at your everyday world. Suddenly you see not just an old chair, but a piece of living history and extraordinary craftsmanship. Collecting antiques introduces you to interesting people. Plus you learn fascinating things, such as the inside story on Mary Gregory and why Chinese chairs are comparatively tall. Each antique has a story to tell, and part of the fun of collecting is gathering those stories.

For the new collector, this book introduces you to the different categories of antiques. But we're not going to just show you the antiques without telling you the best places and ways to get them. We give you the inside story on antique shops, shows, flea markets, and auctions so that you not only know what you're buying, you know more savvy ways to buy it.

For the more experienced collector, this book presents a chance to broaden your knowledge base. We consulted with specialists across the country, searching out the facts and the stories and the tips to make you an even wiser collector.

This is a practical book, designed to help you incorporate antiques into your life. We show you some ways you can bring antiques into your home by suggesting different types of antiques for some of the rooms of the house.

Collecting antiques is like falling in love: You are constantly discovering new and interesting aspects of the antiques. The more you know, the more you want to know. You never get bored with your explorations, and you want the relationship to last forever.

Collecting antiques is also very personal. Each carefully chosen object has its own charm, appeal, and personality, much like the very people who collect. You are matching your personality with the personality of the piece.

How to Use This Book

The more you know about antiques, the more fun you have discovering and buying them. We start out talking about the art of antique collecting and give you tips on developing a buying strategy and becoming a wise collector. From there we move into the basics: furniture, glass, ceramics, and silver. We have a section of how and where to buy. Then we take you into the house so that you can see ways to use antiques in your home. We end with ways to care for your antiques, sell them, and get them appraised. Fakes and frauds are out there, and even the most sophisticated of collectors can be taken in by them. Throughout the book, we give you lots of tips on ways to recognize and avoid falling into fakes.

If you are a new collector, you may want to read the opening two chapters so that you understand the territory you are walking into. If you are eager to get out there and buy, dip into Part II for some shopping advice before you spend a lot of money.

Other than that, read any section you fancy.

Conventions Used in This Book

Every day, some wonderful objects turn 100 years old and become official antiques. Not all the objects we write about are official antiques. We included some antiques-in-waiting. These pieces have age but sometimes fall shy of the requisite ten decades. Because of either amazing craftsmanship or unusual popularity, we included several of these stellar creatures.

Who Needs to Read This Book?

In writing this book, we often thought about you. We envisioned you as a smart, sophisticated person who wanted to know more about antiques. Perhaps you are worried about being taken advantage of. Perhaps you are curious. Perhaps you want to add antiques into your life and don't know how to get started. Or perhaps you are already a collector and just want more information.

We want to make the huge field of antiques as manageable as possible and to give you the tools and resources you need to make your antiquing purchases fun and meaningful and wise.

How This Book Is Organized

This book is organized into parts, each of which eases you into the world of antiques. Each part has chapters that highlight a specific area of antique collecting.

Part I: The Antiquing Primer

This part starts at the very beginning and prepares you for the complex world of antique collecting. You find tips on how to tell the antiques from the stuff that's merely old. You understand the resources available and discover ways to choose the ones that are right for you. You have a chance to analyze the components of a desirable antique.

From there, we move on to furniture. Antique furniture can be as reasonably priced and as functional as well-made contemporary pieces. Chapter 3 shows you the different styles and periods of furniture and ways to distinguish them. Chapter 4 describes dovetails, nails, and other construction elements that give you clues to tell old from new.

Part II: Who's Got the Goods? Shopping for Antiques

Read this section, and you may save yourself a lot of money. Here you get some insider tips on bargaining for antiques. You get a survey of places where you can buy and shopping strategies for each. The information on how to bid at auctions both real-time and online makes you want to get going once, going twice.

Part III: Material Possessions

Glass, ceramics, and silver are fun to learn about and collect. These antiques are frequently reasonably priced, pretty to look at, and great to use. Each chapter in this part surveys collecting opportunities and provides tips on how to identify different items. You also get tips to help you watch out for the unlabeled reproduction. Sip from a glass chapter that's full of collecting ideas and information. Explore the battle to create western porcelain and discover how to add history and romance to your life with antique ceramics. Shine up your life by adding antique silver to your dinner table.

Part IV: Integrating Antiques into Your Home

You don't have to hide your glorious antiques in a glassed-in cabinet. The chapters in this part are full of decorating ideas and suggestions for antiques that you can blend into your household. Make your kitchen more secure by adding a pie safe. Lounge around in Victorian parlor furniture and store your magazines in an antique coal hod. Then travel to the Orient and explore the wondrous aspects of jade, ivory, Oriental ceramics, Japanese woodblock prints, and Chinese furniture. Finally, take an antique out and transform your yard or garden with a few well-placed conversation pieces you never have to water.

Part V: The Care, Feeding, and Deleting of Antiques

This part provides some tips for taking care of your antiques. If you want to get them appraised, you need to know how to choose an appraiser and what to expect from your appraiser. When you want to sell an antique, you can read about the advantages of all the different venues, from estate sales to auctions, from consignment to Internet.

Part VI: The Part of Tens

To be sure the price is as nice as the antique, consult our list of general and specialty price guides. Be up on current antique happenings, from shows to auction results to repro watches, to what someone is willing to pay today, by subscribing to some or all of the periodicals we list. These great publications keep you educated and involved in the ever-changing antique world.

Icons Used in This Book

When you're out there on the collecting trail, these tips help raise your antiquing savvy about specific categories of collecting.

These tips put you on alert and warn you about possible pitfalls.

These paragraphs contain the tidbits you might be tempted to scribble on the palm of your hand when you go antiquing. They remind you of important information.

These paragraphs alert you to possible fakes and frauds and remind you to examine carefully before you buy.

We want you to pursue your antique passion by learning more and more. These are some great additional resources to help you along the way.

Where to Go from Here

You can always learn something new about antiques. This book is one beginning of your journey. As you settle on areas of collecting, you'll want to buy other more specialized books. We've listed many of these books in the text. You'll want to look at lots of antiques, by going to antique shops, attending shows and antique malls and flea markets, and more. "Every day I learn something new," said one of our specialists, who's been in the business for 30 years. That's the pleasure of antiquing: There's always something new to learn.

Part I
The Antiquing Primer

"Gee, Mark– look at this pot. It's obviously quite old, but in wonderful condition..."

In this part . . .

"I couldn't help myself. It was love at first sight."

Of course, you're already experienced in the ways of romance. You know how love can sneak up behind you, flash you a brilliant smile, and suddenly, you are smitten. Antiques are that way, too: One look at them, and you can be head over heels, before you've even been introduced.

In this section, we introduce you to the world of antiques. We give you several definitions, a few admonitions, and a little exposition. We give you a RADAR lesson in ways to evaluate an antique. Then we invite you into our parlor for a stirring story of immigrants and kings and carpenters and queens — the evolution of furniture.

Chapter 1

Stalking the Wild Antique

In This Chapter

- Stalking the wild antique (and recognizing it when you find it)
- Tracking the untamed collectible
- Deciding whether old or new is best for you by looking at antiques, meeting dealers, and reading price guides

The antique supply fluctuates constantly. Every day, fewer older antiques are available, and a few new "just turned 100" antiques become available. Before you buy, look at a lot of antiques, talk to dealers and other experts, and read a few price guides, auction catalogues, and books. Dealers, curators, and collectors all gave us this same advice: Buying antiques is like searching for buried treasure — if you don't know what 16th century doubloons really look like, you may not see the treasure even if you stumble over it.

So how can you stop and smell the doubloons? Finding dealers and other specialists you can trust is one key to successful antique buying. This chapter gives you tips for finding competent dealers and suggests other ways to quickly scope out the antique scene.

Question: What kind of car do you drive to look for antiques?

Answer: An Oldsmobile.

Antiques, Collectibles, and Other Aging Items

Before you buy, you have to get enough experience to figure out the difference between old stuff that isn't worth the lace on your tennis shoes and an antique that you should mortgage your stationary bike over. You need to know the difference between an antique, an antique-in-waiting, a collectible, and an antiquity.

A is for Antique

A "legal" antique is something that is 100 years old. This definition was created so that the customs people would know how to tax things.

Antiques come into the country duty free. You pay duty on pieces that are 99-years-old or less. Besides being 100 years or more, antiques carry with them certain presumptions — presumptions of value, good craftsmanship, and rarity.

Beginning in 1891, the McKinley Tariff Act required that foreign-made imports be stamped or labeled in English words with their country of origin. Ideally, this means that foreign-made antiques created before 1891 will not be labeled and those created after will.

Some items had paper labels and other markings, which may have disappeared by now. Foreign-made pieces that were not made for export to the United States did not have to be marked or labeled.

Stepping up to the collectible plate

A collectible is just about anything people want to collect that is younger than 100 years. Collectibles include items such as Hummel figurines, collector's plates, Depression glass (you know, that thing you drink from when you need to get out of the dumps), various toys, and baseball cards. Really, just about anything is fair game.

You did say you were going abroad, didn't you?

To satisfy customs, you need proof that the object is 100 years old or more. Ask the dealer to give you a receipt that describes and dates the piece. Certain valuable art and antiques from Europe and the Middle East are not allowed out of their own country. Ask the dealer to make sure that you have any information you need so you can get through customs smoothly.

If the item you buy in Europe is less than 100 years old and made in America, you can mark the piece "American Goods Returning" and bring the piece home tax-free.

Those charming pre-century antiques-in-waiting

Just to keep things from being too cut and dried, a certain 20th century crowd exists that is simply too magnificent to accept the word *collectible.* These "antiques-in-waiting" are truly masterpieces and are valued more highly than many antiques. This beauty-before-age syndrome applies primarily to work from the Art Nouveau, Art Deco, and Art Moderne periods in the early 1900s. A Tiffany lamp that goes at auction for a quarter of a million dollars — well, it's definitely an honorary antique.

Digging into antiquities

Finally, there's the stuff that is unearthed. These include work from ancient cultures such as the Roman, Greek, and Egyptian and are called *antiquities.* You might come across these ancient articles: ancient Egyptian/Syrian glass, little pottery jars, bowls and vases from Greece and the Middle East, ancient bronze coins and miniature bronze figures from old Persia, the Middle East, and Italy (not in the excellent quality/condition that the museum pieces are, but collectible and great conversation pieces).

At an antique center, Michael spotted some beautiful opalescent bottles and was told they were genuine antiquities. Later that day, Michael saw more "ancient" bottles displayed at a fancy decorator's shop. He was surprised by their reasonable prices. Still later, one antiquities expert told him that buying ancient bottles was very tricky and that repros were rampant.

Sears or Sotheby's: Deciding Between Something Old and Something New

Contrary to popular mythology, antiques are not necessarily more expensive than newer items. You can find wonderful antique furniture and accessories comparably priced to newer items. Here are a few questions to ask yourself when you're choosing between old and new items.

- **Will this antique get along with you and your house?** Many people proudly describe their decorating style as eclectic. They mix antiques with modern pieces and have a charming and comfortable look. Have you ever tried to introduce a turn-of-the-century wicker rocker to a St. Bernard? Make sure that your antiques can get along with your lifestyle as well as your decor.

- **Is it functional or usable?** Unlike most people, most antiques come from "functional families." You can find plenty of antiques that are as functional as their modern counterparts.

  Just because an antique is old doesn't mean that you have to shut it up in a cloistered cabinet. Think of ways you can use your antique. Think of places where you will see it every day. Many antiques were functional parts of everyday life: Don't put them out to pasture just because they're old enough to get a letter from the president.

- **Can you adapt your antique so that it will be usable?** Armoires are a great example of an antique cross-trained to a new function. Once they were simply closet cases, an elegant way to store clothes. Now we put entertainment centers in these elegant shelvings. The purist won't want to drill a crass hole in a lovely old armoire: Here's where natural shrinkage and old knotty wood come in handy. Sometimes you can "get wired" by squeezing the plug through those slightly loose boards or poking out a knothole. (But save that old knotty wood, in case you ever want to sell the piece.)

  Chinese altar tables are another great example. They were once used for strictly spiritual purposes. Now the spirit moves them to the bedroom for an intricate bedside table, to the living room for a coffee or end table, to the kitchen for a breakfast bar, or to the dining room for a sideboard.

  You can even adapt an antique bed to fit your needs. If you discover the perfect "sleeper," you need to find out if the bed size suits you. Many antique frames were ¾'s today's standard bed size. It's often easy to have a custom mattress made to fit a bed frame size that is slightly out of vogue.

Preparation A: Researching Antiques Before You Buy

Look, listen, and read before you buy antiques. Antique buying is a wonderful and tricky business. The less you know, the trickier it gets. The less you know, the greater chance you have of getting merchandise that isn't what you thought it was and paying prices that aren't the great bargains you thought they were.

Before you enter the antique jungle, ground yourself with firsthand experiences, mentors, and books. You'll have far more fun! Plus you'll have great tidbits to throw into conversations.

Getting firsthand experience in the "field"

Great news for those of us who couldn't sit still in fourth grade: Antique collecting is a hands-on activity. A great deal of your knowledge comes from going out and seeing things, touching things, getting to understand the look, feel, and scent. (You know how important it is to stop and smell the ivory!) If you can't wait to find out how this works, zoom ahead to Chapter 17.

To become an "instant expert," there's no substitute for experience. Getting out there and looking at antiques, handling them, comparing them, is one great way to learn.

For "hands-on" experience, where you can actually touch and examine antiques (although you may want to ask the dealer to assist you), go to antique shops, shows, malls, antique centers, and auctions. To see top quality antiques, for comparison purposes, go to museums and selected national auctions.

Meeting mentors and teachers

Get to know some dealers. Get to know them even before you are ready to purchase. Dealers are part of your training ground.

A *dealer* refers to the person with the most knowledge, often the owner, in an antique shop, or in a booth at an antique show. The dealer is typically also a decision-maker, a person who can inform you, advise you, negotiate with you, and help you find antiques. In this chapter, we tell you how you can get to know dealers, how they can help you, and why you need dealers as part of your antique collecting strategy. Look in Chapter 6 for other ways to find dealers, and check out Chapter 5 for ways to make deals with dealers.

Interview with a dealer

We asked dealers and collectors for tips on how to scope out a dealer. What did they want to know about the people they were doing antique business with? How could they tell if the dealer was reliable and knowledgeable?

Here's a working list of questions:

- **How long have you been collecting/dealing in antiques?** Try to get a sense of the dealer's hands-on experience. Some dealers are part-time hobbyists who, like you, enjoy antiques. Still, even those who collect "on the side" can have great expertise in specific areas.
- **Do you belong to any professional organizations?** Dealers may join dealer's associations, such as the National Association for Dealers in Antiques, appraiser's associations, or organizations related to specific types of merchandise. Extra points for the dealer having credentials as an appraiser.

Depending on the appraisal society, this may mean that the dealer has been required to take various courses and examinations, to present examples of appraisal work, and to practice for a given number of years before being accredited as an appraiser. Each society has various levels of accreditation. Some of the national appraisal societies include The American Society of Appraisers, the International Society of Appraisers, and the Appraisers Association of America. (See Chapter 20 to be apprised of appraisers.)

In antiques, the first or even the third degree doesn't matter as much as the dealer's knowledge and ability and willingness to communicate.

The dealer does not need to be an appraiser or have a certain type of degree or education to have a deep knowledge of antiques. Conversely, just because dealers belong to professional organizations, do not assume that they are going to be as knowledgeable or as forthcoming as dealers not associated with such organizations. As with other professions, each individual is different.

- **What types of items do you typically specialize in?** You are seeking a dealer with expertise and passion in your areas of interest. Some dealers are generalists and can be somewhat helpful in many areas. Others focus on specific areas, such as pressed glass or 18th century American furniture. Most dealers have areas that they particularly love and love to talk about.
- **Do you have any reproductions in the shop?** You want a dealer who is above all, truthful. If dealers have reproductions mixed in with authentic antiques, make sure that the repros are clearly labeled. Some shops have a policy that everything is antique. Some shops carry only reproductions. When shops have a mixture, ideally, antiques and repros each have their own distinct section, or even a separate floor. If the dealer tells you there are repros and they are not well marked, be wary. Some reproductions are so masterfully done, even the experts have difficulty discerning.
- **What do you like about this antique? Why do you think it's a good buy?** The knowledgeable dealer has looked at thousands of antiques and hopefully has a highly developed aesthetic sense. You'll learn from hearing the dealer describe the attributes of the piece and compare it to others of its kind. Design, color, material construction, rarity, historical significance, and condition are all aspects of an antique that the dealer can hopefully illuminate.
- **How do you know this is the real thing?** Listen carefully to the answer. Dealers who specialize can teach you a lot about understanding the real from the repro. A dealer who is knowledgeable and honest is an ideal partner, in your collecting career.

- **How have you identified the antique — by what authority?** "It's in the book," can be a typical response. Don't nod sanguinely and go on. This could be the phone book or a price guide book. A less knowledgeable dealer might use only the price guides to identify things. As you will soon read, the price guide as a single source has its limitations. Ask to see the book. Look at the picture and see whether the dealer's ID makes sense to you. If it doesn't, if the piece looks different, ask for further explanation.
- **Do you guarantee authenticity?** If a dealer is willing to tell you what the piece is, the dealer should be willing to stand behind what he says. If the dealer is unwilling, this doesn't completely disqualify the purchase. Most dealers purchase items without absolute certainty as to their authenticity, and if the price reflects the uncertainty, it may be worth a bit of speculation.
- **What is your return policy?** What if you get home and the person you love most goes absolutely ballistic over the idea of this antique invading your living area? What if your wall is way smaller than you remembered? What if you get home and discover a chip, one that you didn't notice in the store? What if the dealer does guarantee that the piece is of a certain type and then your knowledgeable best friend comes over and tells you that you've purchased something that was born yesterday? What will the dealer do?

  When you make a good-sized purchase, many dealers in shops or malls let you take it home on approval. That way, you can make sure that Oriental rug you want doesn't clash with the orange shag in the hallway. And a truly reputable dealer should be ready, willing, and able to take back anything that was incorrectly represented. After all, the dealer's reputation depends on it.

Once you meet dealers you are comfortable with, tell them you are a new collector, you are learning, and that you want to establish relationships with reputable dealers. Ask if they have time to show you antiques in your area of interest. If they are too busy, make an appointment for another time.

Sure, first impressions are important. But be willing to hang in there for a second or third impression. That's what we learned from walking in (and out) of hundreds of antique shops. Some shops greeted us cordially and asked how they could help. Other shops totally ignored us. Still others looked put out to see us — as if we were walking into their home and interrupting their telephone conversation. Do not be put off by what might seem like rude behavior. Sometimes dealers who initially ignore you can be fabulous sources of information and merchandise if you show a little patience.

What you need to know about repro: Do you copy?

People often use the word *repro* to designate something new that has been made with the intent to deceive. For example, some crafty sly person creates a copy of an original Tiffany lamp. He hopes to sell it to you for the big wonderful antique Tiffany price. (See Chapter 10 for ways to avoid purchasing such a repro.)

Of course, many wonderful reproductions are created with no intent to deceive. Furniture, Oriental porcelains, and artwork have been copied for hundreds of years. Even the repros are now antiques. An original Queen Anne chair was made during the Queen Anne period. (See Chapter 3 for more about the Queen and her furniture.) Still, a 100-year-old repro of a Queen Anne chair is much more valuable than last summer's Tiffany glass knock-off reproduction.

Discovering the antique network

Network with other people who love the same type of antiques that you do. Connect with collectors' clubs, on a local and national level, and groups such as The Questers, collectors who like to share knowledge and tips. *The Questers* is a national organization that started in the 1940s and has chapters in many cities. They meet in each other's homes and take tours of shops and museums usually once a month to learn about antiques, art and collectibles.

Go to antique seminars and meet with people who share your passion for antiquing and who can add to your knowledge.

Many art galleries host antique study groups. The National Association of Dealers in Antiques has memberships for collectors. Collectors can attend educational programs and conventions for reasonable fees.

Most cities have a variety of antique study groups. Some focus on antiques in general. Others are oriented toward a specific type of collecting. Through talking to dealers and other collectors, you can find an antique study group that's right for you.

Price guides and other great books

Remember, Jiminy Cricket's advice: "Always let your conscience be your guide." Antique collecting is one area where you may need a more concrete and specific guide. That's where price guides come in.

Don't be deceived by the practical title *price guide.* These books are not your typical "list of items and how much they cost" books. These books are mini-encyclopedias, filled with technical "bytes" on specific antiques, brief histories, references, compact descriptions, and prices. Price guides give you an ample sampling of antiques — nationwide, sequenced, and organized. Price guides are excellent learning tools.

Here's how price guides work. People all over the country contribute to these guides. They describe the antique and write down the asking prices. Note the disclaimers the price guides use: "There is no variance for condition, quality, location, bargaining power."

You'll want to buy several price guides every year. Prices may vary per each guide, since the information was collected by different people in different cities. Also, different guides list different objects. Just as you want the best sherpas to guide you through the Himalayas, you want the best guides to lead you through the elegant and enticing maze of antiques. Some great guides include Kovels', Warman's, and Schroeder's. (See Chapter 23 for other great guides.)

After you zero in on your passion, you need the specific books and price guides for that specialty. This is how you become an expert in your niche. Beside the price guides, you'll want books that describe the objects of your affection. Some of these books may seem costly, but they are teaching you how to invest wisely.

The information in the price guide may be at least one year out of date when the book hits the market. Use the guides as a general guideline for prices (as well as places to find brief information about all kinds of antiques).

Salute the General: Using general price guides

General price guides help you identify antiques and give you a general idea about price ranges.

Have you ever taken dancing lessons and done really well when the teacher is calling out the steps and informing you "Fox Trot," "Waltz," "Cha Cha Cha." Then you go out dancing, and suddenly, music is playing, other people are gliding about the floor, and you stand there, stymied: With no one calling out the steps, you have no clue what kind of dance it is. You don't even know which foot to put forward.

The price guides can tell you what kind of dance it is and help you take those first steps. Some guides have line drawings or photos showing a range of antiques and collectibles. They succinctly describe each category and give physical characteristics for most pieces.

Here's a description of Bull's Eye pattern glass (for collectors who want to hit their mark, rather than make it) from Warman's *Antiques and Collectibles Price Guide, 32nd Edition* (published by Krause Publications):

> Flint made by the New England Glass Co. in the 1850s. Also found in colors and milk glass, which are worth more than double the price of clear.

A line drawing of the glass illustrates the exact pattern, and then you find a listing of various pieces made in that pattern. For example:

> Bitters Bottle, Clear, $80.00
>
> Cologne Bottle, Clear, $85.00.

With this information, you can waltz (you can at least waltz, can't you) through malls and auctions and target in on this Bull's Eye pattern. If you see colored glass, you know the price is going to be higher.

Price guides are also ideal for helping you get a price sense for antiques and collectibles that have a more uniform quality, such as pattern glass, Royal Doulton character mugs, and Carnival glass. Also use price guides for lower-end collectibles, such as Fiesta Ware (not to be confused with "You say there's a fiesta where?") Use price guides with furniture, oil paintings, and high-end items only as a very general guide. Why? The brief description can't take into account the many variables, such as condition, location, popularity, size, and attractiveness. A huge clunky thing is usually not as valuable and a refinished or repaired piece is less desirable. Use the guides as they advise, to show you the "average" furniture prices. Then form your own private guide by shopping around in your area.

Catalogue shopping: Auctions without going once

Price Guides are based on the retail asking price. To get an idea of how much selling price varies from asking price, treat yourself to catalogues from some of the auction houses, such as Sotheby's, Christie's, and Butterfield & Butterfield. Bask in the beauty of the lavish photographs, which capture the grace and elegance of some of the world's finest antiques.

Auction catalogs often highlight certain items or feature items they expect to do well. They may focus on a certain area. Read the description and notice the estimate range, which might be $25,000 to $30,000 or $3,000 to $4,000. Get the catalogue before the sale and then ask to receive the "prices realized" list, which details what items actually sold for and what items did *not* sell. An item listed for $15,000 to $20,000 may sell for $13,000. An item listed from $5,000 to $6,000 may sell for $7,500. Looking through these auction catalogues is another great way to learn about quality antiques. One thing you learn from auction catalogues: Things are worth what people are willing to pay for them. Prices can skyrocket if the mood is right. Two revved-up people can get things going to previously uncharted heights. And if no one's much in the mood, prices can drop.

Chapter 2

Preparing for the Hunt: An Antiquing Plan of Action

In This Chapter

- Determining your antiquing goals
- Deciding how much you're willing to spend
- Spotting good values for the money

You're going to spend some money on furniture and accessories, so you may as well buy something that can hold its value after you use it. Antiques often have a greater chance of retaining value than new machine-made furniture. Plus, antiques add a sense of warmth, history, and character to your house. (See Chapter 13 for more reasons to decorate with antiques.) Whether you are purchasing antiques because of their beauty, or because you simply love older things, or because you are hoping that they will hold their value, the best rule is to buy what you like.

In this chapter, we give you tips for strategizing your antique purchases.

Antiques have already proven themselves and have established their value in the market place. See price guides for a very general indication of current market value.

Deciding on an Antiquing Game Plan

Before you embark on an antique shopping spree, you need to figure out your goals. What do you want to collect and how much do you want to spend and how do you want the antiques to fit into your home? Your goals may change as you get to know more about antiques and as your own tastes develop.

Why do you need goals to buy furniture and decorative objects, you may wonder. Antiquing is a broad and confusing field, filled with reproductions and fakes so good that even experts can be fooled. Sure, you can plunge in and buy. But we recommend you plunge in with small purchases while you develop your eye and figure out what areas you want to specialize in. The more you learn about antiques, the better chance you have of getting good value and good quality for your money.

The following sections provide some questions to help you define and focus your antiquing interests.

If you're collecting with another person, answering the collecting questions together may help you pinpoint your goals (and avoid fighting over whether you buy the Czech perfume bottle or the Victorian humidor).

Do you want to own few antiques of great quality or more of lesser quality?

Do you want to own a few antiques of great quality or do you prefer to have more antiques of lesser quality? Does your list of favorite things fill a legal pad or a note card? Does your shopping stamina include a series of antique malls or a few little quaint corner shops? Do you like to come home from every shopping excursion with at least a little something?

The way you approach antique acquisitions will probably be similar to the way you approach other purchases. Buying fewer antiques of greater quality implies a tolerance for delayed gratification and a willingness to research your subject and shop around. If you like quick trips with fast results, you may love getting more items that are not as costly. (This also works if you like long shopping trips with lots of instantaneous gratification.)

Your goals may change as you get more knowledge of antiques. Many people start out buying inexpensive things and gradually upgrade their collections.

Do you want to specialize?

Do you want a random selection that suits your whimsy or do you want to specialize in collecting antiques from certain periods or of a particular style? Because antiquing is such a wide field, many people develop areas of specialization or expertise. Your specialties can be as broad or narrow as you want. For example, you may love glass and start out with a collection of antique drinking glasses of different colors, patterns, and/or periods. From looking at all that glass, perhaps you fall in love with cut glass, maybe even a specific pattern of cut glass. And from getting to know about cut glass, you may focus in on the late 19th century Brilliant period of cut glass.

When you learn about specific areas, you can spot good deals. You know what colors are unusual, what price ranges are normal, and what styles are considered most desirable.

Many collectors choose their specialty by the objects they are drawn toward and the types of things they like to study and learn about. Part of developing a specialty is learning about how the object is made, getting hooked up with the collectors' groups, and subscribing to the trade journals. It's "life-long" learning that you can instantly put to use.

Specialties range from concentrating on

- A certain period, such as furniture from the Victorian era
- A type of object, such as boxes or teacups
- A certain category of collecting, such as glass or porcelain
- Works by a specific company, such as Meissen porcelain or Fenton Art Glass
- A certain pattern of a company, such as Lincoln Drape pattern attributed to The Boston & Sandwich Glass Company

For ideas of specialty areas, look at the price guide books, such as *Kovels',* *Warman's,* and *Shroeder's,* which list hundreds of antique categories. Also, you get a lot of information about the categories of antique collecting by looking through trade periodicals such as the *Antique Trader* and the *Maine Antique Digest,* as well as by browsing auction sites on the Web.

Do you want the aesthetic, the functional, or a combo?

You can incorporate functional objects, such as antique desks, chairs, beds, and silverware right into your daily life. It's great fun reading the newspaper, eating your Cheerios with an antique Victorian spoon while sitting on your 19th century Chinese horseshoe back chair. Most antiques bring a beauty along with their functionality.

Some people prefer antiques that are simply lovely to look at and like to display items such as cut glass, porcelain figurines, or miniatures.

Sometimes functionality hinges on the condition of the antique. For example, in Chapter 14, we "pour" on information about how to discover if a tea set can really handle the hot water.

Whether you buy antiques to use or to look at is purely a matter of personal preference and life style. Some people want to use their antique vases to smell the roses and others want to create a display of vases.

You take care of most antiques just as you would any honored object. For more specifics, turn to Chapter 19.

How do you want to budget your antique purchases?

Do you want to set an upper limit on what you pay for one piece? Do you want a yearly cap on purchases? Or do you prefer the random theory of investment: Buy whatever comes your way? One way to decide on your budget for antiques is simply to figure what you would otherwise spend on furniture and accessories.

Whatever your style of purchasing, we advocate starting out small. Every collector (we hope you are the exception, of course) makes a mistake or two. Every dealer makes mistakes. During your "apprenticeship" period, when you are just starting to explore antiques, make less expensive purchases and try to buy from somebody you really trust.

For ways to save money on your antique purchases, rush to Chapter 5, where we give you tips on negotiating and how to work with dealers.

Where do you plan to put your antiques?

If you have limited space and unlimited appreciation of antiques, ask yourself where you plan to put your antiques. Some antiques are rather grand sizewise and resist being squeezed through contemporary doorways. Before you load an ornately carved four-poster bed into your Volkswagen, make sure that you have enough room to make your bed and lie in it. We know collectors who have actually moved to bigger houses because their collections grew so large.

If large hungry puppies roam your house, you may not want to see them teething on a Louis XVI chair. Some tables or chairs may not be sturdy enough for thudding children; others can withstand almost anything. (If they lived through the French Revolution, surely they can live through several years with your family.)

Basically, you want your antiques to have a safe place to live where you can see and enjoy them.

Strategies for Spending Your Antiquing Dollars

We recommend a purchasing strategy that many collectors endorse: Always buy the finest piece that you can afford at the time. The theory behind the strategy is this: As you get more knowledgeable, the flaws in a piece that is not well-made become more apparent. You will get more long-term enjoyment from an antique that is truly well-made and wonderfully designed.

You're generally better off, investment-wise, to own one top-quality porcelain piece than three lesser-quality pieces or even than three quality pieces in poor condition. The finest quality work usually maintains its value and resells more easily. Lesser quality antiques are harder to sell and may not hold up as well physically.

"The best you can afford" does not necessarily mean the most expensive piece. It means purchasing the best example of the type of antique that you love. If you feel insecure about choosing high-quality antiques, consult with a trusted dealer or an antique-loving friend.

Sometimes people weed through their collection, trading or selling pieces of lesser quality. Other people keep every object that they ever buy. Then they have a timeline of antique acquisitions and maybe a story to go with each piece.

RADAR Alert: The Five Signs of a Valuable Antique

We like to tell novice (and experienced) antique collectors to keep their "RADAR" out for values. RADAR is an acronym that stands for Rarity, Aesthetics, Desirability, Authenticity, and Really great condition.

When you find an antique that meets these five criteria, you've probably found an item that's likely to appreciate in value as the years go by.

Rarity

What constitutes a *rarity?* If no one else on your block owns one, you know that it's worth something. If no one in your zip code has one, it might be worth even more. And if no one in your area code has one, chances are, you have a piece that's pretty valuable.

Collectible or dispensable: How do you tell the difference?

Collectibles are more volatile than antiques. If you want a collectible (an item that is less than 100 years old) that can hold its value and grow up to be a desirable antique (more than 100 years old — see Chapter 1 for a more complete definition), you need to determine the following:

- **Is the item readily available or quite scarce?**
- **Is the item still being made today?**
- **How easy is the item to reproduce?**

  The simpler the piece, the easier it is to reproduce. Pieces with a lot of hand carving, pieces with elaborate handmade decoration, are more complex to reproduce. Still, pieces that are valuable enough can inspire reproductive zeal.
- **How desirable is the item?**

  Collector's plates are an example of the trendy versus the tried and true. The early Christmas plates made by Bing & Grondahl and Royal Copenhagen in the late 19th and early 20th centuries were produced in relatively small limited editions, but the size of the editions began to increase as the years went by. Then these companies began to produce Mother's Day and Father's Day plates, and the next thing you know they were serving up plates for every holiday and special event. Soon lots of other companies got into making collector's plates, sometimes creating so-called "limited editions" of up to 100,000 plates! The earlier plates are rarer and thus have a greater tendency to hold their value, while the plates in large editions are less expensive. Because there are so many, it will take longer for them to become desirable as a collectible.

Of course, something might be rare because it just didn't make it in the marketplace. The piece might be too large, too loud, or too ugly. Still, if *you* like it, well, this aspect of rarity can work to your advantage. Turn to Chapter 5 to find out the negotiating strategy when you fall in love with a rare and odd antique.

How do you know if it's rare? Here are a few of the attributes of a rare piece.

- **Few were made in the first place.** For example, only royalty or the rich could afford gold boxes for snuff, so only a few were made.
- **Few of the original pieces remain.** Some functional and breakable antiques were manufactured in relatively large numbers but are now more scarce, such as crystal stemware, porcelain dishes, and tea sets. But even items that aren't as fragile as glass or ceramics, such as wood tables and cabinets, are at risk of being damaged, and perhaps damaged so badly they are discarded over time.

- **A rare or unusual color or design for a particular type of antique.** Many *mold-blown* (glass that is blown into a mold; for more description, break into Chapter 10) early 19th century cream pitchers are clear. Sapphire-colored cream pitchers from this era are rare. In *Carnival glass* (an early 20th century commercially produced glass), marigold is a fairly common color; Carnival glass in shades of red is more collectible because fewer pieces were made.
- **Uncommon subject matter or style for a particular artist or manufacturer.** Tiffany made few *wisteria lamps* (lampshades that featured wisteria blossoms) because they contained hundreds of pieces of very small glass and the process was extremely time-consuming. These lamps are rarer than Tiffany lamps with poppy and daffodil motifs, although no one would call any Tiffany lamp commonplace. (See Chapter 10 for a look at the wisteria lamp.)
- **Unusual size or shape.** These antiques "shaped up" in unusual ways. Some examples of rarities in terms of size or shape include silver spoons or other utensils with a specialized purpose, such as silver *stuffing spoons* used for stuffing a turkey or goose or *marrow spoons* used for coaxing the marrow out of bones.

  A miniature, fine-quality *salesman's sample* of a piece of furniture from the early 19th century, or a large capacity candle mold for making 20 to 40 candles instead of the more common dozen-capacity molds, also are unusual.
- **Reproducibility.** If a piece is not being reproduced or is difficult to reproduce, its rarity increases.

Aesthetics

You may look at a piece, and think "If only that orange line weren't painted down the middle of it . . ." or, "If only that carving weren't slightly off-center. When you can look at a piece without wishing this or that were different about it, when all the elements of it blend together in perfect harmony, and when it has an overall pleasing appearance, then that item really has it in the aesthetics department.

Some folks believe that an object's aesthetic value is a matter of personal taste. On the other hand, some pieces of art and furniture have almost universal aesthetic appeal. Visiting art galleries and museums is one great way to see antique objects of art that are considered aesthetically pleasing. Books on your areas of interest also will show the better pieces. Watch for the Check It Out icons in each chapter.

Desirability

Desirability is defined by what's in vogue in the current market. A few decades after Tiffany created his now-famous lamps, some people thought of them as gaudy, and so prices were steals by today's standards. Now people covet the artistry that Tiffany displayed. (See Chapter 10 for more about Tiffany and about the woman who was his artistic advocate.)

Authenticity

Is it the real thing or is it a mere shadow of the original? Is it from the time period the seller says it's from? Is it made by the artist or company that is indicated? If it's signed, is the signature real? Is it the type of antique the seller says it is?

Part of the mystery and fun of antiques is separating truth from fiction. As technology and the ability to reproduce items become more advanced, identifying the authentic antique becomes more difficult.

We have clues and tips throughout the chapters to help you analyze whether an antique is authentic.

Here are some examples:

- **Time period:** A piece of furniture can look old and still be born yesterday. For example, you can use old wood and create a new piece of furniture. You can hire one hundred people to trample a new Oriental rug and thus, give it that worn in look.
- **Artist or company:** An object with a Tiffany signature is worth more than an object without one. As you will read in the Chapter 10, a signature is not in itself enough to authenticate a piece. Here's where your specialization comes in: You need to know the types of pieces Tiffany made — the texture of the glass, the colors, and the styles — and make sure that all the elements make sense before you can believe the signature.
- **The type of material:** Is that bronze statue the real thing? Spelter, a combination of metals, can look like bronze. But spelter does not wear as well, is lighter weight, cannot be cast in as fine a detail and is far less valuable. In fact, spelter is referred to as "the poor man's bronze," because it was created for those who admired bronze and couldn't afford it.

Really great condition

In an ideal world, the antique you are contemplating buying would be in exactly the same condition as it was the day it was born. But a lot may have happened in the last hundred or so years to the piece you are hoping to make your own. Here's the rule as far as value goes: The less that was done to the original item to alter it, the more it's worth. That is, the fewer the additions or deletions over the years, the better.

- *Mint condition* means the piece is perfect. For example, with glassware, mint implies no chips, cracks, or breaks. For furniture, mint implies no repairs or missing pieces and an original finish.
- *Excellent condition* means that the piece has minor flaws. Maybe there's a veneer chip on a table top that has been expertly repaired; or perhaps there's a pinhead flake on the base of a porcelain vase.
- *Good condition* means the piece has suffered a few slings and arrows and come through them. Perhaps a porcelain figurine's finger has broken and been repaired by an expert.

Damage affects the value of different categories in different ways. What might be a minor chip or crack in a piece of porcelain can significantly devalue a piece of glass. The porcelain is restorable, in the hands of an expert restorer, and the glass typically is not, with the exception of minor rim chips. We share more details about value and condition when we discuss in detail the specific categories of collecting.

It is polite to stare when it comes to shopping for value in antiques. Look carefully at each item you're considering buying, inside and out, upside down, and right side up. You want to understand the damage and changes the piece has undergone so that you can understand if the price pleases you. Also, as you will read more about in Chapter 5, knowing the flaws of a piece can be a negotiating tool.

Look the piece over extremely carefully. Make a note of every flaw or anomaly. Even minor damage can affect the value of a piece.

We cover the subject of condition in detail in later chapters, but in the meantime, here's a quick guideline for the types of flaws you can look out for when examining antiques:

- Scratches
- Breaks and tears
- Dings and gouges
- Chips

- Cracks
- Fractures
- Signs of repair, such as glue, runny paint, mismatched screws or nails, or putty
- Missing parts
- Discoloration
- On figurines, broken noses or missing fingers

The general rule is: How much does the damage bother you? Anytime a piece sustains damage, its value decreases; but a repair job well done (that is, a repair job that you have to look for to notice, that maintains the integrity of the piece) can often increase the market appeal of a piece.

Chapter 3

God Save the Queen Anne: Basic Furniture Styles

In This Chapter

- Understanding the different furniture styles
- Examining 18th and 19th century furniture
- Identifying chair styles
- Distinguishing between American and English furniture
- Looking at furniture with an antiquing eye

Think of antique furniture as a mystery waiting to be unraveled. Enjoy the sleuth-like process of figuring out when and where furniture was made. Every time you see another piece of furniture, you begin the mystery again.

Furniture styles often began in the king's court and spread through Europe and then later, to America. Because there is so much fascinating furniture and so few pages, we focus on the furniture you'll bump into the most — American, English, and a little French. Because many of the great styles are still reproduced today, after you familiarize yourself with the basic styles, you'll be versed in furniture from the 18th century through the early part of the 20th century. (We're not covering the styles that emerged later, such as Art Deco.)

When you know even a little about furniture, you start looking at the sofas and tables around you in a new way. You see a chair, even a plain old kitchen chair, as more than just a place to sit: You recognize it as a piece of history, art, technology, and culture.

Designing Men: Evolution of Style

Furniture styles often began with the ruling monarch. The monarch had designers, often architects, and a host of workers dedicated to creating elaborate and innovative furnishings. Naturally, the original Louis XV chest (known as a *commode*) would be "fit for a king." Decorated with *ormolu* (gold on bronze) hardware and decorative feet and legs, the commode was probably made of fine kingwood, satinwood, and other exotic woods, complete with fancy inlaid designs.

Local cabinetmakers copied the style for their wealthy clients, using the best woods they could get. Eventually, furniture makers from smaller towns recreated the style, using less gilded bronze, fewer exotic woods, and a plainer design. The more provincial the cabinetmaker, the plainer the piece. Even a farmer might make a facsimile of the design with whatever woods and skills he had.

Several years after a style swept through Europe, it began appearing in America. The American versions had their own distinctions (more about that as we move through this chapter).

The styles of the day weren't neatly measured and tidily labeled. Scholars have gone back and calculated dates, styles, and periods to make sense of furniture evolution. *Style* is the way the furniture looks. *Period* is the time period when each style of furniture was originally put into use and offered for sale. The period often corresponds with a royal reign or sometimes with a cabinetmaker whose name was synonymous with the style (as in *Chippendale*). The style frequently continues to be made long after the period has ended (even up to the present day), so styles often overlap. A piece made during the original time period is called a *period piece.* Period.

The Parts of a Chair

Before you continue your furniture odyssey, check out Figure 3-1, which labels the parts of a chair (at least some of them). Understanding these parts will come in handy as you continue reading this chapter.

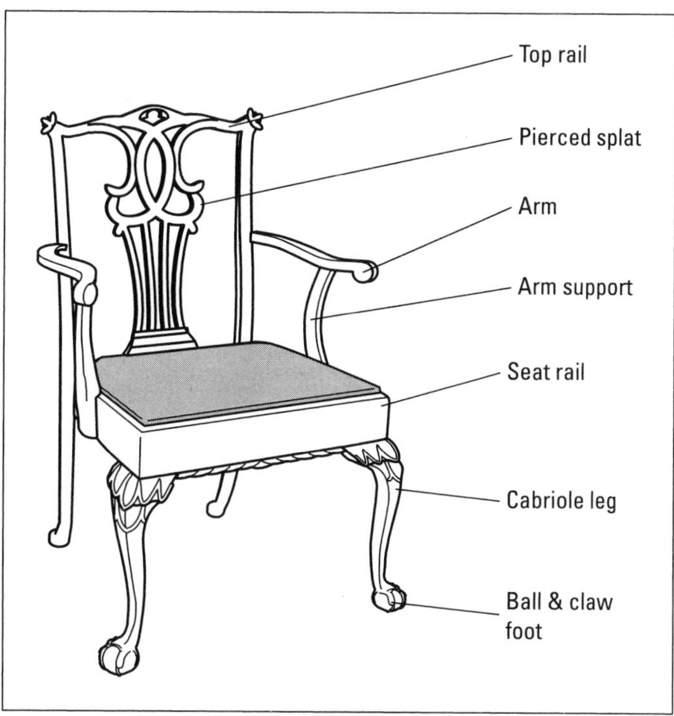

Figure 3-1: Parts of a chair.

Getting a Sense of Style

Because the styles aren't neatly measured and tidily labeled, getting a sense of style in furniture can be confusing. One helpful concept is to notice that styles tend to alternate between the slim, straight, and quietly elegant to the large, curving, and elaborate. Or as some scholars say, styles often move between *Neoclassical* (slim and elegant) and *Non-classical* (larger and more elaborate).

Following is a quick overview of furniture style, starting in the late 17th century. Keep in mind that as you read books about antique furniture, you'll find that different experts use different dates and often different delineations of style. We are giving you one way to look at things, not *the* way.

Note that often you see dates written *c1860.* The *c* refers to *circa,* meaning "about or approximately."

- **Baroque (early 17th to early 18th century):** The Baroque style is heavy and serious. You need several strong people to carry one of these pieces of furniture around. This furniture is carved, ornate, orderly, and symmetrical.
- **Rococo (early 18th century to mid-18th century):** In France, a war ended and people were in the mood to take life with more pleasure. Rococo features sensuous curves with a delightful asymmetry. You see gilding and lots of decorative carvings. The furniture leans more toward comfort and intimacy.
- **Neoclassical (mid-18th century to early 19th century):** Frivolity must meet its balance. Neoclassical moved in to straighten things up. Lines lose their curves, and the golden flowers and ormolu give way to a more mythological bent, harkening back to the great lost days of Rome and Greece. In the Neoclassical period, you can admire a table reminiscent of Greek youths playing their lyres, gaze at a sideboard with ram's head adornment, or sit in a chair with cloven hooves that might have belonged to some mythological centaur.
- **Empire (early 19th century well into the second quarter of the 19th century):** The French version of this style is dramatic and grand, made to glorify the Emperor Napoleon. The Empire period has a military flavor. Some of the furniture is heavy and austere, with rectilinear lines, yet often made with beautiful wood, such as mahogany. The Empire style in England is known as Regency and the Empire style in America is called Classical. The influence of classical design remains apparent in many Empire pieces, especially the formal ones.
- **Victorian, Eclectic, and Revivalist (late 1830s to the end of the 19th century):** Industrialization transformed the world of furniture, making it possible for more people to buy furniture. This period was a time of intense creativity, nostalgia, exaggeration, and experimentation. More was better. The furniture of this period combines the styles of the past and revitalizes them. Within this period, an exciting variety of Revivalist styles, from Gothic to Rococo, emerged.
- **Arts & Crafts (about 1880 to 1915):** Out of the excess, simplicity again demanded its own form. The Arts and Crafts movement decries the overly ornate and bulky Revivalist designs and goes back to basics. This movement touts plain honest lines and reveals construction, showing how the furniture was put together. But simplicity only tastes delicious for so long.
- **Art Nouveau (late 19th century to early 20th century):** Art Nouveau, in a burst of elegant sensuality, emerged to bring back curves. This style is based on natural forms, such as floral and foliate.

Each country interpreted these styles in their own ways. The French were often style setters, followed by the English and then the Americans.

Furniture of the Sweet Seventeen Hundreds

Dating antique furniture (Louis takes Anne to the Sheraton for a nice performance of neoclassical music) is tricky. In the sections that follow, we give you approximate dates in case they help you make sense of things. If the dates are a bore, simply ignore.

Parlez-vous furniture: France in the 1700s

In the 1700s, the French and their monarchs and their monarchs' architects heavily influenced furniture styles. The 1700s waddled in with the Baroque style, which was ponderous, full of bold symmetrical curves and large ornamentation, a style of showing off rather than making comfortable.

The gentler, more graceful Rococo style emerged at the end of Louis XIV's reign, continued to grow during a transitional period, and blossomed during the reign of Louis XV. Rococo is characterized by ornamental curves, asymmetrically arranged, and is rich with carvings of acanthus leaves and scrolled designs shaped like the letters *C* and *S*. The chairs and tables were lighter, more delicate and easier to move around. At last, a person could have a comfortable place to sit.

The wealthy were in the mood for comfort and convenience. They created smaller rooms in their palaces and mansions: a game room, a music room, and a conversation room. The larger furniture that commanded a palatial setting was gradually discontinued in favor of furniture that invited more informal, salon-type conversation.

As the styles changed, the older furniture occupied places of less importance in the court. It might be seen huddled in a corner, instead of displayed in the center of a room. It might be banished to a country estate.

Rococo style

Regence and Louis XV, 1715–1774 (France)

Style changes are gradual. The Regence period between Louis XIV and Louis XV showed the emerging trend to Rococo and the lingering love of Baroque. The cabriole, a gently curved leg inspired by the Chinese, and pictured earlier in Figure 3-1, began to make its way onto furniture, yet the symmetry of Baroque was still in vogue. A carved shell on the apron (the wooden area just below the seat) or on the crest rail on the top front of the chair and turned stretchers between chair legs are other signs of that in-between Regence period.

France led the way in Rococo, with teams of brilliant craftsmen assembled at Versailles by Louis XV. Architects designed the furniture, particularly beds, wall chairs, and console tables, to be part of a grand house. Sometimes, craftsmen painted and parcel gilded (meaning that they only gilded certain areas, usually the raised decoration) the furniture to match the paneling in a certain room. The opulence and ornateness of the furnishings mirrored the opulence of the French court.

Louis' furniture designers popularized the elegant cabriole. If something was "afoot," chances were it was the *sabot,* which was an added bronze cap, often gilded, (covered in gold leaf), and put over the wooden foot.

Rococo pieces are more comfortable and less massive than their predecessors. Yet one wonders: Did Louis have a gilt complex? His furniture factory in Versailles piled ornate gilt bronze on much of his furniture and accessories.

Designer elements on Rococo include:

- Asymmetrical curves and lines with a freer flow (which distinguishes it from the highly symmetrical 19th century Rococo).
- Cabriole leg (an "S" curved leg).
- Acanthus scroll (graceful leaf that often appears on cabriole legs, arm terminals, and bronze mounts).
- S and C curves and/or scroll shapes and designs on knees and feet of furniture.
- Gilt scrollwork.
- Gilt mounts as decorative hardware (to protect the knees and feet of the furniture as they carried it around).
- Marquetry (inlaid figurative designs created from veneer). Sometimes ivory is added to a variety of inlaid woods. *Veneer* is a thin sheet of decorative wood, usually more expensive or rare, which is laid on top of the secondary or support wood.
- Carved flowers, appearing in bouquets on the seat rails or chair crests, or standing out as a single bloom in the floral marquetry on cabinets or commodes.

The chest in Figure 3-2 illustrates some of the characteristics.

An innovation of this period is the bombé (pronounced *bombay*) commode, a real "bombé" shell in its time. This convex curved front was an innovation that demanded master craftsmanship.

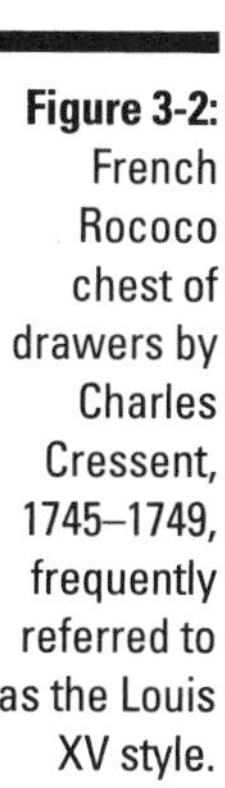

Figure 3-2: French Rococo chest of drawers by Charles Cressent, 1745–1749, frequently referred to as the Louis XV style.

Photo courtesy of the Nelson-Atkins Museum of Art, Kansas City, Missouri.

Neoclassical Style

Louis XVI, 1755–1805 (France)

In one sense, the Neoclassical period straightened things up. After a transition period, Louis XVI shifted away from frivolity and decadence, and tried to restore dignity to the court and glory to the king. Inspired by the excavation of Pompeii, cabinetmakers embraced and enhanced the classical, using exotic woods and carving pillars, brass columns, and mythological creatures. Ovals and ellipses replaced the Rococo curves. Straight lines and symmetry, shown in Figure 3-3, were back in vogue, as were classical tenets such as balance, order, and harmony.

Designer elements in Neoclassical include:

- Rosettes at the top of the legs
- Interlocking circles and cloven-hoofed feet
- Baskets of flowers and bows with crinkly, flowing ribbons
- Corinthian style columns
- Straighter lines and symmetry

In this period, furniture continued its trend toward lightness and featured small tables and writing desks.

Figure 3-3: French Louis XVI ormolu-mounted mahogany commode, last quarter 18th century. Signed by A. Weisweiler.

Photo courtesy of Sotheby's, New York.

The back of a Rococo chair is generally curved. The back of a Neoclassical chair is usually square or rectilinear.

The Guild system was at its peak in France. Although oppressive, these divisions of labor provoked exquisite things. Look for a signature on fine French furniture made in the period from 1743 to about 1789: The French craftsmen were required to sign their work, although foreigners and those working for the government were exempt. Remember, on furniture, a signature isn't necessarily a name: You might find initials, a date, or a monogram.

We include the last few years of the 18th century in the Empire section, coming up after England and America in the 1700s.

By Anne and By George: England in the 1700s

In 18th century England, the cabinetmaker came into his own. In the 17th century, the Guilds controlled furniture making.

As the Guilds lost their power, individual furniture makers were allowed to take commissions from the Crown and from ordinary citizens. With the restrictions lifted, England moved into a creative period in furniture that lasted more than a century.

Baroque to Rococo styles

Queen Anne, 1702–1714 (England)

During the reign of Queen Anne, furniture became simpler and more elegant. Queen Anne furniture is graceful and highlights the natural beauty of the wood. Vase-shaped back splats actually curved to fit the body. Queen Anne furniture frequently features a cabriole leg (with a curve to it) and a pad foot. The primarily walnut furniture is fairly diminutive and reasonably comfortable, not too heavy or overwhelming in size.

Look for a curved top (also called the *crestrail*) on the back of a Queen Anne chair and vase-shaped solid splats in the chair backs (as opposed to the pierced or opened splats that were popular later). *Back splats* are the wood in the center of the chair back. In England, Queen Anne chests were made with thick-cut veneers in figured walnut; American-style Queen Anne chests more frequently used solid woods. (See an American version of a Queen Anne chair later in this chapter.)

Rococo with Baroque

King George I, 1714–1727 (England)

King George I was so Germanic in his tastes and interests that he didn't even speak English. The cabinetmakers during his reign kept the cabriole leg but carved it up. The style becomes more baroque in its approach, with heavy carving taking over much of the furniture. In the late 1720s, the walnut trees were smitten with blight. The Crown let cabinetmakers use mahogany, which had been reserved for shipbuilding. Furniture makers loved the ease of carving the imported mahogany.

During George's era, chairs featured hand carving on the crestrail and on the cabriole legs.

Rococo and Chippendale

King George II, 1727–1760 (England)

Queen Anne first introduced Rococo furniture in England, and George II continued the Rococo trend with an English version that was more restrained than the French. During this time period, Chippendale began his reign, producing elegant carved mahogany furniture, rich with detail.

Chippendale's famous *The Gentleman and Cabinet Maker's Director,* published in 1754, epitomized the Rococo style and its Chinese and Gothic elements and whimsical feel. This collection of design drawings let other cabinetmakers recreate his designs. Some of the designs were so fanciful that they could not easily be made into furniture.

Neoclassical

King George III, 1760–1820 (England)

Although George III lost the American colonies, he presided over one of the golden ages of English furniture making. Along with Chippendale, furniture makers George Hepplewhite, Robert Adam, and Thomas Sheraton designed and made furniture.

The reign of King George III was a time of innovation, overlapping styles, and foreign influence. Robert Adam had taken a "Grand tour" of the Continent as part of his education, and he was influenced by the classical elements he saw in Italy. Chippendale, too, borrowed from other cultures, creating "Chinese Chippendale" chairs, with pagoda shaped backs.

The decorative elements of England's Neoclassical period include:

- Swags
- Medallions
- Shields
- Bellflower inlay
- Feathers
- Exotic woods, such as satinwood, amboyna, and yew
- Reeded legs
- Square chair backs
- Baluster forms
- Pedestal base dining tables
- Inlaid colorful and exotic woods and painting on flat surfaces

When the popular and admired Admiral Lord Nelson died during the 1805 Battle of Trafalgar (which crushed the French and Spanish fleets and kept Napoleon from invading England), England went into mourning. Black bands adorned everything, including the furniture. Black inlay and ebonized furniture became popular during this period of mourning.

During the Neoclassical period, a passion to embrace the past straightened up furniture and gave it a classic motif. English architects and designers followed France in bringing Roman and Greek symbols into buildings, furniture, and decor. Each designer created a look he was particularly known for. Here are a few of the innovations that came to life in this era:

- **Chippendale** created chests on chests and used expensive woods and finishes. Renowned for his chairs, Chippendale designed chairs with a tapered back, wider at the top than at the bottom. He designed numerous variations of ladder-back, ribbon-back, and tassel-back chairs.

  Chippendale is associated with the *ball and claw foot,* derived from the Oriental design of a dragon's claw holding a ball or a pearl (although this foot was in use long before Chippendale came into his own). Chippendale preferred mahogany for formal pieces and also used walnut and maple for less formal furniture. For country Chips (through the late 18th century), pine and oak were popular. Chippendale often featured decorative brass pulls on drawers, shell carvings, and both solid and open carved *(pierced)* fretwork.

- **Robert Adam** had a great influence on England's Neoclassical period. He made classical ornamentation come to life, with graceful lines and attention to detail. As an architect, Robert Adam designed every portion of the building, from the outside structure, down to the doorknobs. Gilded and painted furniture increased in popularity. He still used dark mahogany, but the finer pieces had a satinwood veneer or a veneer of a more golden colored mahogany. Low-relief carving on furniture legs and inlay designs blossomed. Adam introduced the semi-circular commode (a type of chest of drawers).

- **George Hepplewhite** also emerged during this period. His book on furniture making had a worldwide distribution. Hepplewhite designs are slender with little carving. The chairs have a square, tapered leg with open chair backs. Some Hepplewhite innovations include:

  - **Shield back chair.** A shape literally based on the shields carried in classical battles.

  - **Sideboard.** Inspired by a Robert Adam side table, Hepplewhite designed a sideboard that has a center drawer, flanked by a deep drawer on either side. Frequently the drawers had dividers for bottles or lead lining for ice. Used in dining rooms and foyers, people kept serving pieces, tea services, elaborate knife boxes, or a vase of flowers on top.

- **Pembroke Table:** This table had a center section and two drop leaves, which were supported by wooden brackets so that the leaves could raise and lower. The table, shown in Figure 3-4, was named after Lady Pembroke, who supposedly was the first one to order it. Hepplewhite published the design for the Pembroke table in his *Cabinet-Maker and Upholsterer's Guide* of 1788.

  When you look for Hepplewhite, beware of *Boston fakers.* This furniture was made from the last years of the 19th century through the early decades of the 20th century when Hepplewhite resurfaced in popularity. Cabinetmakers bought decrepit pieces of furniture and made *Charles Street specials,* old wood remade into new pieces. Sometimes they changed woods on English pieces to look more American, and thus more valuable. Writing desks were popular pieces to fake.

- **Sheraton's** neoclassical style embraced urns, cupids, gods and goddesses, animals, mythological creatures, and "swag and garland" designs. The legs are predominately turned, rather than tapered. (Hepplewhite tended toward square tapered legs.)

  What would June and Ward Cleaver have done without Sheraton? He developed the twin bed. He also designed square back chairs, with midriff backs, that do not join the seats. And he "revealed the construction," sometimes letting the seat frame show. Sheraton's formal case pieces were often highlighted with inlaid designs.

When you're first studying the furniture of this period, don't worry about distinguishing the Sheratons from the Hepplewhites. Focus on the broader elements of style that characterize this time of honoring the classical.

Pilgrims' progress: American furniture after 1650

By the mid-17th century, the Pilgrims began making their own furniture, which was based on English prototypes. These early furniture makers, known as *joiners,* made their furniture mostly of oak. The pieces were heavily constructed and featured shallow carvings or turned decoration.

To see what kinds of furniture colonists had, look at the public records for the times, which have the inventories listed in wills and probates. These archives give you a fascinating look at what was in the house and what was considered valuable. In general, the furniture wasn't as valuable as textiles, porcelain, and silver during most of the 17th century. In the 1600s, the person of means might have some chairs, a multi-purpose chest or two, and a table of some kind.

Figure 3-4: Lady Pembroke was supposedly the first person to order this "Pembroke table."

William and Mary style

1690–1720 (America)

With William and Mary, furniture "turned" into a more delicate style (see Figure 3-5). The turned legs (meaning the wood was shaped while it is revolving) were thinner, more spindly, and more likely to break. William and Mary style concentrated on applied decoration, rather than carved decor. They used veneers on the fancier pieces and liked to paint the wood dark, to resemble ebony.

By the 1700s, the highboy (a chest on chest with legs) replaced the cupboard as the finest piece of furniture in the house. Even more of a status symbol was a four poster bed, complete with canopy and elaborate hangings. Lowboys and chests of drawers came into use. Tea tables and gateleg tables emerged.

Figure 3-5: William and Mary Bannister Back Side Chair, made in NYC, maple wood painted black circa 1690 – 1700.

Courtesy Bernard & S. Dean Levy, Inc., New York.

When you look at William and Mary highboys, pay special attention to those slender turned legs. When you fill these chests on chests with weighty items, they have the potential for a broken leg. Look carefully for damage, repairs, and replacements.

Queen Anne style

1730–1760 (America)

Queen Anne entered America with a rounded look, less emphasis on applied decoration (decoration added onto the furniture), and increased emphasis on form. The cabriole gave the furniture more of a solid leg to stand on (see Figure 3-6). More pieces survive from this period because they are better built and they were built for more people. The colonists were feeling increasingly prosperous. The American version of Queen Anne included classical and Oriental motifs. The Oriental influence showed up in *japanning,* decorative art that imitated Oriental lacquering style, and in fairly plain brass handles on furniture, which echoed the simple grace of Oriental style.

Figure 3-6: Queen Anne side chair, Newport, Rhode Island, circa 1735.

Courtesy Bernard & S. Dean Levy, Inc., New York.

Here are a few selected examples of Queen Anne in America:

- Tea drinking was a luxury, so having a **tea table** meant you could afford the china, silver, and the tea. The table said, "The people who live in this house have money and taste, and are savvy about what's currently in vogue in London." There are relatively few tea tables available today because fewer people could afford that ceremony.
- The **tilt top table** was great for small rooms, with its "up against the wall" abilities.
- The **pole screen** kept women glamorous and warm at the same time. This adjustable needlepoint screen had a tripod base and moved up and down a pole. It served to shield women's faces from becoming overly heated from the fire (and thus kept their thick make-up from liquefying).
- The **Windsor design** made chairs accessible to more people. Windsors were made using locally grown woods. The parts were easier to "mass produce" and they could be put together later. In America, wheelrights, the craftsmen who were constantly on a roll making wagon wheels, helped make Windsor chairs. Wheelwrights were used to bending wood and chose wood that could be steamed and bent easily. The bows and spindles were usually made of ash or hickory; the legs and stretchers

were most often made from maple. The seat, which was about two inches thick, was usually of soft pine or poplar, which was easy to shape with the hand plane. Seats were also made from chestnut, basswood, and oak. Need more "clues" about Windsor chairs? Go to Chapter 14.

Philadelphia, New York, and Boston became centers of furniture making. New England cabinetmakers favored walnut, cherry, and maple, and New York and Philadelphia artisans stayed with walnut and expensive imported mahogany. Cabinetmakers continued to make forms of English furniture, with American woods and with some American stylistic changes in design.

If you see a style of furniture that you recognize, such as a Chippendale chair with ball and claw feet, and the price seems too good to be true, an alarm should go off. Don't think, "Wow, I'm getting a great bargain!" Think, "Why is this so reasonable?" What are the problems and restorations you're not noticing? Be cautious. Ask the dealer why the price is low. Ask if it is a "period" piece or Colonial Revival piece or even from the 20th century. (See later on in this chapter for more about Colonial Revival.)

Chippendale style

1755–1790 (America)

With the Chippendale style, you see more carving, greater use of the ball and claw foot, and a Chinese influence. The *splats* (the wood that appears in the center of chair backs) of the chairs are generally pierced, with more of a design cut into them. The rounded top of the Queen Anne chair now becomes angular. George Washington really did sit in Chippendale chairs, as you can see in Figure 3-7.

Cabinetmakers from different countries and different traditions, living in different parts of America, made different kinds of feet. When you really study 18th century American furniture, you learn to get a "foothold" on regional furniture making. You can sometimes determine where a piece was made based on its foot.

To really get a toehold on American furniture, get *Field Guide to American Antique Furniture,* by Joseph T. Butler (published by Henry Holt and Company). This book is rich with line drawings on all kinds of furniture and its details, including legs and feet, and gives a good survey of American furniture.

Figure 3-7: Chippendale Side Chairs, Philadelphia, Pennsylvania, circa 1760. From a set of chairs from George Washington's residence at 120 High St. in Philadelphia and the second White House, leased in 1791 by Washington.

Courtesy Bernard & S. Dean Levy, Inc., New York.

Federal style

1790–1815 (America)

The Federal period, referring to the time in America after 1789, coincides with the Neoclassical periods of England and France and includes a variety of styles, such as Adam, Sheraton, Hepplewhite (shown in Figures 3-8 and 3-9), and Duncan Phyfe, who was the first American furniture maker to have a style named for him. During this period, the legs become more tapered, and furniture takes on more delicate proportions and has more adornment with brass mounts, inlay, and veneer.

Because people had fewer rooms with more purposes, furniture was made to go against the wall. That's why the tables fold and tilt. Most dining tables from this period can be collapsed down or put against the wall so that the dining room can also serve as the ballroom.

If you want to purchase quality early American furniture, the Federal and early Empire periods are a good place to start. Frequently, you can purchase good quality Federal era pieces, such as Hepplewhite card tables and Sheraton chairs, for far less than furniture from Queen Anne and Chippendale periods of the same form and quality.

Figure 3-8: Federal sidechair, 1790-1805, frequently referred to as the *Hepple-white style.*

Courtesy The Nelson-Atkins Museum of Art, Kansas City, Missouri.

Figure 3-9: Sheraton mahogany side chair, attributed to Samuel McIntire, Salem, Massachusetts, circa 1800–1810.

Courtesy of Israel Sack, Inc., N.Y.C.

Telling Apart English and American Furniture

How do you tell the difference between English and American furniture? And why would you want to?

The English initially had more furniture. Because there is less high style American furniture and more people who seem to want it, early American furniture usually is more expensive.

Here are some ways to tell the two apart:

- Generally speaking, Americans use solid woods more often. (They had more natural resources.)
- The English use more veneer (as do the French).
- When you are dealing with a case piece (anything with drawers), open the drawers and look at the side construction.
  - English dovetails from after Queen Anne tend to be neat, precise, and small. American dovetails are larger. (As cabinetmaking grew more sophisticated, dovetails from both countries became smaller.)
  - In American case pieces, the interior secondary woods are frequently chunkier than in English furniture. Drawer linings are typically thicker in American pieces because America had more wood. The thicker wood can make American furniture more substantial.
- In the Neoclassical and Federal periods, American furniture tends to be more individualistic, even a little quirky, especially when it wasn't made in the major cities.
- English chairs are wider and squatter than American chairs.
- English makers more frequently used dustboards (thin planks) between drawers, and Americans often did not.
- Both the English and American cabinetmakers were cost conscious and sensible people. They didn't use expensive wood where it wouldn't be seen. They used secondary wood (less expensive) on backs of cabinets, dustboards between the drawers, and all the supportive timber. English used oak for drawer linings and backboards and sometimes used pine. American cabinet makers most often used pine and poplar.

For a wonderful way to learn about the "good, better, and best" features of American furniture, get the current edition of *Fine Points of Furniture,* by Albert Sack (Crown Publishers). This book contains a series of well-captioned illustrations that show you the differences in excellent and good quality furniture. Use this book to help train yourself to look for quality furniture.

Revival of the Fittest: Evolving 1800s and Energetic Early 1900s

A revolutionary society seems to hasten an evolution in furniture. In the early 19th century, France, still leading European fashions, was recovering from the revolution. Previously, there was a time gap between the new styles and when they were adopted in different countries. But with the Empire style of Napoleonic France, the word was getting across the English Channel and over to America in short order. People instantly adopted the new styles.

From the 1830s on, industrialization begins to make its mark on furniture. Some antique dealers specialize in furniture pre-1830, believing that furniture quality is generally not as fine after that date. Other dealers and specialists believe that furniture of these Revivalist eras possess a great deal of craftsmanship and creativity. As you study this time period, you will find that some furniture is totally handmade, some is a combination of machine-made and handcrafted, some is totally machine-made.

Even though the mass-produced furniture with no handcrafting is less valuable than furniture with hand workmanship, many consider it a better purchase than modern machine-made furniture. The furniture still has age, it still has patina and history, and it still has more of a chance of retaining its value.

Vive La Furniture: France in the 1800s

Following the French Revolution, the cache of craftsmen that had worked for Louis XV and Louis XVI dissipated. After Louis XVI lost his head, the guilds dismantled. More people were able to afford furniture. This leavening of society and escalating of mass-production created its own furniture revolution. With industrialization, furniture became accessible and affordable, since more people could produce more furniture for more people.

Directoire to Empire to Restoration to Louis Philippe

1793–1848 (France)

Directoire was a transitional bridge between Neoclassical and Empire, a post revolution period of straight lines, few mounts, and geometric shapes.

Empire, the last great style before the Industrial Revolution, was influenced by the French campaign in Egypt and archeological discoveries in Egypt, Rome, and ancient Greece. Moral values and the ancient and glorious spirit of antiquity were evoked, with objects being large scale and laden with classical mounts, including swans, bees, ram's heads, palmettes, and Egyptian symbols (see Figure 3-10). This was the furniture of warriors. Marquetry and parquetry were forgotten; furniture developed a more austere look, which included large expanses of unrelieved wood, rosewood and dark mahogany veneers, gilt decoration in classical motifs, and brass inlay. Black and gold furniture was popular. People used mirrors to make rooms look larger. Beds were put against walls and surrounded by canopies. Lion's head, claws, and eagles haunted the furniture.

Design elements of Empire include classical, allegorical gilt-bronze mounts, drawn from Greek or Roman sculpture.

Figure 3-10: French Empire ormolu-mounted chiffonier first quarter 19th century, signed by Gamichon.

Photo courtesy of Sotheby's, New York.

The Restoration period, a tame time with little adornment, blends into the Directoire.

During Louis Philippe's era, 1830–1848, machinery was starting to make its mark on furniture production. While in some ways, originality declined, this era still produced some beautiful furniture. Wonderful woods with simple clean lines emerged. You might see an elegant combination of curved and straight lines and wonderfully figured wood. Louis Phillippe's era focused on the natural figuring of the wood as the prime element of beauty. Craftsmen created multi-purpose furniture designed for small apartments, such as chests of drawers that transform into writing desks.

Second Empire style

1848–1870 (France)

During the Second Empire period, France produced some of its most exquisite pieces of furniture. Makers such as Linke kept the quality of furniture lines while adjusting to the industrial age.

Francois Linke made three different qualities of furniture. By adjusting the level of craftsmanship, number of mounts, quantity of inlay, and complexity of form, he could make furniture for the masses as well as custom-make furniture for the elite.

True to the revivalist spirit of the times, Linke created furniture by using elements from Louis XIV, XV, and XVI styles, complete with gilt, mounts, and the works, as well as simpler, less expensive pieces.

During this period of Napoleon III, you will typically not have a maker indicated on French furniture. Most but not all Linke is signed. But just because a piece of French furniture is signed *F. Linke* doesn't mean it's worth a fortune; it could be one of his lesser pieces.

English furniture in the 1800s

In a time period known for its heavy rituals and rules, furniture was exploding with experimentation and creativity. Makers tried new mediums, such as papier-mâché and tole, and gave fascinating twists to the old classics.

Regency style

1812–1837 (England)

King George was too demented to rule, so the Prince Regent took over. This period occurs in conjunction with the American Federal style. It's a time of smaller furniture, elegant lines, brass and ebony, and sphinx heads. As the years went on, the furniture got heavier. George III died; the reign passed to George IV and then to his brother William IV, who ruled until Victoria ascended the throne.

Victorian style

Late 1830s through turn of the century (England)

Victoria ruled until the end of the century. Her style was heavy and fussy. Because of the machine age, the style was also widely distributed.

Victorian is a series of revivals. Many styles come into play. Some scholars describe this as a creative time, a time of simultaneously reaching back to the old and forward to the future.

The Victorian era emphasized etiquette and ritualization: Everything, including houses, their rooms, furniture, and accessories, had a certain purpose. Though the home-shopping channel was not yet a glint in anyone's eye, industrialization meant more goods and lower costs: the birth of the consumer! People could go to the department store to shop or buy things by mail.

During this era, the parlor really came into its own. A seven-piece parlor suite, including a gentleman's chair, a lady's chair, four reception chairs, and a sofa, became popular.

Formal Victorian furniture was most often made of mahogany in England, and occasionally made of rosewood. The style was obsessively ornate and disdainful of comfort, reflecting the severity of the era. Understanding Victorian furniture is understanding an attitude: "You will be decorated and you will be uncomfortable!"

Gothic and other Revivalist styles

1840s onward (England)

Gothic Revival inspired massive, carved furniture, with revealed construction (construction that you can see, such as pegged joints or hinges on the outside, as part of the design). By the 1860s and 1870s, Gothic was reforming, with less carving and a less ecclesiastical feel (that is, less carving of gargoyles and arches, and less of a church-like look). Reformed gothic had a more lean and hungry look, being straighter and more muscular, with less superfluous decoration. Other Revivalist styles includes Rococo and Renaissance. For more about these styles, see the American versions later in this chapter.

Arts and Crafts style

1860s (England)

During the Industrial period, William Morris and Charles Eastlake worried that cheap, mass-produced furnishings would have a negative effect on the human condition as well as the social aesthetic. Morris advocated handmade craftsmanship. But because Morris's furniture was handmade and finely crafted, it was also more expensive. Ironically, only the rich could afford to purchase his finest creations.

Morris's furniture consists of simple forms, often based on earlier traditions. Some of the pieces are decorated with artist-painted panels, a precursor of the "art furniture" movement.

What Americans call Eastlake is typically factory-made, without the same craftsmanship or "honesty" that Charles Eastlake recommended. Eastlake came out against over carved and over curved mass-produced furniture. He was not a great success in England and there is little Eastlake furniture of English origin. But in America, Eastlake was a smash hit (see Figure 3-11 of an American version of Eastlake) and set the trend for the factory production in the Midwest from the 1870s onward. Since his furniture was straight with little carving, Eastlake was the American mass manufacturers' dream. The pseudo-Eastlake (mass-produced) frequently had glued-on molding and inferior craftsmanship. Still, some is well-made, and much is available.

Figure 3-11: This washstand by the Berkey & Gay Furniture Co. circa 1880, shows the influence of Charles Eastlake's design principles as they were adapted for American machine manufacture.

Photo courtesy of the Collections of the Public Museum of Grand Rapids, Grand Rapids,MI.

Here are some easy tips for identifying Eastlake:

- Look for straight lines and flat surfaces. Naturalistic carving gave way to more stylized, geometric, and linear designs.
- Look for construction clues, such as exposed mortise and tenon joints. Many mass-produced pieces have dowel construction with glued on fake mortise and tenon. Mass-produced Eastlake furniture has a lot of extra things, such as spindle galleries and moldings that have been lost or removed. Look for holes. Look for losses.

Aesthetic Movement

1880s (England)

The Aesthetic Movement overlapped the Arts and Crafts movement. Aesthetics believed in integrating art into daily life. They thought people could be improved and elevated by being in a home that was filled with beauty. Whistler was part of the Aesthetic Movement, a fine artist who painted furniture, designed rooms, and did whole interiors. Oscar Wilde traveled through America, giving a series of lectures on aesthetics. Gilbert and Sullivan's musical *Patience,* made fun of these artsy aesthetic types.

Focusing on simplicity of form and honesty of construction, aesthetic designers, such as E.W. Godwin in England, created some of the most original and striking designs. The furniture was lighter than the Arts and Crafts style and used only as much wood as necessary. Like Eastlake, the Aesthetics kept things "straight," not wanting to torture wood into curves. Both styles used design elements based on natural forms, such as floral and foliage elements.

The new Japanese influence spilled into the Aesthetic Movement. People were taken by the extraordinary beauty and simplicity the Japanese designs expressed. This Eastern influence shows up in Aesthetic furniture in ebonized finishes, flat fretwork carving which could be done by machine, revealed construction, and Oriental motifs on "art furniture." Godwin coined the term *Anglo Japanese* for this style of Aesthetic furniture.

Ebonized furniture was popular primarily in the 1880s. Some of the ebonizing may have been removed to reveal its base woods, such as cherry, walnut, and mahogany. If you're looking for something original, look in crevices and crannies to see if the piece was originally ebonized.

A fling with Empire and reviving again: America in the 1800s

In the 1800s, America was coming into its own, furniture-wise. After a flirtation with Empire, Americans went through an intricate series of Revival periods, which ran around the same time as the Victorian Era in England. People had money and machinery, and they were motivated to be bigger and better than their neighbors. This is a catchall period, a series of revivals, filled with energy and experimentation. You will see this time period in America also called *Victorian.* Often, the periods were evolving simultaneously. The dates are approximate.

Classical Furniture or American Empire style

1815–1850 (America)

The Neoclassical focus of the Federal period moved into the American Empire or what people are starting to call Classical furniture. This Classical reign echoed the European fascination with Greek and Roman classical motifs such as lyres, cornucopias, and hairy paw feet.

Duncan Phyfe was important in introducing this style of furniture. Stenciled and "fancy" chairs emerged during this period. Often of Sheraton style, they featured caned or rushed seats and could include patriotic shapes in the structure, such as an eagle back.

The Hitchcock Company mass-produced fancy chairs, with turned front stretchers and painted decor, often marked with the company name. These "knock-down" chairs were widely distributed, because their parts were shipped separately and assembled at the sellers. They often featured gilded paint decorations and stenciling.

Revivalist (Some Call this Victorian) style

Late 1830s through the turn of the century (America)

This is such an inventive, creative, and chaotic time that even figuring out how to label the period is complex. Some pieces of furniture are totally machine-made; others have lots of great hand carving. For this reason, you may see significant price differences in the pieces of this period.

Nineteenth century furniture that's totally machine-made can sometimes be cheaper than today's machine-made furniture and still give you a sense of history and mystique.

Beginning in the year 2000, the earliest furniture of the 19th century becomes two centuries old. As we advance into the 21st century, 19th century revival furniture could become increasingly venerated and sought after, embued with more of a sense of history and romance.

Here are a few ways to distinguish the higher quality furniture:

- Look for tool marks that indicate the human touch. (See Chapter 4 for ways to mark the spots.)
- Look for imperfections in the carving. When you start really looking at hand carving, you'll be delighted to see how easily you can spot the flaws, particularly with the more floral and abundant carvings.

Most revival furniture was really on a roll. Typically, English and American revival parlor furniture, chairs, and even cabinets had casters. If you don't see casters, look for the holes where the casters were attached. If you don't find holes, you might have a repro piece of furniture. Revival pieces from 1920 onwards typically do not have casters.

These Revivalist styles include furniture that often blends machine work and hand work. Scholars are still studying their evolution. The terms we use to identify these styles are art history terms that came into being in the 20th century. The dates indicate the years when the style was at its peak. These styles continued to be produced.

Gothic Revival

mid-19th century (America)

Even though we don't live in a land with ruins of medieval castles, Americans still have inherited a Gothic heritage through European ancestry. American Gothic Revival furniture was inspired by the fashion in London and Paris. This massive and imposing furniture, represented in Figure 3-12, with its pointed arches and finials, mostly held court in the hall and library. Architects designed much of the American Gothic of the period, often for specific buildings. The furniture mirrored the architectural details of its setting.

Nineteenth century Gothic Revival from this period, is typically dark and ponderous looking oak, mahogany, or walnut with a strong ecclesiastical form.

During a second Gothic Revival period, (see the Aesthetic Movement later in this chapter) you see lighter wood tones, more gilt, with less of an ecclesiastical look and more of an architectural sense.

Figure 3-12: American Gothic Revival bookcase designed by Gustave Herter 1852–1853.

Courtesy Nelson-Atkins Museum of Art, Kansas City, Missouri.

Rococo Revival

1840–1865 (America)

The fun and rounded extravagance of Rococo was enormously popular in mid-18th century. Intricate carvings of birds, flowers, and animals gave the furniture a flavor reminiscent of French aristocracy. The original Rococo needed only a hint of carving and was lighter in wood and design. Revival Rococo overflowed with massive carvings and heavier woods.

How do you tell the revived Rococo from Louis XV Rococo? Revival furniture is generally made of heavier wood and has more carving.

During this time, John Henry Belter, a German immigrant who settled in New York City, produced some magnificent seven-piece parlor suites, which no respectable upper-class household could be without (see Figure 3-13). Belter didn't invent lamination, but he used it quite gracefully with his Rococo furniture. Laminated wood features thin sheets of wood, glued together, with the grain at right angles, which makes the wood stronger than a single piece of wood of the same thickness. This strength allowed the wood to be highly carved. Belter featured naturalist designs rather than the S and C curves and created a lot of parlor furniture.

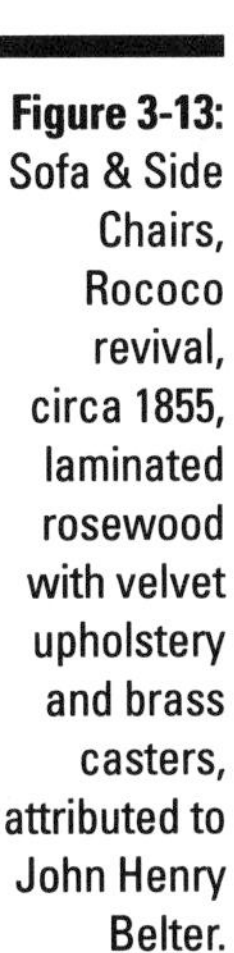

Figure 3-13: Sofa & Side Chairs, Rococo revival, circa 1855, laminated rosewood with velvet upholstery and brass casters, attributed to John Henry Belter.

Coutesty of High Museum of Art, Atlanta, Ga., Virginia Carroll Crawford Collection.

Renaissance Revival

1860–1880 (America)

Enough of curves and asymmetry. Renaissance Revival is more chaotic than the curving 19th century Rococo, more of an eclectic combination of various architectural elements.

Square back chairs, flattened arches, pediments, finials, straight backs, and ebonized surfaces were just some of the features of this massive and elaborate style. Companies in Grand Rapids, such as Berkey & Gay, and other

Furniture for the masses and the maids

During the same period of time these Revivalist pieces were being made, there was a large industry centered around the creation of cottage furniture.

Cottage furniture, 1850 to the end of the century, was factory-made furniture, relatively inexpensive, often painted, and sometimes stained. Like the Windsor chair, cottage furniture was for the masses and the maids: Middle class folk bought it for their homes; rich folk furnished their maids' quarters with cottage furniture — and also their summer houses.

furniture factories across the country, mass-produced Renaissance Revival. This furniture, shown in Figure 3-14, brought together the essence of the Victorian era, with its massive proportions and wealth of details and its admiration of technology. Art historians often define Renaissance Revival by its large scale.

Because of its straight lines, Renaissance Revival furniture was easy to mass-produce. This furniture went through a period of being despised and now it's becoming more desirable. You can find low to mid range pieces at a cost that is often less than comparable contemporary furniture.

Grand Rapids was once hailed as America's "Paris of furniture design." If you are one of the thousands of people who have or want revival furniture, you need *Grand Rapids Furniture: The Story of America's Furniture City,* by Christian Carron (published by The Public Museum of Grand Rapids). This book has great pictures, wonderful hints for furniture ID, and histories of the more than 800 Grand Rapids furniture companies.

Figure 3-14: Renaissance Revival library table, oak, aspen, with gilding, American, probably New York City, circa 1882–1892.

Courtesy of the High Museum of Art, Atlanta, Ga., Virginia Carroll Crawford Collection.

Colonial Revival

1880s–present day (America)

The Colonial Revival began on a small scale after the Centennial and peaked during the first quarter of the 20th century. Though these are not technically Colonial styles, the term has recently been re-introduced. For most of the 20th century, many people inaccurately referred to this furniture as

Centennial furniture. The term "Centennial" is too general because the furniture was not necessarily made at the time of the Centennial and is not necessarily a 100-year-old copy of any particular style of the 17th or 18th century.

Essentially, Colonial Revival features adaptations of earlier American furniture, including Queen Anne, Chippendale, Sheraton, Hepplewhite, and Empire (see Figure 3-15). The more valuable pieces copy the original design of a hard-to-find period antique.

Look at Colonial Revival next to its original and you will learn a lot about telling the differences between machine-made and handcrafted pieces. Construction methods, tool marks, types of wood, and intricacy and depth of carvings are among the clues that let you know the machine-made from the handcrafted.

Colonial Revival Furniture with Prices, by David Lindquist and Caroline C. Warren (published by Wallace-Homestead Books), is a great resource for understanding Colonial Revival furniture. Many detailed photographs point out the differences between machine-carved and hand-carved pieces. You get good pictures and more information about the manufacturers.

Figure 3-15: Desk, in the Colonial Revival style, by R. J. Horner, New York City, 1890–1895.

Photo courtesy of the Brooklyn Museum, Brooklyn, N.Y., Albert T. and Caroline S. Zoebisch Fund.

Aesthetic Movement

The mid-1870s to the early 1900s

The American Aesthetic Movement (some call this the Home Art movement) began around the time of the American Centennial and affected taste at every level of society, from the interiors of mansions, including the White House, to the dinnerware on the table of middle-class homes.

The Aesthetic Movement is both complicated and creative. Inspired by William Morris and the English Arts and Crafts period, the movement began as a modern Gothic Revival, which is different from the earlier Gothic Revival. At first, the furniture followed what Eastlake proposed: straight lines, shallow carving, and minimal inlay. But it became extremely ornate after a few years, with some of the better craftsman from New York and Philadelphia creating real works of art with painted scenes and rich carvings. Daniel Pabst is one of the most noted cabinetmakers of this period.

After the initial modern Gothic phase, the Far East came into play. Herter Brothers of New York City, as shown in Figure 3-16, were among the companies incorporating Anglo Japanese styles. Herter Brothers featured lots of inlay in their furniture.

Figure 3-16: Aesthetic Movement Herter Bros. Cabinet, New York City, circa 1875.

Photo courtesy of The Brooklyn Museum, Brooklyn, NY, H. Randolph Lever Fund

Also watch for these names in innovative furniture: William Wooton and his unique patented desks and George Hunzinger with his line of unusual patented chairs.

Victorian Furniture, by David Lindquist and Caroline C. Warren (published by Wallace Homestead Books), gives you the flavor of this era in an interesting, organized, and informative way. The pictures are well-labeled and help you distinguish one revival from another.

Arts and Crafts: On a mission

Late 19th century to early 20th century (America)

The American Arts and Crafts movement grew from English Arts and Crafts, which was a reaction against the industrial revolution and ornate Victorian designs. You find overlap between the Aesthetic and the Arts and Crafts movement. Honesty, craftsmanship, and simplicity in design were its creed. The movement was a reaction to the mass production of the Industrial Revolution. Arts and Crafts looked back to the aesthetics of medieval times for handcraftsmanship and quality.

One of the most enduring things to come out of the Arts and Crafts movement is Mission furniture. Gustav Stickley was the first person to design a line

100 Years of Togetherness: The Philadelphia Centennial

The 1876 Philadelphia Centennial International Exposition showed America what was going on in the wide world. The Centennial was a 19th century media event, with lots of newspaper coverage and ten million people attending.

Even though the Japanese were already known and admired by many, the Centennial exhibit brought the Japanese style to the attention of a great many more people. Americans were taken with the quiet elegance of the Japanese art and design.

The 1870s was a real time of looking backward at a simpler time. Antique collecting became fashionable. The simple grace of the Japanese, the massive majesty of the Gothic and the handcrafted aura of early Colonial all were attempts to stay in touch with craftsmanship and "easy and better times."

Even then, an increasingly complex society was brimming with immigrants and urbanization; people were on the quest to "simplify their lives." This time period inspired delicate Anglo-Japanese ebonized furniture. Oriental rugs were popular, as was porcelain. The decorating trend was for a complete atmosphere, which included patterned wall and ceiling papers. Things sparkled with iridescent paints in the wallpapers, metals, and mother-of-pearl in the furniture. Herter and Tiffany did entire interiors.

of Mission furniture, which he initially called *the new furniture.* At his Craftsman Furniture Company, he used machines and created a design he felt was simple and honest. The only decorative details were construction elements, exposed joinery such as exterior hinges, pegging, and mortise and tenon joints. Gustav Stickley was influenced by the English Arts and Crafts movement and the simplicity of the Shakers. He embraced the machine and used machinery to relieve the worker's drudgery.

Gustav Stickley tried to get this new style of furniture called *Craftsman* style furniture because he didn't like the term *Mission.* But his terminology never stuck.

Stickley's furniture designs were so popular that by the early 1900s, virtually every furniture company in the country made some version of Mission furniture (see Figure 3-17). Stickley designed his own houses (Craftsman homes), had his own department store, where he sold everything for the home, and published magazines on how to live — he was the Martha Stewart of his day.

Other Stickleys were also in the furniture business. Gustav's brothers, along with the uncle who had taught all the Stickley boys furniture-making, joined the bandwagon and also made Mission furniture.

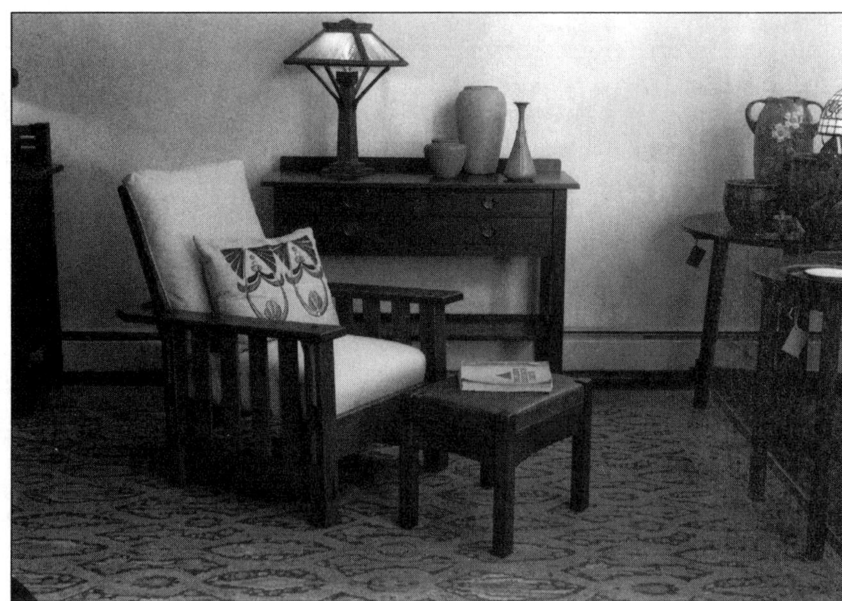

Figure 3-17: Room setting with Mission furniture, including Jim Young Co. Morris Chair, Mission oak lamp, L. & J.G. Stickley footstool, a Stickley Brothers Co. server, and selected American art pottery.

Courtesy of JMW Gallery, Boston, Massachusetts.

How to choose antique Mission furniture

Because so much contemporary Mission furniture is available, it is vital to know and trust your antique seller and to have a guarantee with return privileges.

When you buy furniture, you are juggling form, condition, and maker.

"Gustav Stickley piece" means furniture made in his Craftsman workshop. Look at old Craftsman catalogues and study the furniture styles. Financially, you're better off buying the old, since the old Mission pieces retain equity and new pieces do not. Find these reprint catalogues in bookstores or through antique magazines.

Here are some tips for analyzing and selecting Mission furniture:

- Form affects the desirability and value of the piece.
- Munton Stickley bookcases and china cabinets have *muntons* (strips of wood) dividing the pieces of glass. With lesser makers, the munton look is merely an overlay. Look inside the glass door, to see if wood divides the glass.
- *Slats,* the strips of wood between the arm and the seat, affect the value of the chair. Generally, vertical slats are more valuable than no slats under the arms.
- The classic Arts and Crafts style for a sofa is an even arm, where the arms are the same height as the back.
- A five-leg table, which is four legs plus a center leg, is generally more desirable than the more common pedestal base.
- Look for replaced wood. Check slats, legs, rockers, arms for wood that does not quite "fit in."
- The finishing touches are important when talking about condition. Original finish is most desirable. Refinished takes second place. Look underneath the furniture, under stretchers and edges for drips, stripped areas, or discoloration. (Typically, furniture strippers are in a hurry to finish! They apply stripper to the outside and don't rub underneath the edge. If you turn a piece over, you can see places where the new stain dripped.)

Many contemporary companies are making furniture in a Mission style. L. and J.G. Stickley (a company created by two of Gustav's brothers) switched from Mission to Colonial Revival furniture in 1918. They survived until 1988 when E.J. Audi bought them. Audi bought the rights to use Stickley's name and make reproductions of Stickley designs.

Here is a list of some of the more prominent Mission makers:

- Gustav Stickley
- L. & J.G. Stickley
- Roycroft
- Limbert
- Stickley Bros Company

- Charles Stickley
- J.M. Young and Harden
- Lifetime (Grand Rapids Furniture Co.)

A piece in pristine, original condition often has a mark. Shop marks were frequently water-transferred decals and paper labels, which could come off with heavy cleaning. L. & J.G. often put a large visible mark on its furniture. Sometimes homeowners scraped off those marks!

Woodn't It be Loverly: Learning about Wood

Knowing the difference between cherry, oak, and mahogany helps you in your furniture identification quest. Woods can often tell you country of origin. For example, you will rarely see a curly maple 18th century desk that was made in England.

Better wood often translates into better quality antiques. The type of wood also helps you determine the time period and the country. Some of the more expensive wood includes mahogany, beechwood, kingwood, teakwood, walnut, and rosewood. Burled and other highly "figured" woods are especially desirable. Pine and oak are generally less expensive.

Chairs from the 18th and 19th centuries often include several different woods.

Eighteenth century wood

In France, the fine urban pieces were primarily veneered, with oak as the secondary wood. The provincial pieces were usually oak, cherry, walnut, or yewwood, or pine, with pine, oak, or ash as the secondary wood.

In England, walnut was used until about 1730 and from then on mahogany was predominant. Pine (or deal) and oak were the most common secondary woods.

In America, walnut and mahogany were the main woods for formal pieces. In New England, they also used cherry or figured maple (tiger stripe, or bird's-eye maple). The provincial makers used pine, maple, butternut, fruitwoods, and ash.

Nineteenth century wood

In the 19th century, France favored mahogany, satinwood, beechwood, and fruitwood as primary woods with exceptions for very fancy pieces. Pine, oak, and ash are typically used are secondary woods. For a formal piece, oak is the secondary wood.

In England, furniture makers used rosewood, walnut, and mahogany. Pine and oak were secondary woods.

In America, furniture makers used walnut and rosewood for formal furniture. Oak and pine were secondary woods. Oak got a promotion during the Golden Age of Oak (about 1890 to 1930). Many fancy pieces were made of oak.

How to Look at a Piece of Furniture

How can you tell if you have something old, something new, something nailed, or something glued? Pat Saultman, appraiser and associate of Butterfield & Butterfield, shares the process she uses to look at a piece of furniture.

When looking at the piece of furniture, give yourself enough time to relax and see it overall. Imagine that you are looking at a *bonheur du jour,* a small writing desk. First impressions are important. Ask yourself

- Is it interesting and eye-catching?
- Is it a beautiful form?
- Are the proportions graceful?
- Does it have elegance at a glance?

After you decide you like it, the next questions are:

- What condition is the piece in?
- What repairs has the piece had? And what is the quality of those repairs?
- Look at patina. What is the quality of the finish? Does the wood have a soft glow?
- Examine the components. Look for craftsmanship and attention to detail.

- Look at the mounts. Usually the mounts of period pieces are gilt-bronze. Are the mounts cast clean and finished? If not, the mounts may be later ones.

  Old mounts were sand cast mounts and finished to perfection.

  Later mounts are stamped out with unfinished edges. The faces have only a suggestion of eyes and mouth. The floral leaf has unfinished edges, like a charm you get out of a gum machine that still has the edges of the seam.

  If the mounts are in the right places, but they seem newer, look at other components.

- What is the quality of the gilt? On many pieces, all the gilt has worn off. You see traces only in the crevices. If the gilt is too bright, it may be redone or "refreshed" (which indicates that there is such a thing as refreshing gilt).
- Look at the legs. How light and graceful are the legs? How do they lead into the body?
- How does the desk work? Do the drawers slide nicely? What's the construction? Are the drawers loose? Snug-fitting drawers might have been reworked.
- Take the drawers out and examine them. (See Chapter 4 for details on dovetails.) Earlier pieces have a chamfered bottom; later pieces have a flat bottom.
- Does the piece have a provenance, a known history that is important enough to increase its value?

These are a few ways to get to know and analyze furniture. Of course, the big question is, do you like the piece!

Check out *Miller's Furniture Antiques Checklist,* by Richard Davidson (published by Reed International Books Ltd.). This small book packs in a lot of basic information, including color pictures, line drawings, basic terminology, and basic construction. It contains lots of reminders, check lists, and clues that help you ID different styles of antique furniture.

Chapter 4

Dovetails and Nails: How to Spot the Real Thing from the Fake

In This Chapter

- Looking for signs of aging
- Casing the joints
- Analyzing hardware
- Understanding reasonable repair

Forgeries, reproductions, and secret marriages: Checking out antique furniture can read like a tabloid headline. Don't be deceived by a prettily turned leg or a single cooing dovetail. Don't let someone put the screws to you — the "new" screws, that is. By knowing a little about the periods of furniture manufacture and by looking carefully at the furniture, you'll soon be able to tell the good old guys from the new kids on the block.

This chapter is a hands-on chapter. Remember to pause and examine the wormholes, and stoop to see the shrinkage. But don't stop there: You can't rely on just one, or even two, clues. Look at all the sections featured in this chapter when you examine furniture. When you *use* the hard-hitting stuff in this chapter, you'll feel like an expert in ferreting out old furniture.

Never determine age and authenticity simply by looking at any one place on a piece of furniture.

And now, screw up your courage, nail down your attention, and get ready to hammer out the details.

The Lonesome Dovetail

A *dovetail joint* is the corner joint that brings two perpendicular pieces of wood together. You need to open a drawer to see the dovetailing inside. Dovetailing is one clue that the piece might have some age.

Dovetails alone do not assure age. Some high quality new furniture also has dovetails.

As a rule, the fewer number of dovetails, the older the piece. An early 18th century drawer may be joined with one large dovetail, as in Figure 4-1. As furniture making matured, craftsman generally used between three to five small dovetails on a drawer. They cut each one by hand, so the size of each one and the spacing between them was different (see Figure 4-2).

In the later Victorian period, furniture was made with machine-cut dovetailing, often having eight or more small dovetails on a drawer. These dovetails were quite evenly spaced, as pictured in Figure 4-3.

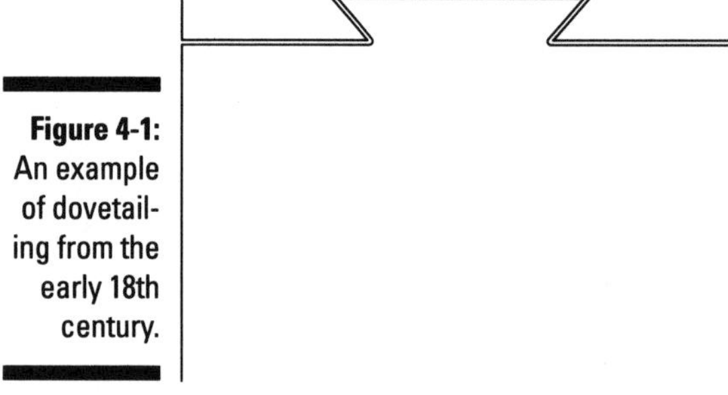

Figure 4-1: An example of dovetailing from the early 18th century.

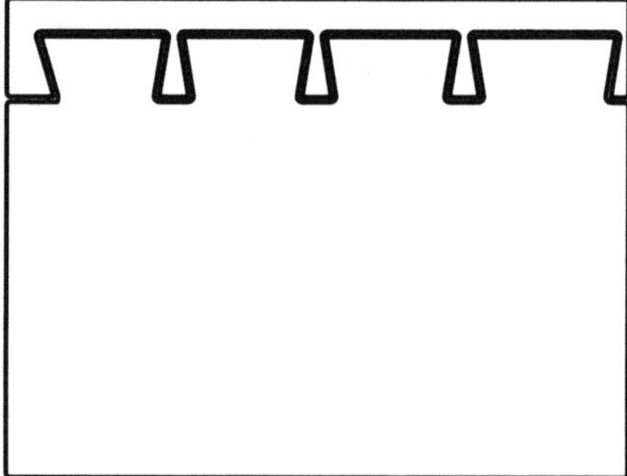

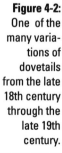

Figure 4-2: One of the many variations of dovetails from the late 18th century through the late 19th century.

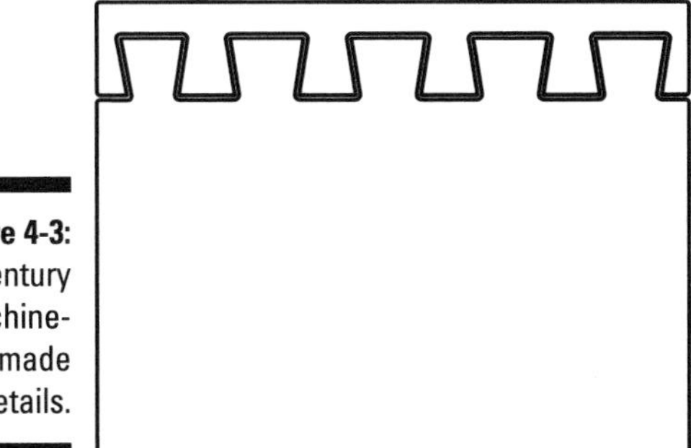

Figure 4-3: 20th century machine-made dovetails.

Mark My Woods: Reading Between the Grain

Everyone knows that you can tell the age of a tree by counting its rings. Well, similarly, you can tell the age of wood by reading its marks. Use the signs discussed in the following sections as tools to determine if you really have an antique in your hands. And if you are holding an antique, use the signs to determine its condition. Remember, much of this wear and tear can be faked. So don't declare your piece a genuine antique after sighting a few wormholes: Press forward to discover other confirming clues.

Saw marks: The cutting edge

Saw marks are the rough-hewn marks craftsmen and sawmills made as they shaped the wood. The handsaw, used almost exclusively until the mid-18th century, left distinctive, straight and uneven marks on the wood. From the second half of the 18th century into the mid-19th century, furniture was often created at sawmills. These saws, which were powered by oxen, water, and people, sometimes moved jerkily through the wood. Their marks are not as distinct as those from the hand saw. With the evolution of power tools in the mid-19th century, saw marks became curved and often less distinct. Power sawing and sanding smoothed away all but the faintest traces of saw marks.

Look for saw marks on the underside of tables, chairs, and drawers, and on the backs of case pieces (such as chests).

- On older handmade furniture, until about the mid-18th century, you see straight and uneven marks.
- On old sawmill furniture, approximately mid-18th to mid-19th century, you often see wavy lines, which may be unevenly spaced.
- On newer furniture, from about the mid-19th century, the marks are rounded and much harder to see.

Use a flashlight to examine old drawers and new drawers side-by-side to get a sense of what you are looking for.

Where are the wear marks

After something has been around for a while, it usually has a mark or two to prove it. *Wear marks* are the natural dents, dings, and wearing down furniture gets from being one of the family.

Chair wear

What a drag. You've been guilty of it yourself: moving a chair by dragging its back legs along the ground. The old wooden, dirt, or stone floors in the 18th and 19th century really gave the chair legs a beating, which makes the legs a great place to look for wear marks and repairs. Old *stretchers,* the pieces of wood that stretch between chair legs, were home to a lot of restless feet. As the unofficial "foot rest," the front stretcher of an old chair should have considerably more wear than the other stretchers.

Even before Lazy Boys, there were lazy boys. Look for shorter back legs from someone creating their own private recliner.

Table wear

The tops of tables sustain most of the wear, although the legs might have endured some restless kicking. Dents, scratches, and splotches all are signs of natural wear. Sometimes the natural look can go too far. Look at the tabletop and ask yourself, how displeasing are the imperfections? If the piece is too beat up, you may need to consider refinishing.

Try to avoid refinishing a table, as this can diminish its value. Some restoration specialists can touch up even areas that look severe, without refinishing the entire surface.

Case piece wear

Question: What do baseball players' uniforms and furniture drawers have in common?

Answer: After years of sliding home, their bottoms and sides can get worn down.

Look for signs of smoothness and wear on the bottoms and sides of drawers. Sometimes, drawers are so worn down that they wiggle around.

If you want a more functional drawer, you may need to consult a restoration specialist. Choose someone who will preserve as much of the original drawer as possible.

Look for signs of repair, such as new wood, on the sides of drawers. Because the repair does not show, if it's done well, it does not greatly diminish the value of the piece.

Stop and smell your drawers. The insides of old drawers have the kind of musty, old scent you notice when you climb a flight of stairs into the attic of an old house. Reproductions smell of lacquer or fresh wood.

Scribe marks: The writing on the wood

The 18th century craftsmen marked their spot with a knife or cabinetmaker's scribe tool. The *scribe marks* are shallow lines cleanly scratched in the wood. You can usually find scribe marks flying out of the ends of dovetails and almost always near joints. Most scribe marks are right at the widest end of the dovetails on the front and rear of drawer sides, which is how the furniture-maker kept the dovetails aligned and as even as possible.

Wormholes: Worming their way out

Wormholes are small uneven holes made by "woodworms," which are, in fact, beetle larvae. The larvae hatch in the wood and tunnel their way to freedom. They tunnel parallel to the surface and exit on maturity, flying away. The holes you see are their exit holes. Woodworms usually avoid mahogany, preferring pine, maple, oak, and walnut.

Old holes are irregularly shaped and winding, so that a pin cannot go straight through them. They are dark, filled with dirt and wax, and free from fine powder. New holes are dusted with sawdust.

If you think a piece is "alive," watch daily for the appearance of small pyramids of sawdust, which means the baby beetles are leaving. If you just moved a piece of furniture, you can get a drift of sawdust out of those holes. Don't worry at a scatter of sawdust; when you see little mounds, it's time to freak out and call the exterminator.

If you can insert a pin straight into a hole, you should be suspicious. Some larger "worm" has faked the hole. Sometimes repro makers use drill bits; occasionally, they use buckshot on larger pieces. Sometimes, repro makers use genuine wormed wood and put it where you can spot the wormholes.

Shrink raps

Over time, wood shrinks across the grain. Here's how to measure shrinkage: On a table that is 36 inches round, measure with grain. The table should be 36 inches, give or take ⅛ of an inch. Then measure against the grain; if it's 100 years or more, it should have shrunk perhaps ¼ to ¾ inches from the original 36-inch diameter.

Inspect wide boards for shrinkage, cracks, and cracks that have been filled. Expect splitting on boards that are wider than 20 inches. For a purist, an open crack is better than a filled one. (Consider the Grand Canyon, for example.) Of course, when the crack is so large that your peas and carrots fall through, you may want to consider restoration work.

Normal wood shrinkage is not warped. Warped wood contracts differently in different directions because it was not aged properly originally, or because the wood got wet, or suffered an extreme temperature or humidity change.

Chinese furniture-makers allowed for shrinkage by using *floating panels.* These wood panels are surrounded by wooden frames, with side and end grooves, so that the centerboard has room for expansion or contraction as the humidity changes. Many good American and European cabinetmakers followed this tradition from the 1600s on. For signs of aging, look for the gap between the center panel of wood and the frame.

Looking for Marriage in All the Right Places

Some people you look at and know they are married. It's more than the wedding rings and the matching T-shirts and pants — it's a look about them, a sense of togetherness. Antiques can be trickier. You can look at them, they can look all matching, so you think, well here's an original. You have to look within, explore the inner shelves, to find out if this piece is really an original individual or a marriage made on earth.

With antiques, single is better. Single means the piece hasn't been tampered with and is still original. A *marriage* is two pieces, joined together by man (or woman) that do not belong together. They may be from different eras, of different woods, from different manufacturers or craftsmen. They also may be from the same era, and possibly even the same maker. Marriages often occur between furniture that has two parts, such as desks with tops or chests with two distinct easily separated parts, or tables with bases. A married piece should typically cost considerably less than the equivalent original.

How to detect a marriage

Antiques from the same era tend to do well together, as do antiques from the same country. The May-December marriage, such as an old bottom with a new top, is usually easier to spot. Examine both the top and the bottom to see if these match:

- **Woods:** Look for the same type of wood, the same grain. If the grain is different top to bottom, the piece may have been restored or married.
- **Wood Finish:** Does the finish have an evenly distributed patina, a mellow color created from years of wax and dust build-up?
- **Dovetails, chamfering, nails, and screws:** Examine the dovetails, chamfering, nails, and screws in the top and bottom drawers. Expect the same *chamfering,* hand planing that shaves the sides and ends and bottoms of drawers so they slide into the grooves.
- **Carvings:** Is the quality the same, top to bottom? Is the style the same, top to bottom?
- **Brasses:** Are the brasses matching and from the same time period and are the holes consistent on both the top and bottom of the piece?
- **Wear:** Do both top and bottom show similar degrees and signs of wear?

Take Two: Remade furniture

Suppose that you find a Victorian spinet (without the inner workings) that has been turned into a writing desk. It's the antique version of reengineering. The piece started life with one purpose, and then someone redefined that purpose. Nothing is wrong with buying a remade piece, as long as you know about it in advance and are paying accordingly. The price should be considerably less than if the piece were original.

Set too, Brutus

There's the married set and the made-up set. The made up set is furniture, which has been grouped as a set that did not come from the same maker at the same time. The pieces can be old, but they don't belong together. The more variation, such as different makers and different time periods, the less valuable the piece. For example, four chairs blended from different makers and the same time period are preferable to four chairs that span a hundred years.

The plainer the furniture, the easier it is to blend together. The closer the match, the closer to the same time period, the better the value.

Hardware, the Old Fashioned Kind

Looking at the hardware is a great way of determining how old a piece is. It's great to have the original hardware. But replacement hardware is common and may not significantly diminish the value. Many old pieces have gone through several changes of hardware, depending on the age of the piece. When you understand the evolution of pegs, nails, screws, and brasses, you can more accurately note the time period of the piece.

The earlier and rarer the piece and the higher the quality, the more important it is to have the original hardware. For a wonderful and more "ordinary" antique, small hardware, such as nails and screws, that has been replaced with skill and a sense of aesthetics does not have a big effect on the piece's value. The larger and more prominent the hardware is on a piece, the more significant the loss of value if it is replaced.

Got you pegged

There's Peg o' my heart and there's Peg o' the joints. Guess which Peg is the oldest?

Craftsmen made their own pegs and used them to attach arms and legs and join together case pieces. The old wooden pegs are imperfect, unlike the smooth new pegs now called *dowels*. How a piece is held together helps authenticate it. Wooden pegs and crude metal spike-like nails were the earliest ways to join furniture. Even today, pegs are an elegant and effective way to join together furniture. Pegs are slower to work with and can protrude as wood contracts and expands. Pegs can be as strong as nails, and they are more aesthetically pleasing.

Question: What did one peg say to the other?

Answer: Let's get out of this joint!

You've got nail

It's easy to tell if there's a screw loose. It's more difficult to tell if the original nails are in a piece. Original period nails are another way to try to date or authenticate a piece.

- **Wrought iron nails:** Older nails are wrought iron with rectangular heads. As the blacksmith made the nail, the blows of the hammer created a petal formation (also known as a *rosehead*) on the flat top of the nail.

  These nails had a thick, rough body tapering to a point. The heads often looked like two nails clinging together. Finishing nails were smaller, had no head, or the head was L-shaped or T-shaped so as to tap into the wood fully, flush with the surface or a bit below.

  Here's what wrought iron nails and people have in common:

  - They are distinctive, even when they are bent out of shape.
  - They're not perfectly round or square.
  - Their heads are irregular.

- **Cut nails:** At the very end of the 18th century, nail-making machines created the first cut nails, made of flat metal, instead of hammered iron rods. In the early 19th century, nails had hammered heads that were thinner than wrought iron and more uniform in appearance.

- **Wire nails:** In the late 19th century, wire nails replaced cut nails. Made from uniform round metal material similar to that used in barbed wire, wire nails had a round shank and a flat round head.

Nails get loose and some replacement is natural. Some restoration specialists have a supply of old nails they use for replacements. They also can replace old nails with contemporary nails made to look old. By keeping the original look of the piece intact, you minimize the possible loss in value. That means, don't let someone replace a hand wrought nail with a shiny new screw or a 16-penny carpenter's nail.

Use the nails as one tool to determine age. Look for nails on the underside of a chair, the inside of a drawer, or the back of a case piece. If there's a mark or a gouge near the nail hole, someone might have substituted a later nail that doesn't quite fit. Of course, this sort of brilliant sleuthing works only if the replacement nail is smaller.

Be cautious of nails with a rusty shank that are in a hole without rust. Sometimes people put an old nail in new furniture. The hole should be rusty and dark.

Question: How fast did the hammer move?

Answer: At a nail's pace.

Turn of the screws

Before 1850, handmade screws had blunt ends, and the slot for the screwdriver was off-center. The hand-cut threads meander a little and were spaced further apart. With modern, machine-tooled screws, the threads are even, more fine, and closer together, and the head slot is centered.

New screws often appear in antique furniture. The old screws fall out. Sometimes, to keep an old piece stable, restoration experts choose modern hardware. They can later replace the hardware with a peg or something more authentic, if the collector is a purist. But the owner might have to be more careful with the piece of furniture.

Open wide: Hinges

The 17th and 18th century *cotter pin* type hinge used a single hole. Craftsmen inserted a U-shaped metal wire (sometimes called a *staple*) through two pieces of wood or metal and bent it back flat against the inside of the drawer or the back of a box to hold things snug. This hinge was easy to make although rather weak. It's also easy to identify: It leaves a single hole and often marks on the wood where the cotter pin was bent back into the wood.

The *butt/butterfly* hinge was made of iron or brass and had two flat pieces with a pin in the middle so that the hinge could swing freely. Two or more screws or nails held each side of the interior hinge plate in place. Similar to the hinges we see in kitchen cupboard doors today, butterfly hinges were standard hardware on desk lids, trunk lids, doors, and table leaves throughout the mid-18th to the early 20th century.

Beware of an 18th or 19th century piece that has hinges with little wear, perfectly centered holes, and no rust or corrosion. Look to see if the fit is right. A large reproduction hinge can cover up original hinge marks, but a smaller replacement shows the outlines of the original.

Get a handle on it

Handles, or *pulls,* are an essential part of furniture and can help greatly in dating a piece. The first half of the 18th century, brass plates were usually thinly cast, and hand-finished. In the later half of the century, they were stamped out by machines and were thicker.

For an extra clue of whether the piece has been refinished, take off the brasses: You'll see the old finish and a definite difference in the color of the wood under the brasses versus the wood surrounding them. You can also look on the interior for signs of filled-in or extra holes that don't align with the holes that are on the surface. Also be sure to look at the back of the brasses. Reproductions of handmade brasses are cut from sheet brass and are smooth in back.

Escutcheons

Escutcheons are decorative brass plates that went around keyholes and prevented the wood from being dented and scratched as the people tried to insert keys by dim candle light or fluid lamps. All but the simplest furniture had escutcheons around the keyhole.

When an escutcheon falls off or is removed, it will have made an indentation in the wood. Look at the wood around the escutcheon for suspicious previous escutcheon marks.

Check to see if the lock has been replaced. Metal locks were usually nailed or screwed into notches, flush as possible with the drawer front. Look inside to see if they chiseled out a place to put a replacement lock. (Locks will rarely fit the hole exactly.)

Knobby needs

Eighteenth and 19th century craftsmen also used wooden knobs on the more "provincial' or "country-made" furniture. Decorative pressed glass pulls were also popular from about the 1820s to the 1850s.

Case Study

Let's say you go into an antique shop that specializes in 18th and 19th century furniture. You see a chest of drawers that might be country Chippendale. Read the tag. It should say country, type of wood, century, and style.

You know the primary wood for country Chippendale in England is oak or pine. See if the finish is nice and even and has a fine patina.

Ask to pull out the piece and see if the backboard (or boards) looks original. It is acceptable to have some replacement of the backboards. The back was nearly always unfinished, since furniture-makers tended to save money and time on the hidden parts. If the backboard is original, you'll see plane marks. If the back is really smooth, it's definitely newer (the back, that is).

Open drawers and look at the dovetailing. Ask the dealer to take the drawer out for you. Look at the bottom. You're looking for dovetails on the back of the drawer, which are usually crude and often fewer than the front. You look at the bottom of the drawer for plane marks and old nails.

Look for additional holes in the front of the drawer, scars or discolorations that might hint of other hardware. Look at the outside hardware and see if the holes match. Then look for repairs and damages. The inside of a drawer will often show where earlier hardware was.

Everything on the piece of furniture should make sense to you. Finally, analyze your findings and see if you're still in love with the piece.

Part II
Who's Got the Goods? Shopping for Antiques

The 5th Wave
By Rich Tennant
ANTIQUING NIGHTMARE
©RICHTENNANT
We'll never get this well finished. This old pottery keeps gummin' up the drill bit.
Try this!
ANTIQUITIES DRILL BIT
"Grinds through ancient artifacts in a jiffy"

In this part . . .

"If you really want to have some fun, bring your flashlight and come at 5 a.m."

You never know where antiques will show up: a third-story bedroom of a midtown estate sale, a well-lit showcase at an elegant shop, a folding table at your neighbor's garage sale, or a bustling booth at a weekend show. The hunt is part of the thrill of antique collecting. Once you find the antique you've been searching for, or that you stumble upon and fall instantly in love with, you want to make sure that the price feels right.

In this section, we bring you (and your flashlight, tape measure, and magnifying glass) to some of the great antique hunting grounds — shops, shows, auctions, malls, flea markets, estate sales, garages sales, and the Internet — and give you ways to survive, thrive, and get really good deals.

Chapter 5

Bargaining Basics: The Price Can Be Right

In This Chapter

- Locating the win-win
- Questioning the price
- Developing negotiating strategies

You've been reading your price guides, your auction catalogues, and your antique trade journals. You've driven down long country roads to find auctions and tiptoed through antique malls, sniffing out sleepers. You've asked questions and handled several dozen antiques. You are ready to buy, so you need to be ready to negotiate.

This chapter gives you some basic negotiating strategies, specific to antiques. You'll get even more specific hints as you journey through the rest of this part of the book, so remember to adapt the techniques to suit your own style.

Preparing for Win-Win: Understanding Dealers

It's important to know who you're negotiating with. So we interviewed a number of antique dealers and asked them what makes them want to give a better deal. They also told us a few things that drive them to the wall (which is, of course, covered with a 19th-century flocked wallpaper):

- **Customer, in a crowded shop, pointing to a Windsor chair and shouting across the room at the dealer, "What's your best on this?"**

  Be discrete when bargaining. Draw the dealer quietly aside if you want to negotiate.

- **Customer, waving a precious vase to get the dealer's attention, and asking, "How much is this?"**

  Handle all merchandise with respect and care. Dealers are more at ease, and therefore more open to negotiating, when they trust you around their antiques.

- **"You've had this bowl since the day I came in this shop. I'll take it off your hands if you chop the price in half."**

  An overly aggressive approach may be counter-productive. Just because the dealer has something for a long time does not mean that he wants to sell it for a cheap price. Antique shops don't always have the turnover that is more common in other retail establishments. Because antiques have an intrinsic value (the value generally holds constant or can increase), dealers are willing to wait for the right buyer.

- **"This piece is just a mess (referring to a piece marked "as is," which means it's damaged or repaired), but I'd be willing to pay (insert here an insultingly low price)."**

  Dealers can feel very sensitive about having their merchandise criticized. "As is" tells you that the dealer knows there are things wrong with the piece. When you need to point out problems with the piece and make comments on its condition, do so in a straightforward and non-accusatory manner.

Dealers are sometimes more prone to negotiate with people who might become long-term customers.

All's Fair: Question the Price

If the price marked on the piece of your dreams is higher than the price guides or higher than you want to pay, ask: "How did you come by that price? I'm under the impression the value of a piece like this is (insert the amount)." A reputable dealer should be willing to explain the price of the piece.

Perhaps the piece is cranberry colored rather than green and therefore more valuable. Perhaps you failed to notice a signature. Or perhaps the piece has decorative elements that distinguish it from its more pedestrian companions.

Or the dealer may say, "I can show you an auction catalog where this sold for $600.00 more." Soon, of course, you will know enough about auctions (or if you don't, zoom ahead to Chapter 7) to know that just because someone got seized by auction fever doesn't mean you want to do the same.

Negotiating Strategies: Getting the Price Right

"Can you explain the price on this candy dish?" we asked a dealer at an antique show.

That one question gave us a fabulous education on Wave Crest glass. The dealer, who turned out to be a long-time collector specializing in this glass, showed us the characteristics that distinguished quality Wave Crest. He told us to hold the piece and feel its lightness and its smooth texture. He told us where to find a repro in the same show just four booths away so that we could compare for ourselves. "Just don't tell them I sent you," he said. Surreptitiously, we went into the booth to scout out the fake. We saw and felt the comparative heaviness and roughness. We also noticed the price on the repro: more expensive than on the authentic!

Getting an education is just one benefit of developing your negotiating strategies. When you negotiate, you learn more about what you are buying, you understand why it's worth the price you're paying, and you often get a more favorable price!

The manners approach

Be polite and discreet. Wait until the dealer is not surrounded by people. Have the piece in hand and quietly ask "Is this the best price?" If you can't pick up the piece, or if there are people all around, say to the dealer, "I'd like you to look at a piece and tell me if that is your best price."

Walk over to the piece. The dealer may then slip you a piece of paper with a new and improved price.

Good better best

If you know the price is good and you simply want to try for a better price, put on a deadpan face. You are holding a poker hand you don't want anyone to get too curious about. Ask, "Would you be willing to do any better on this piece?" After you consider the answer you might gently ask, "Is this your best price?" Or "Would you be willing to take. . . ." Or, "May I make an offer?"

A con-sign of the times

Some shops take merchandise on consignment. This means that people bring antiques to the shop, and the dealer sells those goods for them. The consignor contracts with the dealer for a flat fee for the piece or a percentage of the sale price. Often shops have a sign, stating they take goods on consignment.

In such shops, you might ask, "Is this a consignment piece?" If the answer is yes, you can then comfortably ask, "Do you think the consignor will take less?"

Sometimes the dealer will reduce the price without even consulting the consignor.

Then give a specific price. Now the dealer knows you are a serious buyer; he's been offered a deal, and he may be willing to take it.

Or he may answer, "I can't sell it for $500, but I could let it go for $600."

He's telling you he wants to sell the piece. At that point you can go comfortably back and forth and settle on a price.

The two-fer approach

Negotiate on more than one piece — "Can we make a package deal on these pieces?"

Now you've given the dealer an excuse to give you a discount, because you're buying quantity. Dealers prefer to bargain on several pieces. But sometimes, you can make a package out of two pieces.

The two-fer approach can motivate the dealer to work on a closer markup with you. Dealers appreciate having the chance to do a good day's business with one wonderful customer (you). Plus, they see that you may become an ongoing customer.

The flawed finder

Who put the chip in the Chippendale? Who put the tiff in the Tiffany? Who put the cut in the cut glass? Mimic the great writer Flaw-Bert and find a flaw the dealer didn't mention.

Perhaps there's a break in a table leg or a nick on a cut glass vase that the dealer didn't even know about. Subtly remind the dealer that having the piece repaired will cost you. No dealer enjoys finding out he has inadvertently purchased damaged goods.

This bargaining tool is often worth 10 percent off or more (depending on the nature of the flaw). Once the dealer realizes the piece is damaged, he really wants to sell it. It's not worth as much and he'll have to explain the flaw and apologize for it to future customers.

Selling Uncle Stu and the crew

Remember the time your Uncle Stu came and stayed with you for two whole weeks? Remember how happy you were to see him go, even if you did have to loan him train money to get him out of there? Every dealer has his antique Uncle Stu. (Some dealers have whole families.) These are pieces that the dealer mistakenly invited into his shop, and they've been hanging around, taking up space for way too long. He would love to sell such pieces, even if he has to throw in a little traveling money.

You may totally love the dealer's Uncle Stu. You may have been looking for such a piece for months. So how do you uncover the dealer's unwelcome relatives and make them part of your antique family?

Look for odd jobs

Look for pieces that are unusual, that don't blend into the overall ambience. When you find one, see if you really like it.

Ask the dealer for the history of the piece. This opens the way for finding out how long the piece has been lurking in his shop. Of course, even if the piece has been in the shop since prehistoric times, a smart dealer might say, "Antiques get better with age. The value of this is greater than when I priced it four years ago."

Assuming the dealer is right, you have to decide if you love the piece enough to pay that price. Use your knowledge and intuition: If the dealer overpaid in the first place, you may not want to be the one who bails him out.

The big picture

"Size up" the situation and examine pieces that are oversized. Notice the giant painting in the corner. Look at the huge canopy bed that would be great for you, because you wouldn't have to buy any more bedroom furniture (you wouldn't have room). These pieces may be just right for you but wrong for most everyone else — including the dealer.

Naked women and dead animals

Antiques with challenging subject matter often are hard to sell. Erotic pieces, hunting pictures, bronzes that feature dead animals, devils, or blood — even when the art is great and the craftsmanship superb, the market prefers charming children or beautiful, clothed, women. Hunt around for something that may be on the road less traveled and see where you can go with negotiating.

Throw it in

Even if you weren't born with that silver spoon, here is your chance to get one "thrown in." Suppose that you are interested in several items, and one of them, the spoon for example, is substantially less in price. Calculate to see if getting the spoon free would be a better deal than getting a discount. Or maybe you can have both.

If it feels comfortable, at the end of the negotiation, say, "I'd like to buy the vase, the gateleg table, and the cameo pin. How about throwing in those three spoons?"

If the dealer has a sufficient markup on the other pieces, he may be pleased to offer you this little bonus. If not, he will tell you so and — assuming that you have not been too aggressive in your other negotiations — there will have been no harm in the asking. Use this negotiating strategy sparingly and judiciously.

Adding to the package

You have just put together the ideal package and agreed on a good price. You're looking around while the dealer wraps everything up and you see something else you like. You are in a glorious negotiating position. The dealer is already thrilled with you. Show the dealer the piece and say, "In light of what I've just purchased, can you make me a really great price on this?"

In this situation, you can sometimes get a much larger discount on this item than on the entire rest of the package!

In the interest of interest free

Ask if the dealer has layaway. Layaway is usually an interest free payment plan. Many dealers prefer layaway, because it promotes an ongoing relationship. Every time you write a check, you think of that antique shop. If the dealer is strapped for cash, he may prefer an outright sale. Ask, "If I pay in full right now, would you be able to do a little better?"

Other stuff to negotiate for

- Free delivery
- Repairs that might need to be made
- Having the piece cleaned or polished
- Installations, such as a chandelier, painting, or mirror
- Additional research or documentation, when applicable

When bargaining doesn't work

You've just seen the most stunning spectacular piece. It's in mint condition and your heart beats faster just looking at it. When the dealer has a piece that's totally unusual and unique — or if the dealer has priced it in close to start with — he may not give a discount at all. If it is well-priced and stunning, follow your heart and pay the full price. We have heard more antique collectors bemoaning the piece that got away than the piece they overpaid for.

Don't push the dealer to his discomfort level. If he says, "This is my best," and holds firm, don't press, with "What is your very best price?" You're trying to build a relationship with the dealer.

When you develop that relationship, hopefully the day will come when the dealer offers you a discount without you even asking.

Chapter 6

Meet the Dealers: Antique Shops and Shows

In This Chapter

- Building relationships with dealers
- Working with antique shops
- Showing up at shows
- Practicing good antiquing etiquette

The ceramic tile stove stands in the corner. The dishes reside in an open wooden rack with a trough underneath to hold the pots and pans. The worn refectory table is set with blue and white pottery. A nearby cupboard with carved baskets of flowers and curved molding holds sparkling drinking glasses. It takes the ringing of a telephone to remind you that you aren't in 19th century Normandy; you're in an antique shop specializing in country French furniture.

Going to an antique shop can be like going into another world. It's travel without a passport and without a time machine.

For those who like to do at least two things at once, going to antique shops and shows is ideal. At these locations, you can build a relationship with an "antiques source" (the dealer) while you build your antique collection. Shops and shows are the two areas where the dealers are most often consistently involved. That means you have a good chance of having a knowledgeable person to talk to, someone who knows about the antiques and who wants you to become a steady customer.

Building Relationships the Antique Way

So you want to build a relationship, meet a committed individual who's not afraid of honest communication, and find someone who wants to negotiate through your differences. Yes, you can have your antiques and a meaningful relationship, too. Shops and shows are ideal places to create such relationships.

Here are some other benefits to having a glowing relationship with a dealer:

- **Many dealers have interest-free layaway plans.** This happens more often in antique shops, less frequently in shows.
- **You often can take something home on approval, more frequently at shops than at shows.** Dealers usually require a credit card number or check as a guarantee.
- **Dealers can usually deliver your antique, and if you need, set it up and help you figure out where your new acquisition looks best.** Again, show dealers usually don't have the luxury of this kind of involvement.
- **Dealers can give you a written guarantee of authenticity.** This could include a written description of the object, age of the piece, condition, artist, or manufacturer. This description is good to have for your records.

  If the dealers can't guarantee an expensive piece, ask them to contact an expert who can authenticate it. If they don't know anyone, find an appraiser or knowledgeable friend to look at the piece. Even if dealers say they can authenticate, you may want a second opinion on an expensive piece. If you do, hire an objective, qualified appraiser or a layperson who is a well-known authority. Expect to pay for the help in authentication. Most appraisers charge a flat fee or work on an hourly basis when appraising or authenticating a piece. (See Chapter 20 for more information on appraisers and how to find them.)
- **Many dealers keep customer want lists and are happy to look for a specific piece for you.** Many show dealers happily look for items for their customers and either deliver them at the next area show or mail them (after having sent pictures and gotten the okay in advance).
- **Many dealers will sell antiques for you, either by taking them on consignment or by making an outright purchase.** On consignment items, you agree on either a set amount for the piece or a percentage of the selling price. You do not receive your portion of the money until the dealer sells the piece. Selling on consignment gives you a chance to upgrade your antique portfolio in a hassle-free way. You can weed through and sell pieces you don't want anymore, and you don't have to bother with advertising. You also don't have to field phone calls or deal with lookers.

Eight million old stories

Stories of pieces that have special uses tend to be more accurate. Chances are that a young Chinese couple of economic means probably did spend their wedding night in the intricately carved two hundred-year-old Chinese wedding bed. Claiming an object belonged to a famous person is fairly common in the antique business. Buying an antique is like purchasing any other previously owned object (or adopting a puppy from the pound): The more questions you ask, the more you find out.

If "Queen Victoria sipped tea from it," look for proof. That proof could include a notarized statement, a page from an old auction catalog indicating when and where the piece was sold or bought, and letters by well-known dealers, curators, or "experts." Make sure you get plenty of opinions before you spend a lot for a "celebrity" antique.

Use caution and common sense when someone offers a story and a piece of paper that supposedly ties a piece to a very famous person and raises its value greatly. Signatures and old paper can always be forged or faked by someone trying to deceive.

- **Dealers know where things came from.** Dealers can tell you if the piece came from a recent buying trip or from an elegant local family. You can ask dealers where they got a piece, but don't expect them to give you the name of the former owner. They also probably won't divulge their out-of-town sources.

Curioser and Curioser: Antique Shops

No matter what city you find yourself in, the best starting point for hunting antiques is the good old Yellow Pages. They contain a nearly complete listing of every antique shop in town. When you look at the listings, you'll notice antique shops are typically clustered together. It's fun to make a list of shops by address and cruise the antique districts.

It can be difficult to figure out what a shop is like from reading the Yellow Pages ad. If you're looking for something specific, call and ask if the shop has the type of antique you want. But remember that part of the fun of antiquing is just seeing what is out there.

Some shops list how many years or generations they've been in business. Look for such indications that a shop is established and stable. That way, if you later find out the piece is not what you bought it as, the shop is more likely to still be around to stand behind its mistake.

Making the most of your visit

If you like to sleep late, antique shops are perfect for you. Some shops have the "never on Monday" rule and do not open on Mondays. Antique shops often don't open until around 10 or 11. Call to find out the hours.

Here are some other things to keep in mind that will help you make the most of your visit to the antique shop:

- If you want to spend time with the dealer, find out when he or she is in the shop. Quiet weekday mornings are often good times for you to connect with dealers.
- If you don't see staff when you first come into the shop, try to make your presence known so that you don't surprise anyone.
- If you're in the looking and learning phase, say so. Many shops have specialties, which may be announced on their signs, listed in their ads, or apparent when you walk in.
- If the person who offers to help seems knowledgeable, stick with him. If he can't answer your questions, ask to speak to the manager or owner.
- If you want the dealer to discuss one of your antiques with you, call ahead of time and ask whether you can bring it in. Make it clear that you are asking for information, not for a price. See Chapter 20 if you're looking for an actual appraisal.

Do look back

Tell the shop's staff if you're looking for something specific. If they have it, they can take you right to the piece. If they don't have what you want in the showroom, ask whether they have anything tucked away. An item may be in the legendary back room for any of the following reasons:

- **It's not yet priced.** The dealer often has to do research before pricing an item. If you see an unmarked piece you love, ask the dealer to call you when it's priced. Check "just in" merchandise carefully, since it often has not been cleaned up yet. Ask if you can view the piece in better light or if the dealer will clean the piece a bit (especially if it is a piece of glass or pottery or porcelain) so you can make sure that it has no cracks or chips.
- **It's on hold for another customer.** Sometimes people let go of things on hold, however. Ask the dealer to call you if the person he's holding it for doesn't come through in a timely fashion.
- **It's having minor repairs or being cleaned.** The antique awaiting minor repairs can be a prospective purchase. Selling the piece "as is" can save the dealer time, money, and labor, resulting in a lower price for you.

After you look around, ask what other shops you might enjoy visiting. Most dealers know the kinds of merchandise other shop owners carry and are happy to share names and locations.

It's Showtime!

An antique show features a crowd of dealers coming together for a limited time only. These events are often annual or semi-annual, lasting from a weekend to a week, and are a whirlwind chance to be around a lot of antiques in a short period of time. Sometimes the shows center on a particular theme. In many shows, hundreds of dealers display their wares.

Some promoters may use the word *antiques* when their events feature primarily *collectibles.* (See Chapter 1 for more about antiques versus collectibles.)

Showing up: Finding good shows

When you read publications such as the *Antique Trader* or the *Maine Antique Digest,* you see all the possibilities for antique shows. Shows can be generic, featuring hundreds of dealers with a variety of antiques. Or they can be as focused and specific as an all-postcard show, a music and phonograph show, a doll and toy show, or a show filled with glass made by Heisey. Your local newspaper, trade publications, and the Internet are all great places to find show dates and times. The national sources give you a wider range, so you can plan your travels around a show, if you want, or find shows in unlikely spots close to you.

Of course, word-of-mouth is always a great way to find out more about shows. When you go to one, ask dealers and collectors what other shows they like, and get to know the names of some of the promoters. You may hear comments like "He always puts on a good show," or "She attracts the best dealers," or "That promoter is particularly good about sending around checkers to try to keep reproductions from being sold in the show." Different promoters have different standards for their shows.

Some of the more famous and prominent shows are very difficult for new dealers to get into; some promoters even ask new dealers for photographs and information about previous show experiences before they allow the dealers into the show. Dealers typically try to keep the same location for their booths in a recurring show so that their customers can easily find them.

Show and tell: What you need to know

Find out which promoters run their shows as advertised. That means if you go to a show billed as *antiques,* you should not have to wade through booth after booth of modern collectibles. Even then, don't expect everything to be over 100 years old. Not many shows exclude valued collectibles from the Art Nouveau and Art Deco period just because they haven't reached their maturity as an antique yet.

At a show, you're buying from traveling dealers who may not be back in your town for a year or ever. Here are some tips for getting to know good dealers:

- **Look in trade magazines for advertisements.** Many dealers have ongoing advertisements, which indicates some stability and a desire to create an ongoing clientele.
- **Call and ask the promoters for information about dealers in your area of interest.** Shows usually list the promoter's name. Ask how long the dealers have been in business. Ask about their reputation.
- **Talk to the dealers.** Reputable dealers will provide you with information about themselves, such as length of time in business, professional affiliations, shows or shops where they are known, and where you can reach them. Ask whether they'll provide a written guarantee of what they sell you.
- **Get the dealers' street address, phone number, or e-mail address.** Ask about their show schedule. Chances are they may be near your area again throughout the year. Visit them at other shows. Ask to be on their mailing list. Often dealers coming into an area let their customers know that they will be at a particular show and in what booth.

Making the most of your visit

Antique shows buzz with the energy of hundreds of dealers and collectors crammed into a relatively small space. First take a brisk walk through and see everything at a glance. If you find something you are collecting, be prepared to buy — or be prepared to give it up.

After a blitz through, walk row to row, lingering wherever you want, talking to dealers and looking at antiques. Usually the booths are in no particular order, but the rows are often numbered, so you can keep track of where you've been and where you saw an item that you like.

If you think you're in love with a piece but you're not quite sure, ask the dealers to hold the piece for an hour or two. They may refuse, since this show is their limited chance to get things sold. Do not ask the dealer to hold a piece for you and then leave the show without buying the piece or telling the dealer you've decided against it.

After buying what you really want, go around one more time more slowly. But don't expect to find all your favorite pieces still hanging around. Whoever said "Who seeks and will not take when once 'tis offered, shall never find it more," might have been talking about antiquing and about antique shows in particular. If you see a piece that you love that is properly represented and at a right price, remember the words of that wise old bard.

On the other hand, because you can rarely take things home on approval, you need to be confident and prepared before you buy at a show. You also need to remember that the dealer you are buying from may not be easy to find if you later discover a problem with the merchandise.

Show booths are often crammed with merchandise and crowded with people. Be careful of swinging purses and reaching children. Most dealers want you to pay if you break something.

Curtain calls: Why show biz is great

Shows are wonderful places to soak up information about niche antiques. You can find a booth filled with art glass next to a booth specializing in oyster plates next to a booth of primitives and Depression glass. Many of the dealers are specialists — or at least very knowledgeable — in their areas. Some are collectors whose love of collecting gave them such an extensive collection that they either had to buy a bigger house or start selling. Either way, most dealers love to talk about their favorite subject. If it's your favorite subject, too, you're in luck!

You can linger in a booth and study specific merchandise, if the booth isn't crowded. If the dealer isn't busy, he or she is often available for conversation, so you have a fabulous opportunity to learn from some experts.

Ms. Antique Manners

When you shop for antiques, you are walking among precious, unique, breakable history. You are browsing among the irreplaceable. Here are some common courtesy clues for your time with antiques:

- **Don't bring in food or drink.** A moist glass or an innocent spill can mar the finish on that antique table or put a serious stain in that valuable Oriental rug.
- **Don't smoke.** A hot ash can damage antiques.
- **Don't open a closed display case.** If the case is closed, assume that fragile items are within.
- **Ask for help before you handle fragile items.** But don't be afraid to ask to hold a piece, even if you are only looking.
- **Pay attention to any *Do Not Touch* and *Fragile* signs.** Dealers usually have a good reason for putting up that sign, even if you can't see why.
- **Don't pick anything up by its top or handle alone.** Cradle a piece in both hands, rather than holding it only by the handle. Using both hands helps keep a weak handle from breaking and lessens your chances of banging the piece against something. Always support the bottom.
- **Ask permission before taking photographs.** Not every dealer likes to have pictures taken of the merchandise.
- **Ask for permission and help when using your antique sleuthing skills.** Get the dealer's okay before you:
  - Turn over a small piece of furniture to look at construction
  - Take out a drawer to examine those wear marks
  - Tap glass to see whether it rings that crystalline bell
  - Use your magnet to see whether the piece is brass or iron

If you are at the show to study and learn, let the dealer know. Many of these knowledgeable people will gladly share information with you. When dealers feel that their merchandise is safe in your hands, they feel more comfortable and at ease with you. This relaxed atmosphere makes the time you spend in the booth more pleasant, and it may even translate into dollars when it comes time for negotiating. You are also practicing handling your own valued antiques.

Chapter 7

Sold on Auctions: Going Once, Going Twice

In This Chapter

- Finding auctions
- Speaking auction lingo
- Premiering at auction previews
- Developing bidding strategies
- Plunging into the auction without catching auction fever

It's early and the room is buzzing. Four hundred carefully labeled pieces of antique glassware are spread across the tables. People are consulting their catalogues, examining the pieces, looking for signatures, making notes of what they see. Then the auctioneer goes to the raised platform and everyone takes a seat.

"I'm selling everything as is," the auctioneer says. "You may hear the number 100. That is an absentee bidder. I'll start off with a few things that aren't in the catalogue."

A beautiful piece of cut glass appears on the velvet-lined twirling platform, and the local auction begins.

Auctions are exciting ways to buy antiques. They offer you a look at how prices can get set and an opportunity to interact with a group of antique enthusiasts. One auction can have a variety of merchandise and another may have specialized merchandise. They can be in the heart of the big city or at some isolated outpost in a farmer's field. They can be entertaining and sometimes even thrilling. "Like going on a wild mushroom hunt," says one collector. "Just the adventure is exciting." At auctions, dealers and the public mix as equals and set the market value for that day.

How to Get Going (At Least Once)

Yes, there is an antique grapevine (with those specially aged grapes you read about in *Wine For Dummies*). Part of the fun of auctions is analyzing the ads and deciding which auctions are best for you. Each auction has its own flavor and some specialize in specific types of antiques. The following section shows you ways to find auctions.

Paper chase: Reading between the lines

Your local papers list area and in-state auctions. The more individual items listed, the better the chance of the auction having quality merchandise. The sentence "tons of boxed lots," could easily mean "lots of junk." Of course, hidden in with the junk may be a treasure, if you can recognize it when you see it. (And here's where an auctioneer who doesn't recognize antiques or know their value can let bargains slip by.)

Household/country auctions are often held outside, in a barn or at a rented facility like a VFW hall and can feature an entire household or specific parts of an estate or household. The auction looks like a giant picnic, only there's usually not much edible spread across all the tables. In these household auctions, even the *boxed lots* (stuff thrown into boxes) have potential. Generally, the auctioneer sets up a couple hours ahead of time, so get there early enough to go through all those boxes. Make notes (mental or otherwise) and reference what you want to bid on. Often, the ad lists *preview hours*. The preview gives you a chance to look things over, write down lot numbers of items you want to bid on, along with notes regarding condition, value, and so on.

Estate sale auctions often have antiques that are *fresh,* which means that the antiques haven't been in the marketplace for a long time. ("This chair was previously owned by a genteel lady who only sat in it on national holidays.")

Word of mouth

Talk to people at sales and auctions. Ask them whose sales and auctions they like to go to and why. Many people travel the region and country going to auctions. They can advise you on which auctioneers tend to carry the type of merchandise you are looking for. Then go to auctions and watch how the auctioneer works. Does he mention the damages on items? Does he seem to know his merchandise? Does he sell quality merchandise?

Getting to know your auctioneer is another great way to find auctions. A good auctioneer can advise you about other auctioneers and how they operate. Ask to be put on his auction mailing list.

Going national

When you're ready to "go national," call some of the more prominent auction houses, such as Sotheby's, Christie's, Phillip's, Butterfield & Butterfield, and Skinner's, and get on their mailing lists. The antique trade publications (covered in Chapter 22 and throughout the book) often list national and regional auctions. Or cruise the Internet and check the individual auction sites.

You can access many of these sites by just typing the name of the auction house and **.com.** For example:

sothebys.com

Some national auctions are also slotted to coincide with another antique event, for example, when the Asian Art Fair is in New York, the auction houses are often auctioning Asian antiques.

Preparing for the Auction Block

Before you raise your hand for the first time, familiarize yourself with the lingo and the rules of the game. Here's what you want to know:

- **What are the bidding increments?** *Increments* are the minimum jumps the auctioneer requires to make the next bid. These increments can change when the bidding reaches certain monetary levels. Sometimes the catalogue defines the bidding increments; sometimes you just have to ask.
- **Are there reserves?** A *reserve* is a lower limit, a number unknown to you, the bidder. The reserve is no higher than the low estimate listed in the catalogue. For example, if there is a 60 percent reserve and the item is estimated to sell for $100 to $125, you can expect to pay at least $60.00 for the piece. If the auctioneer does not receive a bid at least that high, he cannot sell the piece. Then it becomes a *bought-in piece,* which means that the auction company returns it to the owner.
- **Is the merchandise sold "as is?"** Or, if you find damage when you get home, can you return it? Many knowledgeable auctioneers try to mark any damage they find. Most auctions sell things "as is." So it's vital to carefully examine the merchandise before you bid.
- **Is there a buyer's premium and if so, how much?** When an auction states a buyer's premium, typically you pay a 5 to 15 percent premium above your closing bid.
- **Is there sales tax?** Sales tax is often listed in the catalogue.

When you're new to auctions, remember all the additional charges as you make your bid. An extra 5 to 7 percent tax on top of a 10 percent buyer's fee can add a hefty amount to the "hammer price."

Catalogue shopping

Auctions often have a catalogue and a preview period. If you're on an auctioneer's mailing list, you get the catalogue in advance. Catalogue descriptions vary in detail from "green lamp shade" to "German glass with yellow and black swirl, 60 year Jubilee, 1908," to still greater detail for the more important items.

For the large national houses, purchase the auction catalogues in advance. These are often full-color catalogues, which include wonderful photographs, detailed descriptions, and the estimated prices the auction company believes each piece will realize.

The estimates are merely that; actual auction prices can be far lower, right within or far above the estimates. Reading these catalogues is a great way to really understand more about antiques and to focus on your goals at the preview session.

Do not use the catalogues to analyze condition. The description is rarely thorough enough. You need to examine the piece firsthand or have someone you trust examine the piece for you. At the major houses, you can call and ask for a specialist who will get you a condition report and answer your questions about the piece.

Auctions that last two to three days give their customers a sale bill that tells which days they are auctioning off which items. For example, the sale bill may read *Saturday — Glassware and pottery; Sunday — Furniture and household goods.* In the larger auction houses, they will often list which lots will sell on what day or *session* by lot number (for example, *Morning Session: Lots 1-250*).

Previews

You've looked at the catalogue and you know what tugs at your heart. Now you're ready to preview the merchandise. For the larger auctions, attending the preview is vital. You need time to look everything over and see what you might be interested in. Then you may need to go research, so that you can decide what items you want and what you're willing to bid.

Auctions are one place where being a specialist, not a generalist, comes in handy. Part of the thrill of auctions is the aura of the "sleeper," the piece you can get for a song when it's really worth the whole orchestral treatment. Just like the prince hacking his way through the bramble hedge not knowing what he would find in the castle, you need patience, knowledge, strength of character, and a fairy godmother or two (or good luck) for your vision of the "sleeper beauty" to come to life.

Talk to other collectors. Talk to the auction personnel. Ask for help in looking at the pieces. Be sure to contain your natural vivaciousness and enthusiasm when looking at a piece that you are interested in. You may be tempted to extol the virtues of your favorite pieces, but wait until the piece is safely ensconced in your home; otherwise, you might inadvertently get someone else interested.

Talk to the most knowledgeable people in the auction house about the pieces you are interested in. Develop a relationship with them. If the catalogue says, *restored, repairs,* or anything else regarding problems with condition of the pieces you like, find out specifically what that means.

Auction houses may not always know how much the piece has been restored, so ultimately you have to rely on your own resources.

Bidders, Biddies, and Absentees

Unseen people affect the auction. It's good to know who's who, in and out of the room.

- **Absentee bidders** send in bids for certain objects, letting the auctioneer know the maximum they will pay. If you have time or travel constraints, or you get restless sitting too long, and absentee bidding sounds like your cup of jasmine tea, make sure that you work with an auction house you truly trust. You need to know the auctioneer will not go up to your maximum when it's not necessary.
- **Telephone bidders** have more control than absentee bidders. They are actually on the phone with auction department staff while the pieces of interest are being auctioned. The representative on the phone consults with them and bids for them so that they can make on-the-spot decisions about how high they want to go.

You need to know and trust the house. Auctioneers have been known to "take bids from the chandelier," which means they are acknowledging bids that aren't really there, thus, falsely raising the ongoing bidding.

- **Auctioneers** don't have to know anything about antiques to auction them off. That's why it's wise to get to know the auctioneer, particularly in a local setting, and to learn which have antique expertise. The role of the auctioneer is to inspire the bidding, keep it moving and get the most for the piece. Because of this, you might feel more secure with an auctioneer who knows how to note damages, identify pieces properly, and estimate market prices.
- **Spotters** stand next to the auctioneer or roam around the room, looking for raised fingers and subtle bids.
- **Clerks, cashiers, security, or ring men** may carry the merchandise over to show a potential bidder. At some auctions, staff helps the bidders pack up the pieces and load them into their cars.

Strategic Planning: Taking Action in the Auction

Contrary to mythology, you can scratch your head during an auction without the auctioneer thinking you are bidding. You may want to watch several auctions before you consider bidding. When you are ready to buy, use these guidelines to map out your bidding strategies.

Front row or back wall? Where to sit

The first decision you need to make is where to sit. Many seasoned bidders find a low-key approach works well. Here are three good options for where to sit:

- **The front row:** In the front row, you can bid by holding your finger up to your chest, and no one but the auctioneer will see you.
- **The back row:** In the back row, you get the grand overview, the chance to watch the whole scene unfold before your eyes without being easily observed by everyone else.
- **The center aisle:** From the center aisle, you can hold the bidding paddle or your hand down and out to the side, making it less obvious to most of the room that you are bidding.

In the action and out of the limelight

Perhaps you enjoy going to auctions and thrive on the notoriety, but want to come and go with as little fanfare as possible. If so, here are some bidding tips for you. If not, these tips let you know what others might be doing around you.

A touch to the eyebrow, a subtle finger, or a nod of the head will be picked up by a sharp auctioneer. If you want to remain as anonymous as possible during the bidding, you may choose to make a gesture as subtle as a wink. If you do, be sure either the auctioneer or a spotter is tuned into your cue so that you are not left out of the bidding.

These techniques can prevent others from tracking your bids. However, some auctioneers point out the bidder by saying "The bid is now with the lady on the aisle" or "The gentleman in the back row." When the bidding is over for that piece, the auctioneer may point you out yet again, this time as the successful bidder.

Should you wish to uplevel your anonymity, you can resort to write-in bids, phone bidding, or sending a friend. Some people choose one of these methods and then sit quietly in the back of the room and watch the action without being directly a part of it.

Bid by bid: How to bid

The bidding process requires some assertion on your part. Here are some common ways you can bid:

- Raise your bid card, which could be a scrap of paper or a paddle
- Raise your hand, or your forefinger
- Establish eye contact with the auctioneer and nod
- Agree in advance with the auctioneer on a subtle gesture you will use

Raise your hand and raise the bid

The auctioneer often leads the bidding by suggesting the next number. If no takers are in the room, you can raise your hand and either call out your bid or hold up a finger.

For example, suppose that they are auctioning off a marvelous Wave Crest box. The last bid was $225.00.

In the action and *in* the limelight

Here's a bidding strategy for the extrovert in you. Raise your hand definitively when you bid. If you hesitate, you let your competition know that you are indecisive and could back down. To show your seriousness, you can even bid over the auctioneer's incremental amount. Your assertive manner could quiet down the house and save you a few dollars.

If you are really into intimidation, raise your hand or paddle and leave it up until you get the item or you reach your limit.

In a large room, when you try to get in after bidding is well under way, you may need to be bold. We saw a man raise his hand several times, only to go unnoticed by the auctioneer. Finally, after the gavel had sounded, he stood up and said, "I was trying to bid." The auctioneer graciously reopened the bidding, but it was at his discretion whether or not to do so.

"Do I hear $250?" the auctioneer sings out. You want to bid just $10.00 above the last bid, so you wait, hoping no one else will bid. The room is silent. Then you call out "$235." The auctioneer can accept or reject your bid. Depending on the house rules, the auctioneer may or may not have the discretion to take a bid for less than the next incremental amount that he has called for. Often your bid will be accepted, so there is no harm in trying.

To avoid potential embarrassment, ask in advance if the auctioneer accepts bids for less than the incremental amount.

If only a few people are bidding, the auctioneer will look to you after each bid, to see if you are still in the game. When you have reached your limit, you can lower your head and break eye contact or simply shake your head when the auctioneer looks at you.

Before you go into the auction, set limits on each item you want to bid on. You can take aspirins for an ordinary fever, but for auction fever, preventive medicine is best. Here's how to prevent this fever from taking you over and wiping you out: Decide on a price ceiling. Give yourself an additional 10 percent, just to allow for a slight auction temperature. Stick with the ceiling, no matter what.

Bidding your time: When to bid

Some auctioneers ask for a starting price. If there are no takers, someone might offer a lower price or the auctioneer might lower the starting price.

If you are interested in a piece and no one opens the bidding, make your first bid low. Assuming that there is no reserve (or that you have met the reserve), you can buy the piece for a low amount, if nobody else bids.

One strategy is to let others get the bidding going. Watch how things go; otherwise, you may be fever pitched into a long bidding contest, joining a crowd of people all blurting out their bids simultaneously, thus raising the temperature of the entire room. Keep a cool head and wait until the bidding wanes before jumping in. Then, as a general rule, raise the price by small increments.

As your expertise grows, you may spot a valuable piece the less knowledgeable auctioneer did not properly identify. This puts you in a great bidding position, since many of the other bidders will also not know the value of the piece. (Unless, of course, they've read *Antiquing For Dummies!*) If you notice damage the auctioneer did not note, you could actually be at a disadvantage if you want to buy the piece despite the damage. Other bidders might think the piece is perfect, and they might bid unnecessarily high.

The Wrap Up: Cash and Carry

Some auction companies take credit cards or checks from people "known to the auction company." For others, you must have cash, traveler's checks, or a letter of credit from your bank.

At the end of the auction, it's your responsibility to pack up your merchandise and get it home. So carry packing materials in your car.

Good News and Bad News

The RISES theory gives you some pros and cons of auctions.

- **Risky:** Typically, you cannot bring things back. You need to deal with auction houses you trust and/or know what you're doing.
- **Investment in Time:** You can stay all day, and still not get anything. Dress comfortably, take food if you need to, and prepare for bad weather if the auction is held outdoors.

- **Sleepers:** The possibility of sleepers adds a delicious thrill to the auction hunt.
- **Equal chances:** You have as much chance as anyone of getting this great merchandise.
- **Special merchandise:** Special merchandise is sometimes sold at auction, stuff you might not otherwise see. Museums sell off various collections; movie stars sell their stuff; Grandma Schwartz's estate goes into the auction. Talk about a journey into another world: Where else can you see — and potentially buy — the contents of an Iowa farm house or a snuff bottle collection of a great museum or a private collection of antique American furniture?

Chapter 8

Cruising for Fabulous Finds: Antique Malls and Flea Markets

In This Chapter

- Milling around antique malls
- Getting the best buy at antique malls
- Scratching the surface at flea markets
- Ferreting out the thrift stores

Some people think unearthing buried treasure requires shovels and maps. Others find malls and flea markets an equally good way to uncover treasure. Most people find a delightful spontaneity comes with sifting through the complex jumble of merchandise at antique malls and flea markets.

These days, fascinating malls and fleas pop up everywhere. The sections that follow give you tips for making the most of your mall and market expeditions.

A Mall and the Day Visitors

An antique mall (or *collective,* as they are called in some areas) hovers by every other highway exit. Inside, you find glass cases and wooden shelves, where dealers of all kinds can leave their merchandise. Some malls require each tenant to work the floor every so often. Others hire managers to deal with customers.

Some malls are elegant and refined. Others are squatting on asphalt. Still others are tucked into barns, houses, and pre-fab buildings.

Malls often advertise by the number of dealers. You can sometimes get a sense of the quality of the mall by looking at the ad. Some malls simply use the word *antique* to mean any old stuff. The merchandise inside malls tends to be as varied as the buildings themselves.

Malls can feel overwhelming. The following sections provide some ways to make the most of your time and your money when you're cruising for antiques.

Finding an antique mall

Finding an antique mall that takes seriously the word *antique* can sometimes be a challenge. Both malls filled with various types of "old stuff" and malls with a high percentage of antiques and collectibles are fun and can yield grand and surprising things. If you want to target your mall experience to searching out antiques, call before you visit and see if you can get a sense of their merchandise.

Finding one antique shop or mall can often be your ticket to finding others in the vicinity. Here are some places to look for malls:

- **Signs on the road:** Drive-by antiquing is a great way to discover something wonderful. Look at the billboards as you speed along the highway. You can find antique malls right off the freeway.
- **Yellow Pages:** Often you find malls listed under *Antiques.* Some list the number of dealers; others include their square footage. Still, you can't judge the antique quotient by the size of the mall: Big malls with many dealers can give you more chances of finding something good or can take you more time to figure out there's nothing there.
- **Antique shops:** If there's an antique district around, start your search there. Antique shops often know about other antique areas. Some dealers have a shop and a booth in a mall, as well.
- **The Internet:** You can also do a mall crawl through the Internet to get the location and size of various malls. Use a search engine such as Lycos and enter antique malls and then sift through the information. You can find malls by state or specific Web sites, such as `www.showcaseantiquemall.com`, which describes the Showcase Antique Mall, a 300-dealer mall in Toronto, Canada.

Before you travel, look at the antique mall ads in the applicable trade periodicals such as the *Maine Antique Digest* and the *Antique Trader.* Many large malls advertise in the periodicals, complete with lists of dealers and pictures of merchandise. (See Chapter 22 for a more complete listing of periodicals.)

The Alliance Guide to Antique & Craft Malls: A Traveler's Companion by Jim Goodridge (published by Alliance Publishing) provides a state-by-state guide to 2000 antique and craft malls.

Pre-mall prep

Get ready for the mall before you even go in. Divest yourself of purses and backpacks: Many malls ask you to leave any satchels, purses, or packages at the front anyway. The fewer items you carry, the less you have to worry about knocking into merchandise. You may want a pen and paper, a tape measure, and your flashlight.

When you enter the mall, stop at the desk to ask the "rules." Here are some questions you might ask:

- Do you offer discounts?
- If I want to get into a showcase, do you have people around to help me? (Some malls are quite large, so knowing how to get help can save you a lot of time and running around.)
- Is there a restaurant or snack bar?
- How many floors are there?
- Do you take bids or offers?
- Anything else I need to know?

Cruising the mall

When you first enter a large mall, you can have that moment of panic: How can you see everything? Ask yourself, How much time do I have? Are you looking for anything specific?

If you have limited time and are on a quest for the perfect teacup, ask the front desk if they know of any teacups. The person at the front desk should be able to answer your question. If he can't help you, ask to speak to the manager, who may be more knowledgeable, and in some malls, may even get a percentage of sales.

If you have time, wander through the entire mall and look at everything. This is a great way to get familiar with what the different dealers carry and how they price things. Simply walk quickly through, letting anything catch your eye. Then walk more slowly and deliberately. Be sure to look under the tables for merchandise that is kept on the floor.

One booth may look like it contains all lunchbox memorabilia and Smurf glasses and yet the antique that you've been looking for may lurk on the lower shelf between the Santa candle and the old Hershey's advertising tin.

If you see something you like, carry it to the front desk and ask them to hold it for you, assuming that no floor clerks are around. If you see something you're thinking about, make a note of the booth number and location. In a large mall, you can easily forget which booth is where, especially when you get tired.

Note the booth numbers that carry objects from the period you like or that carry the types of things you like so that you can check in on them next time you come to the mall.

An added bonus: Malls (and flea markets) can be great places to find used and reasonably priced books on antiquing.

Making the price right: Negotiating at malls

As with any small business, each mall is managed differently. Some malls have steady managers, who know the dealers and where most of the merchandise is. Others have a rotating staffing system, with lesser knowledge of what's in the stalls. Managers who are willing to work with you and make calls to the dealers give you a better chance of experiencing a real negotiation.

The following sections describe the way the mall negotiating system often works.

Asking for the best price

Often, each dealer has filled out a form that outlines his or her "conditions of sale." The form includes information such as the discount they are willing to give and whether he or she accepts bids. So if you ask, "What's the best price on this?" the clerk can simply look at the dealer's form and tell you the percentage discount.

An exception to these conditions is something that is marked *firm*: That means the price indicated is the dealer's lowest price.

Because the dealer is typically not around, bargaining is often as simple as accepting the discount or not buying the piece. The clerks often don't know much about the individual pieces and generally have no negotiating powers over and above what the dealer has put on his form. If you really want to discuss the piece, or want it for a lower price, ask the clerk to call the dealer for you.

In some malls, only dealers with a tax ID number get a discount. But more frequently, anyone who asks for a discount will get one. So it's worthwhile to ask if they give discounts.

In some malls, you get a discount only on items of a certain dollar amount. If you find an item you really like that's under the dollar amount, keep looking around in the same dealer's booth. If you find something else you like, you can combine your two items and receive the discount.

Bidding your time

Many dealers accept bids on pieces. Some malls have a minimum dollar amount for bidding, such as the piece must cost at least $50.00. Other malls don't accept bids on pieces that are already reduced. If the discount doesn't suit you and you really want the piece, see if you can leave a bid.

Sometimes the clerk can reach the dealer right then. She tells the dealer your bid, and the dealer accepts or rejects it or makes a counter-offer. Other times, the clerk has to leave a message with your bid.

The usual protocol is not to bid less than 75 percent of the marked price. After your bid has been accepted, the dealer expects you to buy the piece.

The good news about bids: You can often get the piece for a reduced price (particularly if it's a piece they've had in inventory for a while). The bad news: Often you have to make a trip back to the mall to pick up your piece.

The Greatest Flea Circuses on Earth

Flea markets have a buzzing, electric energy. You can find them in fields, in old buildings, on street corners, and in lean-tos by the side of the road. Some flea markets appear every weekend, and some, such as Brimfield (one of the country's great outdoor flea markets in Brimfield, Massachusetts), are seasonal. Some are monthly; some are only on summer weekends.

Some flea markets are upscale with lots of antiques, and others are open to anyone at $5.00 a table (and you can set up the day of the market).

Finding flea markets

To find flea markets, look in newspapers and in national antique magazines and papers. Inquire at antique shops. Ask people who love to hunt for things about their favorites. Many periodicals, such as Warman's *Today's Collector,* and the *Antique Trader,* list flea markets. Keep a list, for when you travel.

Every flea market has its own time frame and hours. Ask dogged flea shoppers for tips on what's what and what markets have the best antiquing possibilities. Expect to pay a modest entry fee and sometimes a parking fee.

If you want a fun and functional guide to flea markets, flea market shopping strategies, and flea market prices and categories, check out any of the following books:

- ***Flea Market Treasures,* by Harry Rinker (published by Wallace Homestead Books).** Provides great pricing information, a price guide for all kinds of fascinating things, as well as great tips for making the most of the flea shopping experience.
- ***Flea Market Trader,* by Sharon & Bob Huxford (published by Collector Books).** Provides a good price guide, listing thousands of items, with brief descriptions for each category.
- ***The Official Directory to U.S. Flea Markets* by Kitty Werner (published by House of Collectibles Press).** Gives you hundreds of flea markets, listed by state.

Even the Net has fleas:

- `www.fleacountryusa.com` offers a partial directory of flea markets by region. Many list addresses and phones, but no times or hours.
- `www.fleamarketguide.com` lists American and Canadian flea markets.

These lists may not be complete, but they are a good starting point. Some markets list directions, hours, phone numbers, even booth prices. (So you know how much money the dealers have to bring in each month!)

Flea markets are everywhere. But not all fleas are equal. The following sections describe just a few great flea markets.

Brimfield

Some flea market aficionados say, "You haven't lived until you've been to Brimfield." Brimfield is a seasonal market held in Brimfield, Massachusetts. The market is held for six days in May, July, and September. The smaller markets open early; the major markets are open only Friday and Saturday.

Brimfield began in 1959 with 67 exhibitors spread across the family field and now hosts more than 4,000 dealers spread over more than 20 fields. Some of the dealers, such as J & J, sell only antiques and collectibles. Plan as though you are going on a long and amazing journey (because you are). Bring all-weather gear and read the survival guide in *Flea Market Treasures* before you go.

Dates may vary. You can call J & J Promotions (the founders of Brimfield) at (413) 245-3436 for more information. Or go to `www.brimfield.com` on the Net.

Kane County Flea Market

Kane County Flea Market bills itself as the "best in the Midwest or anywhere." It's held the first Sunday of the month, and the preceding Saturday, in St. Charles, Illinois.

More than 30 years ago, Helen Robinson started this market with 14 dealers. One hundred people attended the first market. Now, 1,400 dealers, including Helen, show up during the summertime, attracting up to 25,000 people on a Sunday! This indoor/outdoor flea market continues in winter, with 400 to 800 dealers, depending on the weather.

Call (630) 377-2252 or visit the Web site at `www2.pair.com/kaneflea`.

Renningers Extravaganza

Three times a year, Renningers hosts the Antique & Collectors Extravaganzas at Kutztown, Pennsylvania. Held every April, June, and September on the last Thursday, Friday, and Saturday, these shows feature over 1,200 dealers from 42 states. Call (877) 385-0104 to find out more.

After the extravaganza, spend Sunday in nearby Adamstown, Pennsylvania. Open every Sunday 7:30 a.m. to 4 p.m., Renningers Adamstown hosts 350 indoor dealers. Want some really exciting shopping? Bring a flashlight and show up at 5 a.m.! Call (717) 336-2177.

Renningers also has markets and extravaganzas in Mt. Dora, Florida, and holds a mid-winter classic in King of Prussia, Pennsylvania. Find out more by going to `www.renningers.com` or call (610) 683-6848.

Dogging the flea markets

For outdoor flea markets, you want to be ready to weather any weather. You want comfortable, good shoes that are happy in the potential mud and dust, packing materials, and a list of things you are looking for. Also stash a few of your favorite price guides in your trunk, in case you need a quick consultation.

You'll notice that many of the exhibitors are sitting around snacking on wonderful looking food. They probably brought this food with them. Many flea markets have carnival-type cuisine. (Or as Elvis might say, "You ate nothing but a corn dog. . . .") If you're making a day of it, and you're not into chips and dogs and cola, bring some nutritious backup.

To prevent unwittingly getting "lost in space," write down where you parked your car. After you get into the flea market, pick a meeting spot, in case you separate from your group. Many markets do not page for lost children or adults. ("We'd be paging all day," one promoter told us.)

Take a quick walk through to get the lay of the land. (Sometimes, this is quite literal; you'll be walking in grass, over mud, and through ruts.) If you see something you want, but you want to price shop a bit, you can ask the dealer to hold it for you for an hour or so. If they won't, don't be offended. Things sell fast at markets. Understandably, the dealer would like to have a sure sale, not just a "maybe."

The sellers run the gamut, from someone who's been collecting a long time and wants to weed out their collection, to someone who's just doing this for fun to the dealer who makes his annual income from doing flea markets, mall shows, and garage sales. You need to be your own expert here or take one with you.

Flea bargaining

Bargaining is acceptable and often expected at flea markets. It's easy to ask, What is your best price? Sometimes you can ask on one item and get a good price. Then look around the same booth. If you find another item, ask for the best if you take both pieces.

Training grounds

Dealers-in-training often get started with a booth at a mall or flea market. For example, Judy had a little penchant for cut glass. She studied avidly; she bought judiciously. When she could no longer use her dining room table, because it was covered with cut glass, she figured it was time to sell something. She rented a case in a local mall. Then she had to rent another and finally, she rented a whole booth. Today, she still has a booth there. She makes her living traveling around to shows.

Many malls and fleas have reasonable rates that make them ideal selling grounds for both collectors and dealers. So you may be buying from a professional antique dealer or from a hobbyist or collector. And should your dining room table start flowing over with antiques, someone may be buying from you.

The Accidental Antique: Sifting through the Thrift Shops

Antiques do surface in thrift stores, occasionally. If you already like thrift stores and would look there anyway, you might as well also be on the alert for the misplaced antique.

Salvation Army and Goodwill are common thrift stores. Many charitable organizations run thrift shops, as do hospitals, churches, Junior Leagues, and cultural groups, such as the symphony. Simply look in the Yellow Pages. When you're traveling, ask around for people's favorites.

In thrift stores, you can find everything from well-worn clothing to real antiques and collectibles. Many of these places have only volunteer help, so you're on your own if you have questions about something. If you're serious about tracking antiques, go on weekdays and go early. If not, just enjoy the thrill of the hunt.

Chapter 9

Doing a Little Legwork: Estate and Garage Sales, Classifieds and Cyber-Buys

In This Chapter

- Being the first in line at an estate sale
- Trolling the garage sales and yard sales
- Scouring the want ads
- Surfing your way through the Web of antiques

How can you keep up with the Jones's if you don't even know what they have? Garage sales, estate sales, and the want ads provide a firsthand peek at what others have for sale. Plus you can get a jump on everybody by being the first in line at a sale or the first to call on an ad.

Poking around through a stranger's stuff can be thrilling for those of us on the hunt for that special something. And it's sometimes a great way to find fascinating things at rock-bottom prices.

You are the expert when you buy from individuals. You have to rely on your own judgment and powers of observation. Things are sold "as is," and sometimes you have only minutes or hours to decide on your purchase. You have no guarantees of authenticity and no recourse if you are later dissatisfied. The buck, and hopefully a buck that has been well spent, stops at you.

Even if you're uncertain of your antique expertise, you can still have lots of fun at estate sales and garage sales, and answering want ads and surfing online auctions. Simply buy things you love for a price you are happy to pay. That way, if the antique writing desk turns out to be younger than your teenager, you won't be unhappy.

Wise and Wherefores of Estate Sales

It's 5 a.m. on a Thursday morning, and already the line extends for half a block. Impatient hopefuls are guzzling coffee and swapping tales of marathon waits. "Five hours," says one. "In subzero temperatures," says another. "Eight hours," says another, "and it was in pouring rain." These aren't loyal Deadheads talking; they're estate sale aficionados.

Individuals hold estate sales for a number of reasons. Perhaps someone died and the heirs want to sell the personal property. Maybe someone is seriously downsizing, moving from a large home to an apartment. Or maybe someone just read a book on simplifying his or her life.

An estate sale is really just an upscale clearance sale. The estate sale is often held in the home and features a household full of furniture and other objects. Most of the time, the unstated sales goal is "everything must go." The pricing and schedule of an estate sale typically goes something like this:

- Estate sales usually last two to three days. On day one, generally little or no bargaining is allowed and prices are not reduced. On day two, prices may be reduced as much as 25 percent.
- During the last day or the final hours of the sale, you may find items marked half-price, depending on the policy of the estate sale operator and the arrangements made with the client.
- In many cases, the liquidator (the person running the estate sale) sells everything that is left over for a lump sum. Some liquidators have salvage dealers come in at the end of the sale and make bids on buying the remains of the day. The highest bidder gets everything.

State of the art estate sale strategies

Some liquidators are open to polite bargaining. Stating your offer with a question such as, "Can you take $50 for this?" is preferable to saying "I'll give you $50 for it." The amount of markdown depends on the individual liquidator.

If bargaining doesn't work, ask the liquidator if she'll accept a bid. Some liquidators keep bid forms on hand. That way, you can write down your offer for that lovely crazy quilt. If the quilt doesn't sell the first or second day, the liquidator will call you before the markdown on the final day. Your bid may be far less than the original asking price and far above what they will get from a salvage dealer. This is one of the advantages of buying in an "everything must go" market.

How estate sales work

Estate sales are typically held in the home, and estate sale auctions are typically held off-site. The estate sale auction is conducted like any other auction. To find out how to make a bid, read Chapter 7.

Here's how the estate sale works:

If individuals decide to run their own sales, they set the prices, using whatever criteria they can figure out. They might visit antique shops or other estate sales to get an idea of market prices.

Often a professional liquidator runs the sale. Ideally, the liquidator knows the marketplace and sets competitive prices. Sometimes a liquidator with no particular expertise in antiques might be hired to run a sale that features some antique items. This is good news and bad news. You can find bargains shopping a sale where a liquidator might miss or misprice an antique. You can also find things incorrectly labeled and too highly priced.

Some liquidators are also appraisers. This means that they should have a definite feel for the prices and will research items as necessary.

Reading between the ads

Get in the habit of combing the classifieds in your daily newspapers and the weekly free "shoppers" for notices of estate sales. Take special note of their locations. Some estate sale experts say the higher-quality items tend to be found in the more affluent neighborhoods. But the hunt is part of the fun of estate sales. You never know where you will find a wonderful antique.

Some ads promise a shopping bonanza with the catch phrases "house packed" or "whole house." That means you'll find many opportunities to buy, since much or all of the household (excepting the kids and the dogs) are for sale. Some ads list the more desirable items for sale.

If you haven't had enough experience to know if the prices are "right," bring a more knowledgeable friend with you. Or before you go to the sale, look up the listed antiques in your price guides. Remember, the price guides compile prices from auctions, dealers, and other sources across the country. Use them only for a general idea of price.

When you become a regular reader of the estate sale ads, you can gain information about various *liquidators*. After you go to a sale, reread the liquidator's ad and analyze his or her advertising strategy. Were the listed items described accurately? Was everything listed in the ad present in the house (assuming you got there right at opening time)? Were the prices fair? Did you find anything wonderful that wasn't listed (indicating the liquidator didn't know what it was)? By asking other estate sale goers, reading the want ads and going to sales, you can learn each liquidator's specialty and expertise. This helps you decide which sales to go to.

On your mark, get set, get in line

Estate sales operate on the basis of first come, first served. With great sales, estate enthusiasts may camp out in vans overnight so that they can be the first in line. If you're serious about acquiring certain advertised merchandise at an estate sale, make sure that you get there early. Bring your own packing materials, just in case the supply is slim. Some sales accept only cash; others take credit cards and checks, as well.

When you arrive, don't be surprised if you see a number of people peering in windows to get an advance peek at what's inside. While you're standing in line, ask the other folks their opinion of the other liquidators who run estate sales. You want to know if their pricing is fair, their areas of expertise, and if they allow pre-sales.

Some buyers try to avoid liquidators who have a reputation for *pre-sales,* which means letting a select group of favored customers into the sale prior to the stated hours.

Here are a couple reasons a liquidator might have a pre-sale:

- The house is so crammed with merchandise that there is worry over breakage or thievery.
- The merchandise is of such quality that the liquidator feels the general public won't appreciate it.

On your mark, get set, buy

In the opening hours of an estate sale, buying activity can move at the speed of a Concorde. The liquidator has set up the items throughout the house, and typically a "sales crew" is around to watch over things and answer questions. Some items are labeled with a brief description; others may just show the price. When liquidators are knowledgeable about antiques, they may note damage or repairs on antique items. Still, it's best not to count on this.

During the opening hours of an estate sale, you often don't have time to mull things over. You need to know your stuff and be prepared to act. Typically, you walk in, fall in love with something, pay for it, and get out. If you see something you want, carry it with you until you see a staff person. The staff person takes it to the cashier. Be careful with fragile items, as you might be responsible for any damage. If the item you're interested in is the size of a four-poster bed, find a salesperson to mark the item "Sold" with your name on it.

If you suddenly decide not to purchase yet another antique rocking chair, tell the cashier right away. That way, the staff can put the chair back on the floor.

You don't have to be caught in the buying frenzy. If you want to take your time and examine things, come in the *remains of the day,* the late afternoon or the morning of the second day. The fierce buyers have rushed through and plenty is still left. This is a great way to take your time, browse, examine items, and test your ARE (Antique Recognition Expertise). You can walk in anytime during sale hours.

If you're confident in your antiquing abilities, check in advance with the liquidator to see if you can come equipped with sticky notes with your name on them. Then you can run through the rooms and tag everything you want. This gives you a tremendous advantage over the rest of your competition.

After you've tagged everything, let the sales staff know which items you have posted. In the frenzied and chaotic atmosphere of the opening moments, your carefully placed note could be "jostled" (yes, it is a jungle in there) and a piece that you specifically came for could end up in someone else's hands.

The mother of all estate sales

There are estate sales and then there are the mothers of all estate sales. One of our favorite liquidators, who is also an appraiser, recently held a grand estate sale. She began with a wine and cheese invitation-only preview party. To get into the party, each person had to donate to the client's favorite charity. At the preview sale (not a presale, but just a place to get a look at the wonderful antiques) she handed out numbers so that people would know what order they could come into the sale the next day. Why the donation? The house itself was so gorgeous, she wanted to eliminate the house gawkers. She hoped this strategy would lure top buyers to the preview — and afterwards to the sale.

Finding Antiques Parked at a Garage Sale

Carolyn owns a turn-of-the-century American oak chair, which she found at a garage sale across the street from her. She almost didn't spot the chair because it was stacked with flowered sheets and accounting textbooks. The price was a mere five dollars. She now has a beautiful antique chair in her dining room and a story to go with it.

Although you may visit many garage sales or yard sales before you find something you love, when you do find that special piece, the price can be very right. If you know your antiques and the seller doesn't, you have a chance to score wonderful bargains.

A strategic game plan

Going to garage sales and yard sales can be an entertaining experience, particularly if you invite other people to go along with you. Choose people who are interested in searching for a variety of things. With different types of collectors in your group, you have others who can help you scout out the things you're looking for without adding to the competition. In addition, you can learn from them about other collectibles and antiques. Plus, it's simply more fun to have companions when you search for your treasures.

Once Upon a Garage Sale by Lisa Rogovin Payne (published by Clover Creations), gives you the inside story on garage sales from a veteran sale-goer. The book tells you how to have great sales and also helps those going to sales. *Rummagers Handbook,* by R. S. McClurg (published by Storey Publishing), is lots of fun for buying, selling, and fixing up treasures.

Garage sales and yard sales have one major drawback: Because many garage sale ads don't list a phone number, you frequently can't call ahead and ask questions in order to save yourself some legwork.

Finding the right garages

Find garage sales by looking in the classified section of shoppers and free newspapers under *Garage Sales.* The sales are usually broken down into sections of the city. Some garage sale enthusiasts even line up to get an early newspaper. That way they can plan their strategy, mapping out sales by area, so they can cover the most territory in the least amount of time.

Military bases are good places to look for garage sales. Sometimes the entire base gets involved. You can acquire some unusual pieces (along with run-of-the-mill garage sale fare) because military personnel often travel the world and bring a variety of stuff back home with them.

Neighborhood associations, schools, and churches frequently have giant garage sales where you can cruise through loads of merchandise presented all in one place. Multi-family or block garage sales save you driving time and energy.

Sailing through the sales

When you're driving by garage sales, stop at those with lots of cars and people crowded about. That's usually a sign of a good sale. Ask the other buyers what other sales they've been to that day and if they recommend any of them.

The homeowner is pricing the merchandise and may be simply guessing on price. They may put a lofty price on something they consider old or a cheap price on an antique they know nothing about.

Garage sales are good places to bargain. Use the techniques described in Chapter 5 to try to get a more favorable deal.

If you can go during the week, instead of on the weekend, you'll miss some of the crowds.

You just paid cash for a wonderful Victorian chest of drawers you found at a garage sale. In order to get the chest home, you have to borrow your former brother-in-law's pickup truck (and your former brother-in-law). To be on the safe side, take one of the drawers with you. That way, the seller won't be tempted to sell your treasure to a bounty hunter.

Classic Stuff in Classified Ads

While you're sipping your morning coffee, you may as well peruse your local newspaper's classified ads to see if any desirable antique items are up for sale.

The classifieds add up

Shopping for antiques through the classified ads has its advantages:

- **Convenience:** You don't have to give up your day job to pursue antiques. You can usually make appointments after work or on weekends.
- **Bargaining:** If you are alone with the seller (generally preferred), you may have a better chance to wheel and deal.

When bargaining, point out specific work you would need to do to fix up the piece, such as reupholstering, refinishing, or re-gluing. You can start by saying, "I like the piece but I have a problem with the amount of work it needs. Given your asking price and market prices, I don't feel I can pay full price." Say it politely, but with conviction, and then wait for the seller to respond. The seller may be tired of making appointments and having strangers trudging in and out and be ready to offer you the piece at a lower price.

Down sides of classifieds

Some disadvantages of antiquing through the classifieds include:

- **The risk involved:** You have no money-back guarantee and you have to rely on your own expertise.
- **You need to supply cash or check on demand:** No credit cards are accepted and no lay-a-way plans are available.
- **No deliveries:** You have to pick it up and schlep it home yourself.
- **Time and energy expense:** You may end up wasting a lot of time and energy and not buy anything, especially if you drive a long distance to see only one or a few things instead of a large selection.

Write a check whenever possible for any classified ad purchase. That gives you a little protection in case the majolica vase you bought turns out to have a repaired crack that the 25-watt light bulb in the owner's house failed to reveal.

Ad hoc questions

Want ads often give a fair to good description of an item for sale, the asking price, and a phone number to call. If the ad says "Queen Anne Chair circa 18th century," it's possible that the advertiser knows exactly what he or she has. It's also possible that the chair is an early 20th century copy of a Queen Anne the seller thinks is a couple hundred years older than it really is. In this case, it pays to call and ask the seller if the chair has been authenticated or if they have some actual proof of its age.

The more questions you ask over the phone, the more time and energy you'll save in want ad wonderland. Here are some questions you might ask:

- **How did the seller acquire the piece and how long has he had it? Did he buy it himself, and if so, when and where?** If you get solid answers to these questions, you have clues as to the age and authenticity of the piece. Plus, you can feel secure that you are not purchasing something that has been stolen. If an item is stolen, sellers often hedge and are evasive in their answers.
- **How much did the seller pay for the item?** Use this as one more clue to the piece's value. Some advertisers may honestly not remember what they paid for an item, or the piece may have been a gift. Others will tell you right off and have a receipt to prove it. But a receipt doesn't mean that the item is worth what they paid for it or what they're asking.
- **What does the phrase "good condition" add up to? Have there been any repairs or refinishing to the piece, or does it have any obvious flaws, such as chips or cracks?** Some people might describe an Oriental carpet as being in "good or very good condition" even when there is a hole in one corner. Wear of this sort greatly diminishes the carpet's value. The more specific details you know about a piece's condition, the more likely you are to avoid a wasted trip. Condition also helps you evaluate the price and gives you ammunition for negotiation.
- **Will the seller negotiate?** The term "$500 or best offer (OBO)" means that they will negotiate. "Serious inquiries only" often means that they may be tougher to deal with on the price. Don't let this deter you from calling or from going to look. Keep in mind that they probably know what they have and don't want a lot of curious people poking around with no intention of buying.

Don't be swayed by the remark, "That belonged to my grandmother." You don't know how long it belonged to grandma. Those grandmas may have had that piece as a teenager or they may have bought it yesterday.

National want ads

Another way to shop the want ads is through the national trade papers, such as *Glass Collector's Digest, "The Bee,"* and *Warman's Today's Collector.* Some items, such as a pattern glass pitcher manufactured by a particular company, are more straightforward to describe than a one-of-a kind hand-blown and hand-decorated art glass vase. The vase has more variables: The pattern glass is mass-manufactured and therefore more consistent in the way it will look.

Some sellers will send you a photo of an item you're interested in for a small fee. If you send a check for the piece, private sellers often wait until your check has cleared before they ship your piece. Typically, the buyer pays the seller for shipping and insurance; the seller will pack the piece for shipment.

Ask the seller how he is packing the piece for shipment. You don't want to end up with a broken piece or insurance that won't be honored because the piece wasn't properly packed.

Surf City: Antique Shopping on the Net

You can wander through a world of antiques without ever leaving home. Try surfing the Internet to learn about antiques. Visit online shops, malls, and museums and buy and sell at auctions.

Part of antiquing online is having patience and a willingness to explore. If you're new at surfing, ask a friend to come and guide you through your first foray. Expect to stumble around a little: That's part of the process.

Ask your friends what sites they like. Once you tell people you're interested in antiques, those who love surfing will e-mail you lots of sites. Get online and just explore. New sites are emerging all the time.

Here are some fun places to visit:

- `www.delphi.com/antiquefreaks` This Web address brings you to the Antique Lovers Forum, a chat room with message boards. They also invite questions.
- `wwar.com` This site concentrates on the arts. You can access stores, the names of museums, and a host of other things.
- `www.collect.com` This site is aligned with Antique Trader publications. It is a fount of antique information, including samples of well-written, researched articles from their magazines, as well as auction opportunities, pricing information, publication information, and more.
- `www.glass.co.nz/links/links.htm` This Web address links you to all kinds of museums, publications, collector's organizations, and more so that you can immerse yourself in glass. It's sponsored by the publication *Antique Week*.

The virtual gavel: Online antique auctions

Visiting an online auction house sounds like a dream job description. Choose your own hours, night or day. See the world (or at least some of the items in it). Wear what you want to. Do it alone or with a group.

Shop the auction sites to see what services each offers. Spend time looking at what's for sale and how much things cost before you bid. When you first bid, bid on something that is inexpensive so that if you make a mistake and pay too much, you can laugh it off. For basic information on auctions and bidding, see Chapter 7.

To find auctions, simply search for "antiques auction." Here are some sites:

- `www.ebay.com` This site includes a chat area and is a great place to get introduced to auctions. It has many auction listings and is an organized and well-run auction. Have fun comparing the differences between the formal auction houses, such as Sotheby's and Christie's, and the online auctions by the people for the people, such as ebay. For example, at Sotheby's, you might read about a Chippendale chair, circa 1782, and at ebay, you see "very old oak chair, "although more detailed descriptions are becoming increasingly common.
- `www.auctionuniverse.com` is an auction site that features antiques and a host of other interesting things.
- `www.ehammer.com` is a site devoted to the online auction of antiques and collectibles. The site was created by two long-time antique dealers.
- For a change of energy, try `www.christies.com`. or `www.sothebys.com`. You can get tips on buying and selling, see their calendar of events, get auction results and visit specialty departments. Search hard: You probably won't find pictures of "really pretty vases" for $15.

Spotting the best auction sites

When you visit an online auction, look for the following features:

- **Feedback on buyers and sellers.** Some auction sites offer feedback on sellers in the form of e-mail comments from people who have dealt with them. Look for the *feedback* link. Some links are available that say *View Seller's Feedback* and *View Buyer's Feedback.* This is a way for you to "know the seller," and learn from the experience of others. When you see sellers who have 150 positive notes, it is hopeful that they are reliable. The buyer information is useful if you are going to sell online.

  The comments may say something like, "Reliable. Merchandise as stated" or "Had problems with the shipping. Had to phone three times to get it straightened out."
- **Numerous categories.** The more specific the categories of antiques, such as pattern glass or cameo glass, the quicker and easier your search.

Even if a seller has "0" listed by the number of comments, look at the actual feedback. The seller may have 11 positive and 11 negative remarks.

- **Quick response time.** You want the pictures to come up quickly, so you're not wasting time. Although quick response does not have anything to do with the quality of the site, it makes your life easier.
- **Responsive and organized administration.** You want an auction house that responds quickly to your e-mails. If you want to get in touch with a seller personally, you may need to get his or her phone number from the auction company.
- **Tracking Screens.** Some auction sites feature a screen that tracks all the objects you are bidding on. The screen tells you when you last bid, if you're still the high bidder, and what time the auction ends. On www.ebay.com, the screen allows you to track all the auctions that you are currently bidding on (even if you are not the current high bidder).

Bidder beware: People do get stung at online auctions! Read the contract you agree to before you bid. With some auction companies, the contracts require that you handle any disputes involving a court in a particular state. The auction company is probably not legally responsible — so if you send in your money, and don't get the item, often you can do little about it, without considerable expenditure of energy and money. If the item you bought is not as described, you also can be stuck.

Talk to the sellers before you buy and try to size them up. One collector, who loves auctions and has been stung a couple times says, "If they aren't willing to give me an actual telephone number, they don't want my actual money."

If you have any doubt about a seller, protect yourself by using an escrow service to hold onto your check until you receive your item in good condition. The catch is the additional cost: a 5 percent fee.

Bidding your time: The buyer's process

Suppose that you are at an auction site, such as www.auctionuniverse.com, looking for K.P.M. porcelain, which is a type of porcelain along the lines of Meissen. Enter the search term **K.P.M.** If you enter "K.P.M." and get nothing, try entering **KPM**. If that doesn't work, type a description such as **German nineteenth century porcelain figurines.** Remember, the sellers enter their own descriptions. You may see misspellings and incorrect labeling. You may find items listed by either name or description.

Sometimes searching by using a general description, such as *glass* instead of *cut glass,* leads you to treasures. Someone might have a piece of glassware and not know exactly what it is. When you see the photo and read the description, you may recognize a nice piece of art glass that the seller hasn't identified.

Suppose that you find a site advertising a K.P.M. porcelain figurine. The site features only one picture and you can't see the mark (the indication of the maker). You want to know more, so you send the seller an e-mail. (Most sellers list their e-mail addresses on their Web pages.) If you prefer live conversation, ask for a phone number when you send the e-mail.

Here are some questions you may want to ask in your e-mail or over the phone:

- **Are any more pictures of the items available?** You want to see the mark and the piece from all sides to determine if it's really something you want to buy.
- **What is the condition?** (If not fully described.) Ask the seller to describe any flaws, chips, flakes, cracks, and so on. When you have photos, you can help determine condition for yourself.
- **Is there a *reserve* and if so what is it?** The *reserve* is the lowest price the sellers will take. The sellers must tell you if there is a reserve amount. But they don't have to disclose the actual amount. If they disclose the reserve, knowing that dollar amount helps you decide if you want to bid. But you can still successfully bid, without knowing the reserve.
- **Who pays for packing, shipping, and insurance?** Find out if you are responsible for these costs and then find out how much these charges add to the price of the item.
- **What is your return policy?** Some dealers guarantee their merchandise; others sell it as is and allow no returns. No returns means no refunds or exchanges.

The more you know about the seller, the more you can analyze their antique expertise. Some sellers are dealers; others are hobbyists. Some are selling antiques very sporadically; others are making a business out of it. A novice seller is more likely to make mistakes in identifying and describing antiques.

After you get the pictures and information you requested, you're ready to decide if you want to bid on the item. Each item is on the auction block for a given number of days. Some buyers like to watch the auction site for a couple of days to determine what the interest is in the item. Because these auctions can last for days, you can get a good idea of how many other people are bidding on the item and what their levels of interest are.

The seller sets the opening bid. As a bidder, you can enter a ceiling amount, the highest amount you want to pay. How do you find your ceiling? Spend time looking at similar items in online auctions and look in price guides, such as *Antique Trader's,* before you bid. The auction company automatically keeps you in the bidding by raising your bid the minimum amount every time someone else bids. This automatic bidding lets you be in the auction without being attached to the computer screen. If someone bids beyond your ceiling, the auction house e-mails you. If you want to raise your ceiling, you can get in the bidding again.

Sneaking up on snipers

Some bidders remain out of an auction until the last few seconds. Then they enter the contest, flashing their high bid to take the piece. These "snipers" are violating the rules of auction etiquette. It's fine to take some days to look things over and get into the bidding; it's not fine to appear at the last moments. According to the rules of some auction houses, if the house can determine who they are, the snipers can be kicked out of the auction. Meanwhile, you may have to deal with them.

An expert on dealing with snipers developed the following strategy: If you're bidding on a piece you really want, be sure to be in front of your computer for the last minutes of the auction. Pull up two Internet windows side by side. On one, you watch the bidding. On the other, you enter your bid (that is, your maximum bid and the most you are willing to pay), your user ID, and any other pertinent information. Then your bid is ready to go, with the stroke of a key, should you need it. If a sniper appears, you can instantly put in your bid and still get your antique.

Part III
Material Possessions

In this part . . .

"It can get to be something of an obsession," one glass collector told us. He has not eaten a meal off his dining room table in two years because it's filled with an array of beautiful cut glass. Talk about magnificent obsession: You could study all day and night for 17 years and still not know all the fascinating stuff there is to know about antique glass, ceramics, and silver.

But in case you want an introduction, enough to get you started on a wonderful obsession, or collection, of your own, this section is for you.

Chapter 10

Glass Conscious: Glassware and Crystal

In This Chapter

- Telling what glass has the most class
- Distinguishing old glass from new
- Discovering early mold-blown glass
- Getting the pressing news about pressed glass
- Sharpening your cut glass skills
- "Buying into" late Victorian era art glass
- Getting to know Art Nouveau era glass

This chapter has lots of great information that will help you "break into" glass collecting. Glass blowing is an ancient art form, and understanding how glass is made helps you identify and value it. We are focusing on American glass, with forays into English and French. We are including glassware that technically is not yet antique (that is, it is not yet 100 years old). This early 20th century glass is so artistic and collectible that we did not want to leave it out. We're also including some glass as recent as the Depression era that features great prices for good quality pieces.

Glass is a rich, varied subject that, as many collectors will tell you, can become something of an obsession. We're introducing you to just some of the many wonderful types of glass. We leave you with the glass half full, hoping you'll want to drink in more.

Glass Collector's Digest is a bimonthly four-color publication that brings you right into the world of glass collecting. Read informative articles by some of the top glass people, absorb auction news and repro news, and become part of what is going on in the glass collecting community. To find out more, check out the Web site at `Antiquepublications.com` or call (800)-533-3433.

When you want your glass to runneth over, here are a few museums with magnificent glass collections:

- Corning Museum of Glass, Corning, NY
- Chrysler Museum, Norfolk, VA
- Metropolitan Museum of Art, New York, NY
- Toledo Museum of Art, Toledo, OH

Something Old, Made by Whom: Tips for Glass ID

To understand the properties of antique glass, get to know the nuances of the new glass you're drinking from right now. Then you can compare. Use these tips to help you distinguish the old sets of glasses and to analyze their condition.

- **Flake Off:** Just as you can identify a homemade pie by its flaky crust, you can often find flaking around the rim of antique glass. A *flake* is a small flat piece without much depth.
- **Nick:** Nicks are about the size of a pinhead and are even less serious than flakes. Nicks keep the piece from being mint.
- **Chips:** A chip can be a real problem. A chip has some depth. On a small piece, such as a goblet, anything as big as an eraser on the end of a pencil can really decrease the value.
- **Missing parts or cracks:** When you get down to missing parts and cracks, the value of the glass diminishes drastically. Cracks and dings can make the piece almost worthless, unless it happens to be a museum piece. Take the glass into the light and look for hairline cracks.
- **Rough spots or breaks:** Run your finger around the rims and bottoms of glassware, looking for rough spots or breaks. If you buy a set of twelve drinking glasses, be sure you give each glass the run around. Watch for "as is" tags. Reputable dealers will note a flaw.
- **Signs of wear:** Old glass typically has scratches on the bottom. Hold the glass up to the light and look at it in different angles. No fine lines, no slight signs of wear, is a strong clue that the piece may not be antique. Use a *loupe* (a jeweler's magnification tool) to look at the scratch marks. Old glass has marks in many different sizes going in many directions. With "faked" age, the lines go only in a few directions and are often similar in size.

Avoiding the grind

There's more than one way to repair glass. Some say grind away, when you encounter a chip or slight flaw. But Chrysler Museum Curator of Glass Gary E. Baker believes that grinding into antique glass is the equivalent of repairing an antique statue that is missing one arm by knocking off the other arm to make both sides match.

"You are not repairing the glass," he says. "You are simply inflicting further damage."

Baker is one of many museum professionals who advocate keeping your antique in its most original state. "Instead of grinding down the glass, consult with a conservator about a plastic implant that repairs the glass in a gentler way."

After you determine whether the glass is old or new, use the following characteristics to help you ID the glass itself:

- **Trademark:** Is the glass signed or marked?
- **Technology:** How is the glass made — blown, molded, or pressed? Technology helps you identify the kind of glass and gives you clues as to its value.
- **Style:** What style is the glass in? What period do you think it is from? This helps you date the glass.
- **Pattern:** What is the pattern (if the glass is pressed or cut)? This helps you figure out the company and helps you date and value the glass.

In the real universe, many glass pieces are not marked. Styles overlap. You need to look carefully at a lot of glass to really distinguish the different methods of making it.

These are also some of the reasons that glass collecting is so much fun: You get marvelous, historic, functional pieces, and you get to research and analyze along the way. (Of course, you can also just enjoy the beauty of the glass and not worry about knowing exactly what you have.)

Glass is shaped in these basic ways: by free-blowing, by blowing into a mold, or by pressing into a mold. Blown glass is one of the earliest of the art forms, and of course, continues through this day. Knowing how the glass is shaped, and later decorated, can help you determine the type of glass and its general value.

Thar he blows: Blown glass

Free-blown glass is one of the earliest methods of glass creation. The skilled glassblower has no mold to fall into and is challenged to control the symmetry and form. The glass must be hot enough to work with and not so hot that it's too liquid. Breath control is vital. (See Figure 10-1 for a glimpse into glassmaking.)

Most blown glass features a *pontil mark,* the mark made when the craftsman separates the glass from the pontil rod, a solid iron rod used for holding a glass object during manufacture. Some companies ground down pontil marks very smoothly; with other companies, the sharp or raised pontil mark is a great way to easily and quickly distinguish blown glass. You can often see carefully smoothed pontil marks on fine pieces of art glass. Less expensive pieces, such as bottles, often didn't have the pontil mark polished away. In the 18th and 19th century, you paid less for a "marked" bottle and more for a bottle with a ground pontil mark.

Some call glassmaking America's first industry. It took a while for the colonists to get their glass act together. Glassmaking, like porcelain making, required a level of technology that was not readily available. They needed craftsmen who knew enough about furnaces to maintain the high heat, moldmakers who could create the molds, chemists who could create the formula, and artisans who could blow the glass.

Figure 10-1: Glassblowing Toledo Factory, from Libbey Glass Co. *Facts On Cut Glass,* Toledo, OH, B.F. Wade Co., about 1893.

Photo courtesy of The Corning Museum of Glass, Corning, NY

Although some tried to create a glass house at Jamestown, Caspar Wistar, created the first successful American glass factory in 1739. This entrepreneurial German immigrant, trained in the art of brass buttonmaking, began by making the bottles and window glass the colonists needed. His factory in Alloway, NJ, was located near the ideal mix of natural resources: even-grained, good quality sand; pine forests for fuel; salt marshes filled with "hay" for packing the fragile glass; and small rivers for shipping. There were tariffs on imported glass. Caspar's son Richard was one of the first to advertise "This Glass is American made. Buy American glass."

In the 1920s and '30s, all sorts of early glass was attributed to Wistar. Most of these pieces were actually Germanic imports. Though the few pieces that scholars identified as Wistar glass are in museums, you can occasionally find other early American glass on the market. You also can still find those Germanic imports around.

Here's some interesting trivia: Ben Franklin bought glass tubes from the Wistars for his electrical experiments. Ben was enormously pleased with the quality of these tubes. Ben asked his son, who was to report to Britain on the status of the glass industry in the colonies, to play down the Wistar glass company so that the Crown wouldn't know how successful they were.

Pressing the Glass and Cutting the Cost: Pressed Glass

These days, we talk about "breaking the mold." In the early 19th century, there was more concern over "making the mold." Although molded glass dates back to antiquity, a new mechanical pressing technique developed in the 1820s that used a plunger to push glass into all corners of the mold. This new technique made mass production possible.

With the new improved technology, the skilled glassblower was no longer essential for the production of glass. Here's the way glassmakers used the new mechanical pressing machine to hold a mold.

Imagine you are working in an early glass company. The year is 1830. You are one of a hundred men who work in this "glass house." Talk about a hot spot. The building has thick walls to help keep it cool and dim lighting. You see the blaze of fire through the *glory holes* (the openings cut into the walls of the furnace).

The mold masters

Making the mold is no small accomplishment. As glass making became less dependent on the glass blower's skill, the mold maker became more important. Big companies had their own mold makers; smaller companies relied on independents.

To design and create metal molds, the craftsman needed to be a metal worker and a problem solver. Making a mold could take days, as the mold makers chipped away, creating the intricate patterns in molds, which may have as many as seven pieces.

Imagine glass the consistency of honey. The gatherer has a six-foot iron pontil rod with a solid iron ball the size of a cue ball on the end. He dips the ball into the melting pot of molten glass, and some of the glass adheres to the ball. This glass is known as the *gather.* He keeps turning the ball in the melting pot until he has a large enough gather. If he gets too much, he'll waste glass, and if he gets too little, the piece will be no good. Then, still turning (so that the glass won't drip), he swings the rod over to the mold, which is very close by. He stops the twirling and holds the hot gather of glass over the mold.

The glass flows by gravity into the press mold and the presser cuts it off with a pair of shears. The presser has only a moment to snip off just the right amount of glass. Then the presser pulls a lever and a plunger comes down and forces the glass upwards and into the mold. The pressing mold has a ring around it, which gives the rim of the piece its shape.

Pieces were immediately placed in a *lehr,* a cooling oven, where they gradually cooled for 24 hours. This technique is referred to as *annealing.*

Because of the development of this mechanical glass press, thousands of families who couldn't afford cut glass could have glass on their tables.

Collecting pressed glass from this early period, prior to the 1860s, is for those who love the hunt and who adore learning, studying, and unearthing things. Few companies marked their glass, and companies often copied from each other, so patterns might overlap.

Much of the glass is *flint glass,* with a high lead oxide content, which makes it heavier. Learn the patterns. In the years after the Civil War, non-flint pressed glass (soda lime glass) replaced flint pressed glass. You can often find the later patterns, after the 1870s, in the trade catalogues that the various companies produced.

The following sections provide a brief sample of a few of the types of early American glass you might see.

Early players: The early makers of pressed glass

The Boston and Sandwich Glass Company and the New England Glass Company were both prominent early glass companies that produced a great deal of pattern and other glass. Both companies also produced great blown glass, although not as much of it is around today. Boston and Sandwich concentrated on tableware and lighting devices. Over the years, they made everything from candlesticks to oil lamps to electric lamps, so you can pretty much discover the evolution of lighting by studying these glass products. You can still find pressed glass made by the Boston and Sandwich Glass Company.

Linking early American glass with a specific company can be difficult. When a pattern became popular, many factories began making it. For example, Bellflower and Ashburton were both made by several different factories.

To get more information about Boston and Sandwich Glass and see more than 6,000 pieces of this glass, visit the Sandwich Glass Museum, in Sandwich, MA (508) 888-0251.

Lacy glass (mid-1820s to mid-1840s)

Blazing industrial trails isn't easy. Using the new molds created many technical difficulties. This was back in the old days, before they had *Glassmaking For Dummies.* They struggled figuring out what glass recipes worked best in the molds, how much glass to shear off into the mold, and how to have a long enough cooling period. The early pieces are small, for that's what the new machines could handle, and they often have ornate patterns on them to mask some of the flaws. In the early 20th century, collector's dubbed this glass *lacy.*

The Boston and Sandwich Glass Company made a lot of lacy glass (see Figure 10-2). Some of the lacy glass you might see includes cup plates and salt dishes. In the early days, tea drinking included a deep saucer to pour the tea into so that it could cool, and the cup plate, to hold the dripping teacup. A cup plate is basically a coaster for a teacup.

Salt dishes (small dishes sometimes called simply *salts*) held the coarse ground salt of the time. Other lacy items, such as sugar bowls, are rarer.

Figure 10-2: Lacy plate, hairpin design, and candlestick.

Photo courtesy of the Sandwich Glass Museum, Sandwich, Massachusetts.

The early cup plates are made of glass with a high lead content. When tapped gently with a pencil, the glass rings with a resonance. Look for imperfections in the early pieces. You might see an indented swirl on the inside center, called a shear mark. You might see light cracks, where the glass cooled too quickly, and other imperfections. You might see excess glass between the scallops of a plate from a glass overrun (too much glass poured into the mold).

If the piece looks perfect, it may be a reproduction. Lacy glass feels heavier than it looks. Generally lacy glass in color is rarer and more expensive than clear.

Early American pattern glass (1845–1865)

Even though we were way beyond the colonial era, these patterns have been dubbed *Colonials* by 20th century collectors. Knowing the patterns and types of ware made helps you pinpoint the possible dates of the glass.

There are 17 main patterns of the so-called Colonials. Each pattern has a name, such as *Ashburton, Four Petal,* or *Sandwich Star.* These patterns are relatively simple, as you can see in Figure 10-3. (They copied expensive cut glass patterns of the period.)

Figure 10-3: The "state" of early American pattern glass: Kansas, Bellflower, and Wyoming patterns.

Here are a few of the designs:

- **Thumbprints**
- **Indented circles or ovals**
- **Plain long panels** (flat narrow vertical side panels)
- **Ribbed patterns** (Some ribbed patterns appeared first in flint and then in soda lime, with the flint being the more desirable.)
- **Bull's eyes** (a series of round circles)
- **Diamond**

Many of these wares were made to toast with: Use this pattern glass to celebrate your good fortune with early goblets, wine glasses, and cordial glasses. You can also find footed compotes, decanters, sauces, creamers, and other tableware.

Some people collect by pattern and try to put together sets of tableware. Horn of Plenty and Bellflower patterns were made in extensive services, and you can find wines, goblets, sugars, creamers, spoon holders, pitchers, bowls, open compotes, salts, clarets, and jelly glasses. Some people collect by item and try to get a goblet or salt made in every pattern.

Here's one of many ways to set a vintage table for a reasonable price: Bellflower pattern goblets with ironstone dishes and pre-owned sterling silverware!

Need some more information before you make any "pressing" decisions? You'll enjoy reading Kyle Husfloen's *Collector's Guide to American Pressed Glass 1825–1915* (published by Krause Publications). This book presents a clearly written account of the evolution of pressed glass. The book is well-organized and interesting, complete with good black-and-white and color illustrations. This book also has a good bibliography and a great list of collectors' clubs.

The Colorful Post Civil War Days: Pressed Glass in Color

When you have a soda with a lime in it, you are mirroring a big breakthrough in 19th century glass. Until the 1860s, glass tableware was generally made with a high lead content, which produced a heavy clear glass with a bell-tone ring. During the Civil War, glass manufacturing was not considered an essential industry, so companies couldn't get the lead they needed, and glass got more expensive.

In 1864, William Leighton, Sr., working for Hobbs, Brockunier & Company of Wheeling, West Virginia, perfected a glass formula that used soda lime instead of the more expensive lead. Leighton's formula created a bright glass that could be pressed into ornate designs. Soda lime glass cooled faster, so companies could produce more pieces in a shorter period of time.

Question: How did Leighton's foreman inadvertently help him discover this new formula?

Answer: When Leighton was standing around, pondering chemical properties, the foreman told him to "Get the lead out!"

During the 1880s, pressed glass burst into living color. People were hungry for the new and exciting. As people got more money, and pressed glass got more affordable, a middle class family could obtain sets in dozens of forms. Lots of glasshouses (glass factories) popped up, and pressed glass was everywhere.

We're describing some of the popular types of this Victorian era pressed glass. Pressed glass is great fun to collect. You have lots of choices of patterns and styles that are relatively easy to find. You can start out relatively inexpensively, collecting a tumbler from different periods or patterns. Before you spend much, make sure that you educate yourself on the repro issues. New repros are being discovered all the time. Many of the trade journals have regular repro columns. Of course, joining a collector's club makes repro detection even easier, as you'll have club newsletters and people to discuss this with. Many of the types of glass have their own collector's clubs, such as Carnival glass, Depression glass, Fenton, and more.

A typical first glass love story

Barbara had four little kids, and she needed a hobby. Her mother gave her a book on pressed glass as a birthday present. She read the book and fell in love with glass. On the way to the grocery store, kids in tow, she stopped at an antique shop. She learned about different kinds of glass and began to buy.

She allotted herself $25.00 a month to start collecting. Soon, that money was simply not enough. "Maybe you better start selling off some of this stuff," her husband suggested. And so a business was born. She went to flea markets, she sold, and she bought. Now Barbara owns a successful antique store.

The vast majority of pattern glass pieces can be purchased for well under $100, with some pieces as low as $10 to $15.

Milk glass, for all it's worth

Europeans loved the porcelain of China and wanted to emulate it. So they created opaque white glass called *Opal* (later dubbed *"milk glass")* as early as the 18th century. This milky white glassware sometimes has opalescence on the edges, which gives it a splash of fiery color.

Milk glass became popular in the United States in the 1870s, as a substitute for the more expensive china. Atterbury and Company of Pittsburgh made a line of animal dishes and mustard jars that caught the public's fancy. (With these animals, the glass eyes were an extra option.) Such dishes as rabbits and ducks have the patent date on their base.

The unusual shape or subject matter is most valuable, such as covered dishes, "figural" pieces, and large pieces in perfect condition.

If you know what you're looking for, you can spot this milk glass in garage sales, flea markets, and even newspaper ads. You also can find this glass at country and local auctions, as well as antique shops and shows. You can find milk glass mugs, tumblers, bowls, and vases in good condition in the $20 to $75 range.

Milk glass is one of the most reproduced glasses and one of the trickier glasses to determine old from new. Some companies bought old molds and made milk glass from them. Look at a lot of glass and buy from reputable dealers, particularly if it's an expensive piece. The old glass has sharper detail. The newer glass can be a brighter white. Still, it's best to know your glass or know your dealer.

Custard's continuing stand

Custard glass is creamy and custard-colored. It originated in England in the 1880s and then traveled to America. Harry Northwood, son of a famous English cameo glass carver and designer, captured the American market and helped make this glass wildly popular. Heisey and Fenton also created custard glassware.

Some experts categorize custard glass as art glass, and other experts say it is "on the art glass fringe." Custard glass is often more expensive than other pressed glasses. The pieces were sometimes decorated and painted at the factory and often featured gold trim. The better the condition of the paint and trim, the higher the price of the custard glass (all other factors being equal).

On a ride with carnival glass

This inexpensive, iridescent American pattern glass began its life around 1907 as a way of spreading the Tiffany look to the masses. A mythology developed that boxcar loads of Carnival glass were given away at carnivals.

Carnival glass is pattern glass sprayed while hot with an iridescent mineral salt formula. Produced until around the 1930s, this glass comes in more than a thousand different patterns. (See some examples of these patterns in Figure 10-4.) Its bright and decorative presence stood out during a time when the country was in war and in a depression.

Carnival glass features a regular midway of wares, including glasses, water sets, dishes, creamers and sugars, rose bowls, figurines, powder jars, and decanters. And then there are the nappies, which some people say is a short rest and others say is a diaper and still others, those who collect, describe as a shallow dish that holds candy. A single nappy has one handle and a double sports two handles.

Carnival glass is a great place to hone your intuition. Like milk glass, the field is littered with good reproductions, where the weight of the glass and the marks are the same. The iridescence on newer Carnival ware can be weak, and the patterns are often not the same. So look at lots of Carnival glass before you buy, and buy from someone who won't take you for a ride.

Some companies make their own designs out of Carnival glass today. They may include some pieces of old patterns, but they are not copying the early carnival wares.

Figure 10-4: The price was right with this Fenton iridescent glassware (circa 1920).

Courtesy of the Fenton Art Glass Company

Even the glass felt bad: Depression glass

During the late 1920s and '30s, Depression era glass was abundant. Department stores, service stations, and theaters often gave Depression glass away with a purchase. Five and Dime stores sold this glass. During its prime, it was free or inexpensive, the plastic of the day.

Green, pink, blue, red, yellow, amber, white, ivory, and crystal are the basic palate of colors. Each color has different shades, and there are hundreds of patterns. (See three of these in Figure 10-5.) When you get hooked on Depression glass, you'll need a book that details the different patterns.

Even though prices have gone up from the 1960s and '70s, when you could get a whole box of glass for $5.00, Depression glass is still a great and affordable collectible. You can find some small plates for just a few dollars and glasses and cups for slightly more.

These dishes were used, so you'll see glass that is scratched or chipped. Try to pass them up, even if they are inexpensive. You can find pieces in good condition if you keep looking. And to keep the pieces in good condition, handwash them. Guard the lids; they make a big difference in the resale value.

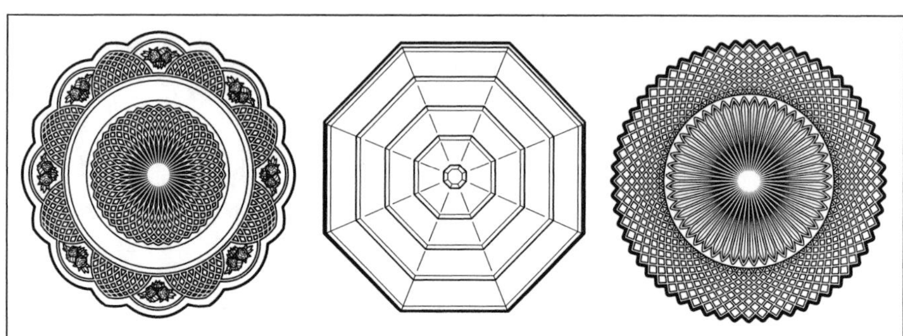

Figure 10-5: Three Depression glass patterns: Mayfair, Federal Glass Co; Tea Room, Indiana Glass Co; and Miss America, Hocking Glass Co.

As with any other area, you need to look at a lot of glass so that you can tell the difference between the real Depression glass and the repros. The color is typically off on repros (the glass is usually greener), and when you look carefully at the pattern, you'll usually see something amiss.

Some dealers aren't familiar with the values placed on different colors and patterns. When you know your glass, you can often find bargains.

When you want to know more about Depression glass shows, conventions, and prices, subscribe to *The Daze*. This periodical is also a good place to find pieces to add to your collection, especially hard-to-find pieces. E-mail them at `DGDAZE@aol.com` to find out more.

For a great book picturing and describing Depression glass, turn to Gene Florence's most current edition of *The Collector's Encyclopedia Of Depression Glass* (published by Collector Books). This book is full of tips on rare glass and buying strategies. It also has prices. Or try *Fifty Years Of Collectible Glass 1920-1970* by Tom and Neila Bredehoft (published by Antique Trader Books). This book is organized by motif, so you don't have to know the name of your pattern.

Glass's Cutting Edge

Cut glass was long popular in Europe and England. American cut glass began its emergence in the early 19th century and burst into full bloom during the latter part of the 19th century. This period is known as the Brilliant period (from circa 1880 to 1915). Nineteenth century manufacturers marketed this glass as "rich cut glass."

Cut glass is a great beginning point for a glass collection. You can find a variety of good, small pieces, often for well under $100.

During the American Brilliant period of cut glass, cut glass reached new levels of beauty and craftsmanship. Some say that the American cut glass craftsmen of the Brilliant period produced some of the finest glass in the world. (See one example in Figure 10-6.) The accolades include a consistent ability to create

- Better quality glass
- Fancier cutting
- Better designs
- Sharper details
- Higher lead content leading to more "brilliance"

Figure 10-6: Cut glass punch bowl from the American Brilliant period.

Today, some glass artisans cut glass using the same skills but more modern techniques. They create their own designs and sometimes incorporate motifs from earlier cut glass patterns. Be aware of modern copies of some rare old cut patterns.

If you want to find out more about cut glass, check out the American Cut Glass Association, P. O. Box 482 Ramona, California 92065-0482,760-789-2715. They publish 10 issues a year of their magazine *Hobstar,* with educational articles on glass, want ads, a calendar, and local chapter news. You learn about glass and get connected with a community of wonderful people, many of whom are willing to answer questions and mentor you as you learn.

How to buy cut glass

When you buy cut glass, start small and buy glass that is in good condition. With time and experience, you'll figure out what you can have cleaned and repaired without altering the piece. For example, you can often successfully clean bottles that are cloudy.

During the late 19th century, more than 100 American glass companies were making cut glass. Some of them were in business only a short time.

While some companies catalogued their patterns, styles, and shapes, identifying patterns can be hard, because few records exist. To further complicate things, there were plenty of independent cutters out there, transforming blanks into vases and glasses.

You can find cut glass in all sorts of places. Enjoy searching antique shops, thrift stores, flea markets, shows, and malls. American Brilliant period cut glass bowls can begin in the low to mid-$100s, but you can find some smaller dishes, like nappies, for less. In cut glass, rarity is a combination of the type of pattern and how many of the pieces were made—and condition is always an important factor. Pieces with unusual patterns and fine signatures that are in good condition run substantially more.

The more you know about cut glass, the better chance you have of recognizing wonderful pieces at reasonable prices. *Identifying American Brilliant Cut Glass* by Bill and Louise Boggess (published by Schiffer Publications), includes a value guide, rates the condition of the glass, describes different shapes, types of patterns, and companies.

Before a show, some dealers might spray their *sick* (cloudy or milky) cut glass with a mixture of baby oil and water. The oil residue makes the glass shine with a lot more brilliance and masks the cloudiness. Look for residue or moisture, so you can be sure the "brilliance" is from the glasscutter and not from a bottle.

Signs of the times

During the late 19th century, many cut glass companies signed their glass pieces. These acid signatures, which were usually applied with a rubber stamp, can include company name and/or logo. They often appear on the bottom of the glass, but you might find them on any flat surface or inside a bowl. It's hard to notice the faint white signature unless you hold the piece at just the right angle in the brightest light source available. Some collectors carry dark scraps of velvet to place the glass on. The dark background can help reveal that illusive signature. Often, the signatures, which are not deeply etched, can get scuffed so badly you cannot read them. A signature can add greatly to the value and authenticity of the glass.

Acid signatures were used only on cut glass of the late 19th and early 20th centuries. Before that, only a few glass companies made any kind of markings.

Judge glass by quality and pattern desirability rather than the mark or signature. During the last 25 years, rubber signature stamps have been widely reproduced, and anyone can get one and dip it in acid. Feel the mark. New marks are often raised up and old marks are flat, indistinguishable in feel from the glass. With old marks, you often have to look to find them. Some makers signed their wares in odd places (not just on the bottom). A mark that's bright and easy to see might be new. Sometimes new marks are smudged and don't have the clarity of the old acid marks.

Cut ups: Distinguishing cut glass from pressed glass

Cut glass is nearly always more valuable than pressed glass. Here are some ways you can distinguish cut glass from pressed glass:

- **Let your fingers talk to the glass.** Cut glass has a more defined pattern and sharper detail. Pressed glass is smoother when you touch the facets. The difference can be as dramatic as the experience of the sharp cragginess of the Rocky Mountains versus the worn-down, venerable old mountains of New England.
- **Let your eyes tell you.** Cherchez la pattern. Pattern glass almost always reveals its mold marks. Exceptions are the more expensive pieces, where they took the time to remove the marks. You'll find no mold marks on cut glass.
- **American Brilliant period cut glass is heavier.** Cut glass simply hasn't "gotten the lead out," and the extra mineral content makes it heavier.

- **Cut glass has more brilliance, and depth of cutting.** Hold the glass up to a bright light and notice the brilliance. The heavily leaded pieces are "crystal clear" or show a touch of blue in their brilliance, and their facets sparkle.
- **Cut glass "sings" more (actually rings) when you gently thump it with your fingers.** Typically, pressed glass from the same period simply doesn't know the words — or the tune.

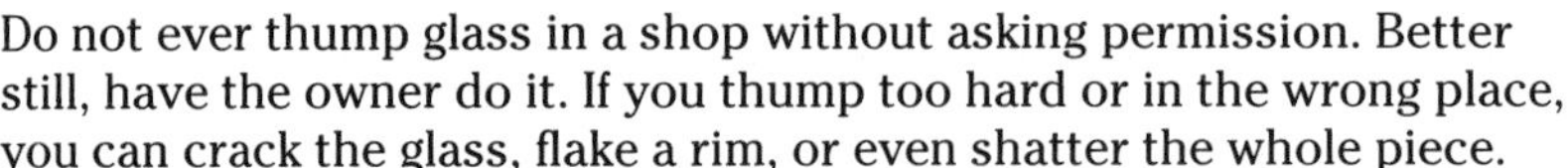
Do not ever thump glass in a shop without asking permission. Better still, have the owner do it. If you thump too hard or in the wrong place, you can crack the glass, flake a rim, or even shatter the whole piece.

Sniffing out damage and repairs

Examine cut glass carefully before you buy it.

- Look for damages, such as chips on the rim or handles, or chips on the sharp protrusions. The more elaborately cut the piece, the more carefully you need to look, because damage is frequently hard to see.
- Look carefully at the proportion of the glass piece. Cut glass pieces usually feature a clear non-cut area of 3/8 inch to one inch on the rim, before the pattern begins. If a bowl's rim nearly touches the cutting, this can mean the top was chipped badly and then ground down and polished.
- Carefully examine the pointed portions on the rim of the glass, often called the teeth. The greater the damage on a tooth, the lesser the value of the glass.
- When it comes to scratches, some people like to leave the glass original and unsullied, because scratches are an indicator of age. Others believe in removing scratches that detract from the pattern.
- Look for *sick glass,* where the inside of the vase or bowl has a milky color from having water in it. If you love the piece, ask the dealer to clean it for you. If the milky color doesn't diminish with cleaning, the value of the glass does.

If you love a sick piece and it's not too expensive, buy it and try to "heal" it with mild dish soap, denture cleaner tablets, or a 35 percent hydrogen peroxide solution. If that doesn't work, ask your dealer for the names of professional cut glass cleaners. Be warned, however, that not all cloudy-looking glass comes clean.

We can see the headlines now: "Blacklight reveals secret marriage." Yes, it's true, married glass (a two-part glass piece, such as a cut glass lamp) may show different colors under a black light.

Cleaning up with cut glass

Ken bought a small, cloudy-looking miniature carafe at an auction. He had it cleaned and turned a $95.00 investment into a $200.00 piece of cut glass. He later bought a rare cut glass decanter that looked milky and sick. He was able to have it cleaned, and now it's worth four times what he paid for it.

Cut to the chase: Spotting repros

Careful study helps you distinguish old from new. Whenever possible, work with a dealer you trust. Look at old and new side by side so that you can really experience the differences.

Here is what to look for:

- **The wheel thing:** Look at the wheel marks. Glasscutters in the Brilliant period used steel or iron wheels and smoothed the cuts at stone wheels. The Brilliant glass is typically smooth, with any lines being choppy rather than long and straight. The new, mass-produced cut glass is made with diamond wheels, which move much faster than the old iron and steel wheels. Diamond speed wheels leave long parallel marks with little pits between the grooves.
- **Cutting your teeth on glass:** "How sharp your teeth are," Red Riding Hood remarked to the wicked wolf. If Red was a contemporary cut glass collector, she could be talking to the wicked repro man. The teeth on new cut glass are often very pointed (sometimes painfully pointed) and sharp. The Brilliant period old glass has squared or rounded teeth. After all, this glass was made to be used, and those painfully sharp teeth are not user-friendly! You can easily knock them off.
- **Banking on blanks:** Old things being equal — getting familiar with the thickness and feel of old tumblers and plates helps you recognize the feel of the new. The new glass can vary more in thickness throughout individual pieces than does the old.
- **Done with art:** When you look carefully, you see the workmanship on the old is superior to the new. The old was carefully made, and the patterns were complicated, with attention to detail and art. The new was zoomed out at high speed, so patterns can be off-kilter and cuts can overlap.

For quick, great, and thorough tips on avoiding new cut glass, get the February 1977 issue on repro cut glass from *Antique & Collector's Reproduction News.* Mark Chervenka, the editor of this great newsletter, has written a piece that will keep you from costly mistakes. Send $5.95 postpaid to ACRN, P.O. Box 12130, 408 Foster Drive, Des Moines, Iowa 50312. For more about ACRN, see Chapter 22.

Caring for cut glasss

Every time you wash your cut glass, you risk damaging it. Some specialists advise: the less handling, the less cleaning, the better for the glass.

When you do want to clean it, handwash cut glass in lukewarm water (never hot or cold). Dry with a soft lint-free cotton cloth. Some people use a vegetable brush to clean the cuts — pat dry and then push the cloth into the cuts with the brush to absorb all the water. That keeps the glass sparkling.

If you're using a cut glass vase, don't let the water sit for a week. Keep changing the water. If you get a little discoloration, let a little denture cleaner rest inside the vase overnight.

Works of Late Victorian Era Art Glass

People have varying ideas of how to categorize art glass. We're presenting you with a buffet of the art glass world: quick tasty nibbles of varied and delicious and collectible types of glass. There are so many more on the menu. And when you connect with the types you like, you'll want to indulge in a full-blown meal, complete with books, tours to working glass factories, and forays into collectors' clubs.

Art glass is vividly colored. It is more attractive and decorative than functional. The glass is typically mold-blown, which requires lots of individual handling and artistic development from the glassmaking team. Art glass often includes hand painting and hand finishing. It was expensive to produce and definitely aimed at the prosperous middle class as well as the "carriage trade." The creation of art glass flourished in the late 19th century and continues on through today.

For a great sense of how art glass was created, watch the video produced by the Fenton Art Glass Company. Fenton continues the tradition of off-hand glassmaking. You'll be fascinated at the intricacy of this art form and the coordination and teamwork glassmaking requires. This complete tour of the factory and museum is great for anyone interested in art glass. Call (800) 319-7793 for more information.

Pass the Cranberry glass

How did cranberry colored glass get created? One story talks about a glassmaker impressing everyone by throwing a gold coin into the molten crystal glass. Another tale says the glass worker's ring slipped off into the molten glass and presto! the glass turned this wonderful cranberry color.

Glassmakers only wish it were so easy. There is indeed "gold in them there glasses." (Even today, companies such as Fenton and Pilgrim use pure gold.) But the transformation isn't quite so dramatic. The gold is dissolved in a mixture that includes nitric and hydrochloric acids. This amber liquid is poured into the batch. The glass becomes red when the formula is reheated — when that happens, the glassworkers say, "it strikes red."

Other examples of red glass that you might see include:

- **Flashed glass:** A thin layer of red glass on the outside, which gives you the impression of solid red glass.
- **Stained glass:** Red stain painted on clear glass, which makes its beauty only "skin deep"—and thin-skinned at that. You can distinguish this less expensive version of red glass because when the glass is scuffed, you will see the clear glass underneath.

Many varieties of antique cranberry glass tumblers are readily available at prices from $50.00 to $100.00. More unusual designs and enamel decorated tumblers go up from there. Cranberry glass vases start at around $100 to $125.

Repros of cranberry glass are plentiful. Get to know the shapes and styles characteristics of the old factories. New cranberry glass is typically thicker than the older glass. Still, you need to look at a lot of glass to see the distinction.

The mysterious Mary Gregory

Some people have their allotted 15 minutes of fame, and some, like Mary Gregory, luck into decades of fame. Mary Gregory did work for the Boston & Sandwich Glass Company for a couple years in the 1860 to 1870 period. Her namesake glass features white enamel painting of children's scenes on clear or colored glass and was actually developed in Bohemia (see Figure 10-7). The scenes are often whimsical, alive with butterflies and children rolling hoops and swinging. Often the glass comes in pairs, one with a girl's scene and the other with a boy. Mary Gregory is one of the glass world's unsolved mysteries: Why was Mary chosen to title this glass?

Figure 10-7: A typically decorated Mary Gregory tumbler.

Cranberry-colored glass decorated with the white enamel is the most desirable and usually most expensive, but Mary also shows up in clear, green, blue, and amber colors, which are less desirable and less expensive. You can find Mary Gregory vases, wine decanters, colognes, pitchers, and more. Some of the more desirable forms include hinged dresser jars and patch boxes (for your beauty patches, my dear).

Patch boxes make a great and "beautiful" collection and take up little space. You can find them in lots of different kinds of glass and in porcelain, as well.

It's all in the details. Modern Marys abound, and although companies try to replicate the older art, they typically flounder on the attention to detail. Look carefully at Ms. Gregory. Hold her up to a light: Repros sometimes show a stenciled form of the figure beneath the clothing and you can often see the mold mark on the glass. The older glass has a finer intricacy in the hand painting and is typically lighter in weight. Here's another place where it helps to learn the shapes, styles, and characteristics of decoration of the older pieces.

Forever Amberina

Amberina is one of those "salts of the earth" glasses. It's a *heat-sensitive glass* (it changes colors with added heat) with a sprinkle of gold in the mixture. Amberina emerges from the melting pot an amber color, and then the glassmakers stick part of the glass, usually the top part, back into the glory hole (an opening cut into the wall of the furnace). That extra jolt of heat causes the heated area to "strike," which means it turns the glass a rich red color. The quality of the color is important: The color should be a deep wine red.

The New England Glass Company developed this glass in the early 1880s. They made all kinds of glassware from Amberina, in both blown and mold-blown formats. At the same time, Mt. Washington came out with the same type of glass and called it Rose Amber. These companies sued each other, and finally decided that they could share the market. These very similar glasswares are now lumped together under the term Amberina.

On older pieces, the amber color tends to be a true amber, while in newer pieces, the color is often a bold yellow. The red on the newer pieces has an orange tint, while the colors for the older range from peach to fuchsia. Also watch for a sharp line between the red and the amber: This indicates a Continental imitation (which can be old and interesting in its own right, but that's another story).

Those satin dolls

You can feel the difference with satin glass. This late 19th century Victorian glass has a satiny, matte finish, caused by using an acid treatment after the glass was made.

Satin glass comes in many colors and often has applied decorations (applied on the surface) that are fired on after the main piece has cooled. Colored satin glass may have a white lining. Unusual color combinations or patterns are particularly desirable.

You might find *bride's baskets* (traditionally, bowls of various sizes often displayed in a fancy silver plate-handled frame), perfume bottles, vases, *rose bowls* (a Victorian innovation — a dish you put on your dining room table and floated a rose in), candy dishes, and *fairy lamps* (a small lamp with a candle and shade, used in the bedroom, like a night light). You might see ruffled edges, candy striped designs, or silver mountings.

Many companies made satin glass, and many companies have made reproductions. The matte finish and the velvety feel are great ways to identify satin glass. Repro glass can have a chalky feel to the white lining or have handles that look too spindly. Some repros can be rough to the touch, but other repros feel surprisingly like the real thing. Spend some time with a dealer you trust and get to know the nuances of genuine satin glass before you buy.

Mother-of-pearl and the glass that made her

In America, the Mt. Washington Glass Company first made mother-of-pearl satin glass. This pastel-colored glass was blown into a mold, which left a raised, air-trapped design on the surface of the glass. Then it was sealed with a thin second layer of glass, producing an overall design such as Diamond Quilted or Herringbone. Some mother-of-pearl glass is further decorated with gilt or enamel.

Here's an area where 20th century repros abound. When you see a profusion of mother-of-pearl satin glass, be wary. The older pieces are rare, and some of the reproductions are of excellent quality. This is another good area to really trust the person you're buying from.

Putting on the Crown Milano

Free-blown or blown into molds, Crown Milano, made by Mt. Washington Glass Company, looks like porcelain but takes only half as long to make. This ivory-colored decorative glass was made to compete with the porcelain companies. Some of the pieces had satin finishes.

Crown Milano was highly decorated with painted enamel flowers. One artist painted wildlife, such as ducks and birds, on Crown Milano pieces. This wild life is unusual subject matter.

Burmese, if you please

In America, Mt. Washington invented Burmese and patented it in 1885. Burmese soon became extremely popular in England, and Mt. Washington licensed Thomas Webb & Sons Company of England to produce Burmese for the English market. The Webb product is often referred to as Queen's Burmese. Both Webb and Mt. Washington added etching and painted or enameled decoration to their pieces. Burmese was made in vases, candlesticks, lamps, and toothpick holders, sugar dishes, and *epergnes* (multi-leveled decorative containers that hold flowers).

On repros, the colors are more garish and don't have the fine velvety finish of the original Burmese. Many repros have shapes that do not duplicate the original shapes. Learn the Burmese shapes by looking at the genuine thing. The old pieces are hand blown, and generally have a carefully polished pontil mark on the bottom. Repros are usually heavier. In Burmese, the genuine pieces are light to medium weight.

Collectors pay a big premium for enamel decoration. Many of the genuine Burmese pieces that originally were not decorated suddenly "got decorated" in the 1950s or '60s.

Catch the Wave Crest

C.F. Monroe Company of Meriden, Connecticut, made Wave Crest, which is a form of decorated milk glass. Wave Crest is highly decorated with colorful designs. Florals were a common theme, as were portraits of people. Some pieces have ornate ormolu handles and brass trim. The early pieces were often signed with a black mark and later, C.F. Monroe used a red banner mark or paper labels. Wave Crest is a great example of ordinary glass being turned into "art glass" by a beautiful decorative treatment.

If you really get into Wave Crest, be on the look out for its close cousins, Kelva and Nakara, also made by C.F. Monroe.

Pretty as a Peach Blow

The story of Peach Blow begins with the sale of the fabulous 18th century Chinese peach bloom porcelain vase from the Mary Morgan collection. This vase was sold at an auction in 1886 for the sensationally high price of $18,000. Hobbs Brockunier & Company, of Wheeling, West Virginia, was one of the first companies to produce a replica of this vase in glass. Their Wheeling Peach Blow, which shades from red to amber, has opaque white casing on the inside. Nearly all the major glassmakers had their own version of Peach Blow. Mt. Washington Peach Blow, which shades down from pink to pale blue, is one of the more expensive types of Victorian art glass.

Figure 10-8 shows a Peach Blow Morgan vase. The pressed glass stand imitates the Chinese carved wood stand for the peach bloom vase.

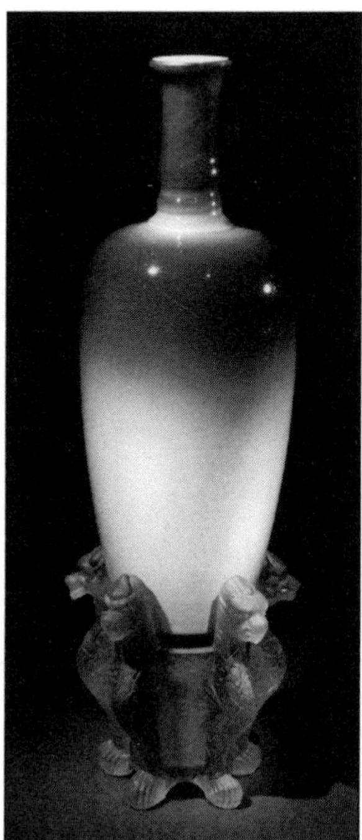

Figure 10-8: This Peach Blow "Morgan Vase" made by Hobbs, Brockunier & Co., Wheeling, W. Va., circa 1886-1891, imitates a famous eighteenth century Chinese "peach-bloom" porcelain vase.

Photo courtesy of The Corning Museum of Glass, Corning, N.Y.

Raving over Royal Flemish

Royal Flemish is a transparent enameled glass, designed so that the light shines through the color. Made by the Mt. Washington Glass Company, Royal Flemish has a stained glass appearance and features geometric sections of color with raised gold borders and typically other raised gold decorations, such as a dragon or coins.

Sometimes people remove paper labels from relatively minor pieces of glass and put these authentic paper labels on much more important pieces of glass that may or may not have been made by the same company. Paper labels can easily be reproduced or stuck on pieces of glass that are not old and authentic.

Another way to get the hang of distinguishing old from new is to study the repros. If you can, go to outlets, warehouses, craft shows, and showrooms where they sell new things. Look at the bottom of the pieces. Look at the workmanship. Look for any signs of intentional aging and notice how that aging is done. Look at the marks and labels. (Often repros have removable labels.)

For a wonderful survey of art glass, look for *Nineteenth Century Glass: Its Genesis and Development,* by Albert Christian Revi (published by Thomas Nelson & Sons). Even though this book is out of print, you can find it at libraries, estate sales, and through book locators. It includes great photos and good descriptions of the glass and their makers.

The Artistry of Art Nouveau Era Glass

Art Nouveau era glass is colorful and artistically daring. Although some of this glass is just now reaching its "antique maturity," the prices can sometimes be stratospherically high. Don't let high prices scare you; you can find lots of great pieces in lots of different price ranges.

Even if you don't start out collecting Art Nouveau era glass, you'll appreciate looking at this glass and understanding the astonishing creativity of the period. This era invited experimentation and gave us some of our most collectible glassware.

Forged signatures and reproduction issues come up often in Art Nouveau era glass. An unsigned Art Nouveau era piece may have the name of a famous maker etched on it. People can simply buy an acid etching pen and sign away. Some of the reproductions are amazingly good. Even knowledgeable dealers often get second opinions before they buy.

Handle as much of this glass as possible to understand fully the genuine thing. Know your dealer. Look at the old and new side by side to really "feel" the differences. This is an area where it's easy for even a knowledgeable collector to make expensive mistakes.

Tiffany: Seeing the light in a new way (America)

For many people, every time they see a beautiful piece of glass with that shimmer of iridescence, they wonder whether it's Tiffany. Every time they pass a leaded lamp, with beautiful stained glass panels, they think "Tiffany." Louis Comfort Tiffany is one of the big names in Art Nouveau era glass. He made it all and used glass in revolutionary ways. He was a great artist and a pioneer in the creation of glass and color. His long list of creations includes windows, tiles, desk sets, lamps, amazing blown glass vases, bowls, and more.

In 1946, Tiffany's own collection of his glass was sold at auction. The most expensive piece was a leaded glass ceiling light 6 feet in diameter that sold for $275.00. Even into the mid-to late 1960s, Tiffany lamps were underappreciated. Few people respected them, and the lamps were not yet anywhere near becoming an antique. Considered too gaudy and even ugly by some, you could often buy these lamps for just a few hundred dollars. Even at those prices, they frequently sat around in antique shops looking for a home to illuminate.

From the 1970s to the 1990s, the Tiffany boom really exploded in America. In 1997, Tiffany Studios pink lotus lamp sold for $2,807,500 at a Christie's auction. This spectacular sale established a new world auction record for Tiffany.

There are lots of ways to see the light when you become a Tiffany collector, from looking at his early stained glass windows, his all-glass lamps, and his lamps that combine both metal and glass. Some say Tiffany lamps are the finest electric lighting fixture ever made. Figure 10-9 shows a Tiffany Wisteria Lamp.

When Tiffany lamps were new, they were made with the finest quality materials, and they were expensive. They are again today, and deservedly so. They have also inspired a whole genre of "Tiffany style" lighting.

Figure 10-9: Wisteria Lamp, Tiffany Studios: Leaded glass shade in a Wisteria pattern on a bronze table base in the shape of a tree-trunk.

Photo courtesy of Lillian Nassau, Ltd. New York City.

Tips for the true Tiffany

How do you sort out the real Tiffany from the many imitators and fakers? Start by reading books on Tiffany, looking at pictures, looking at genuine pieces, and talking to dealers and collectors. Examine enough pieces so that you feel comfortable that you can recognize Tiffany's iridescence and a good Tiffany signature. Listen to the stories dealers and collectors all have about "the Tiffany that wasn't." Even for the knowledgeable, discerning a Tiffany is sometimes difficult. Buy from a reputable dealer who will guarantee the merchandise.

Here are some additional guidelines:

- Never be fooled just because something is signed! The fake "Tiffany" is almost always signed. Don't base your purchasing decision on a signature.
- Learn which patterns Tiffany made. This can help you eliminate the repros that didn't copy a Tiffany pattern or didn't copy it properly.
- Watch out for big "bargains." Be wary of the dealer who says, "This sold at Sotheby's for $6,000 but you can have it for $2,000." Many good, smart, educated, savvy people have paid way too much for such "bargains." Make sure that you are dealing with a reputable dealer who will guarantee the authenticity of the piece.

Even though Tiffany lamps and vases sell for thousands today, you can still buy a piece of real Tiffany for several hundred dollars. Salt dips and shot glasses are frequently in the low hundreds. The quality control on most Tiffany is excellent, so even a small piece of genuine Tiffany has the mark of his quality as well as his maker's mark on the piece.

The woman who brought you Tiffany

When Lillian Nassau opened her antique shop in New York in 1945, her merchandise was mostly European eighteenth and nineteenth century porcelain, glass, and objets d'art. In the late 1950s, Lillian bought her first Tiffany lamp, a Wisteria, for $200.00. Intrigued by its beauty, she began buying other works of the Tiffany Studios, and added other objects from the Art Nouveau period. Within a few years, she completely changed her shop's inventory. Her passion for the work of Louis Comfort Tiffany sparked an interest in decorative art collectors. Gradually, the handmade lamps and hand-blown glass regained favor with the collecting public. Gone were the days when Tiffany lamps were smashed on the sidewalk so the copper leading could be gathered and sold as scrap metal.

Today you can view a resplendent collection of Tiffany at the New York shop that bears her name.

Favoring Favrile

Favrile is Tiffany's trademark name for the glass he made. He derived the name from the Latin word "faber," which means, "to make."

One of the most famous kinds of Favrile is Tiffany's gold iridescent glass. He was trying to re-create the effect of weathered ancient glass. To do this, he sprayed a special metallic salt solution on glass while it was still in the kiln. The result was the creation of a marvelous iridescence.

Often, the word *Favrile* is alongside other markings placed on the glass before it was sent out to the showroom. These marks, which are engraved, often include some form of the Tiffany name, such as "L.C.T" or "L.C.Tiffany," and sometimes even a number. If the number is not a forgery, it can help you identify the date the glass was made. All Tiffany markings, from his Favrile to his name and numbers, can be faked. Some forgeries can be extraordinarily well done, depending on the expertise of the faker and the quality of his acid etching pen. If you find a mark, use it only as one clue that this could be Tiffany.

It pays to be "on the mark." Learn the different marks and signatures Tiffany used for different types of objects. Sometimes forgers make mistakes. They sign a lamp like a piece of glass would be signed. So you're not only looking at the signature, but you're looking to see whether it makes sense for the object.

Steuben (America)

Frederick Carder created every aspect of the Steuben Glass Company. He designed the factory and the furnaces; he created the glass formulas and designed all the products. From 1903 to 1918, Carder also directed the manufacture and the distribution.

Carder created *Aurene* (from the Latin word for gold), an iridescent glass with a variety of rich golden or blue tones. The creation of this glass, which is equivalent to Tiffany's Favrile, boosted the popularity of Steuben. Later he created more colors. Some Aurene colors are similar to Tiffany's, particularly the gold and the blue.

Start small and you can find affordable Steuben.

Emile Gallé (France)

Emile Gallé is often described as the father of Art Nouveau glass. He composed love poems; he thought women the most beautiful things in the world. He was highly literary and well versed in scientific knowledge. He adored nature and created in a style that was contrary from the functionalism of Arts and Crafts. Gallé made furniture, pottery, and dinnerware for the kings and queens. He was so into nature that he made butterflies, bumblebees, and insects on the plates. Somehow, that didn't go over very well. It's rumored one of Gallé's clients said, "Please, don't bug me."

Gallé was a businessman as well as an artist with a factory that employed 600 people and sold merchandise all over the world. His hand-painted glass, originally inexpensive, was wildly popular. His cameo glass creations are brilliant and innovative (see Figures 10-10 and 10-11). Sometimes he used five layers of glass on one piece.

Although Gallé died in 1904, the Gallé factory produced and signed glass until 1928. Pieces made after his death generally have a little star on them, to commemorate his death. Gallé is among the most wonderful and the most expensive of the cameo glasses.

Figure 10-10: Gallé cameo cut banjo-shaped vase.

Photo courtesy of Brookside Antiques, Kansas City, MO.

Figure 10-11: Sample Gallé signature.

Photo courtesy of Brookside Antiques, Kansas City, MO.

You really need to know your dealer when you buy Gallé. Some of the reproductions are extremely poor, but others are so excellent they even fool knowledgeable collectors. Some current reproductions of Gallé often include the letters TIP (which indicates an eastern European reproduction). beside the Gallé signature. But it's easy for people to grind off that TIP.

Daum, Nancy (France)

The Daum brothers started out in other professions and got called into the family business. They were remarkable artists and businessmen, innovative in their art as well as their management. They began their factory in the city of Nancy and signed their pieces "Daum, Nancy." The Daums began with gold ornamentation and later utilized an Egyptian motif, decorating their glass with scrolls and leaves. They are most known for their cameo and enamel glassware. Like Gallé, nature was their inspiration. In their works, they often move into abstract and surreal forms.

Like Gallé, Daum's pieces are often signed, and the signature typically incorporates the cross of Lorraine (a double-barred cross).

Cameo appearances

Cameo glass harkens back to the stone or shell cameo, where craftsmen carved back into the shell. Cameo glass uses an acid etching technique and at least two layers. Craftsmen blow one layer and then while the gather of glass is still hot, they blow another. After heating and cooling (called *annealing*), they add a layer of wax that resists acid and etch a design into the wax. Then they dip the glass into an acid bath, which eats away the unwanted glass. Where the wax is, the outer glass remains. Where the wax is scraped away, the under layer of glass is revealed. The acid leaves the glass with a slightly rough feel. They repeat this process from layer to layer. Where appropriate, a polishing process smooths out the roughness created by the acid baths.

Due to the various layers of glass, some of Gallé's five acid cutback landscape vases have a remarkably wonderful three-dimensional quality, especially when lighted properly. In France, Gallé and Daum were the big makers of cameo glass.

Question: What do you say when you see a great cameo?

Answer: What a relief!

You can find cameo glass pieces made by dozens of lesser-known companies, not prominent enough to have warranted the creation of forgeries. When you can look them up and verify they were of the period, you have yourself a piece of glass that is pretty repro-proof — at least for the moment.

Schneider (France)

The Schneider brothers worked for Daum before they opened their own glass works. They have a broad and imaginative range of production from Art Nouveau to Art Deco. They did applied work, internally decorated work, and metal mounted work. Schneider is also known for their monumental pieces (pieces exceptionally large in scale). Some of cameo work is signed *Le Verre Francais* and some is signed *Charder* (contraction of *Charles*, the more artistic of the two brothers, and *Schneider*).

Lalique (France)

René Lalique began as a jeweler of fabulous Art Nouveau pieces who became fascinated by glass. Lalique had a genius for creating elite and beautiful glass objects by using mass production techniques. He manufactured scent bottles for Coty and other perfumers. For the first time, Parisian women with little money could afford delicious scents in beautiful bottles. Lalique's magic with glass, like Tiffany's, is far-reaching.

When you look at Lalique, look at the quality of the work. As the molds get older, the impression can become less distinct.

You can buy some lovely small pieces of Lalique in clear or frosted glass, such as small vases, perfumes, and various tabletop pieces in the hundreds of dollars. The scarcer pieces of Lalique, such as early large pieces in color, are among the highest prices of all Art Nouveau items.

If you want the eye appeal and aren't worried about the artists, look into the lesser makers. In France, Sabino, Verlys, and Etling created in the Lalique style. In America, the Consolidated Lamp & Glass Company and the Phoenix Glass Company made glass during Lalique's reign and adapted some of Lalique's designs. These American pieces are marked with a paper label, rather than signed. A dancing nymph vase from Lalique might sell in the mid - to upper thousands, while a Consolidated dancing nymph, which looks like Lalique, sells in the mid-hundreds.

Several of Lalique's contemporaries felt free to copy his style. Later, fakers added a signature. Know your dealer. If in doubt, ask the dealer to show you the piece in Lalique reference material, as Lalique is well-documented and still in production.

Webb & Sons (England)

Thomas Webb & Sons were premier makers of cameo glass. Webb's top layer is frequently white. The underlayer is often a pastel pink, blue, or yellow. Webb often used a butterfly for his signature. You might see a vase with leaves and flowers and a butterfly.

Webb did a lot of wheel carvings, which created the extraordinary intricacy Webb was so great at. The acid bath, in his case particularly, was only the bare beginning of the process, and utterly incapable of creating the minute details that came from the hands of the Webb craftsmen. The vases are flower enough; use them for decoration.

Pieces that are signed by George Woodall are exceptionally desirable, with very good cause, because they are some of the greatest pieces of glass ever created.

Loetz (Austria)

Loetz was primarily known for iridescent glass, similar to that of Tiffany. Loetz produces a high-quality glass that holds color extremely well. In terms of iridescent glass, Loetz had one of the widest ranges of production of any glassmaker. Loetz experimented with color, pattern, and form.

Sometimes people polished off the mark because they thought Loetz wasn't as good as Tiffany. However, few Loetz pieces were signed. Judge the piece on its overall qualities and not by the presence or absence of a signature.

The Paperweight Chase: A Weighty Matter

Imagine an entire world encased in a clear refracting glass. This world is created from hundreds of miniature glass rods, some with even more miniature silhouettes at their ends. Each rod is distinct and they fill the glass with an intense design and color that is breathtaking. *Millefiori* (a thousand flowers) is one of the popular paperweight motifs. Though the millefiori technique has been around since Egyptian times, it was revived and refined in the mid-nineteenth century.

Antique paperweights can range in value from the mid-hundreds to $258,000, the highest price paid to-date.

You can learn a lot about paperweights by reading paperweight books and visiting paperweight collections. If you're not near a collection, call the International Paperweight Society at 800-538-0766. They can connect you with private collectors. Many of these generous collectors willingly talk to you about their collection and let you hold and examine the weights.

For a great introduction to "weights" as they call them, get *All About Paperweights,* by Lawrence Selman (published by Paperweight Press). You'll get a good grounding in the art form from the well-done text and the inviting pictures. *The Encyclopedia of Glass Paperweights,* by Paul Hollister, Jr. (published by Paperweight Press), is also a great introduction to paperweights. When you get deeper into the topic, try George N. Kulles' *Identifying Antique Paperweights* (published by Paperweight Press). This book gives you in-depth information on companies and their "canes."

Types of paperweights

Some of the more popular types of weights you'll see include:

- **Millefiori:** A mosaic pattern, bringing together pieces of glass of different colors and heating them until they are welded without the colors bleeding. These millefiori weights are made of "canes" (drawn rods of glass), all bundled together.

- **Flowers:** Either a single flower or a bouquet of flowers.
- **Sulphides:** Cameo-type white clay figures inclusions in the weight. These generally feature historic figures, such as Napoleon and Queen Victoria.
- **Fauna:** Snakes or lizards or butterflies or other types of insects.
- **Fruits and vegetables:** Fruits and vegetables tend to be fairly realistic miniatures, often displayed against a latticework background.

At the end of the glassblower's day, there would be some leftover glass and the artists would play with creating paperweights. These weights made on spare time were called *whimsies, friggers, scrambles*, or *end-of-day weights.*

The paperweight heavy weights

During the prime paperweight years, from 1845 to 1860, Baccarat, Saint Louis, and Clichy were the most esteemed French producers.

One child's school art influenced paperweight art. Emile Gridel was cutting out silhouettes of animals in school. His uncle, the manager of the Baccarat glass factory, was intrigued. He decided to take these silhouettes into the glass canes that create the design in the paperweight. Watch for "Gridels" (canes with black silhouettes) when you look at millefiori paperweights made by Baccarat. Other companies use the silhouettes, but only Baccarat calls them Gridels. (The young nephew grew up to be a famous painter.)

Some Baccarat weights are dated (the date appears in the canes), and some have a *B* on the end of a cane. Saint Louis had a more limited array of canes than Baccarat and had few dated canes. Clichy often features a distinctive rose on its canes and seldom uses silhouettes in its canes.

American weights

Two major producers of American paperweights were the Boston & Sandwich and the New England Glass Company. They made fruit weights.

The Boston & Sandwich Glass Company was also known for its flower weights, particularly the poinsettia.

Mt. Washington had beautiful rose paperweights and rather unnatural-looking butterflies.

You can collect paperweight-related items as well, such as millefiori vases, bowls, lamps, and jewelry.

Worth its paperweight in gold

Joe doesn't really like fruit paperweights. But he knows what they can be worth and he recognizes one when he sees it. He saw a pear weight marked $18.00 at a flea market. Joe got it for $15.00, sold it for $800.00, and used the money to buy millefiori weights for his own collection.

He also saw a small, very beat-up weight for $15 at an antique show. The dinged and scarred weight looked like it had served time as a hockey puck. Still, Joe felt it had possibilities. He bought it for $10, had it ground down and shaped into a beautiful pendant for his wife.

Gaining the right weights: How to tell old from new

Here are some clues for telling old weights from new:

- The old are heavier, because the glass has more lead content.
- By studying the canes in the weights, you can determine the different factories and eras.
- Old paperweights have more bubbles, because the artists didn't have as much control over heat as modern artists do. Unless bubbles are intentional, they are not desirable.
- Check for scratches on the bottoms of old weights. There should be marks!
- Check the top rounded surface in different lights and angles for surface scratches. Scratches are common and, if minor, they detract very little from the value of the paperweight.
- Old weights are seldom artist signed. The modern weights done by artists are often signed and many are also numbered editions as well.

Some real heavyweights

When you're ready to see some great weights, as well as other marvelous glass pieces, go to:

- Chicago Art Institute, Chicago, Illinois
- Bergstrom-Mahler Museum, Neenah, Wisconsin
- Museum of American Glass at Wheaton Village, Millville, New Jersey (Sometimes you can make your own paperweights here!)

Chapter 11

Dishing It Out: Porcelain, Pottery, and China

In This Chapter

- Finding the secret formula for porcelain
- Familiarizing yourself with the language of ceramics
- Looking for marks
- Discovering old versus new, and battle-scarred versus intact
- Knowing who's who and what's what in ceramics

When ale was the common breakfast beverage, drinking from a pewter tankard was great. ("Hop to it," they used to say every morning.) But when tea became popular, well, pewter simply destroyed the subtle flavor of the fragrant black leaves. Exotic foreign drinks demanded exotic foreign drinking cups, so the story goes. And so *ceramics* — porcelain, china, pottery, stoneware, and earthenware — came into prominence.

In this chapter, we tour some of the more popular types of pottery and porcelain. This chapter takes the smorgasbord approach; you get small bites of a lot of makers. When you get avid about a particular type of ceramic, find books on that specific maker. We've listed items by manufacturer or type of ware in a loose version of chronological order.

Ceramics: Collecting Options

You have so many collecting options with ceramics.

- **By factory**
- **By specific type of vessel from different factories,** such as a collection of teacups and saucers

- **By types of ware,** such as Creamware, Pearlware, or Majolica
- **By country**
- **By century**

Take a historical perspective: Try to get several examples from different time periods and paint a historical panorama of a factory. Wedgwood, Worcester, and Meissen are all heavily collected.

Finding the Secret Formula

Today, you think nothing of drinking from a porcelain teacup or dining on china dinnerware. But European porcelain was born out of desire and intrigue, in the quest for power and status. In the 18th century, having porcelain tableware was a sign of status. Porcelain was the inspiration behind many types of antique ceramics. Knowing the story of porcelain helps you understand the evolution of European and American ceramics.

When porcelain came to the West from China and Japan, people were intrigued, mystified, and enamored. They wanted some of this expensive and precious substance. Europeans didn't know how it was made: Had it been buried in the ground and then struck by lightning? Esoteric theories on how to create porcelain abounded.

By the 1700s, porcelain was sought after. Many wealthy individuals commissioned their cabinetmakers to create a court cabinet or cupboard (*court* is short for *French*) to display their porcelain or other treasures. Of course, only the rich could afford this luxury. European companies struggled to reproduce the formula that created such lovely teacups, dishes, and decorative pieces.

Augustus the Strong, Elector of Saxony, didn't like how much he had to pay for imported porcelain. One day, J.F. Bottger, a self-proclaimed "alchemist," presented himself in court and bragged that he could discover the porcelain formula. Augustus promptly held Bottger captive so that Bottger could make good on his promise.

Many experiments later, the alchemist stumbled on the formula by mixing china clay (*kaolin,* a special type of clay) with china stone *(petuntse).* Soon after, Augustus established the Meissen Porcelain Manufacture. Because Meissen was originally created just for the king, the court tried to guard the formula. Even though sharing the secret of porcelain held a penalty of death, word spread, and by the mid-18th century, many European factories were making porcelain. Meissen was highly prized back then and is still among the most valued porcelains today.

Pasting Together Porcelain Particulars

The body of the porcelain is referred to as *paste*. The paste is often covered with a glaze, which is usually a transparent substance. The glaze seals the porcelain and often can decorate it, as well.

Chinese porcelain is created from *hard paste,* which is a combination of china clay (kaolin) and petuntse, which is china stone. The minerals in this clay mixture fuse at a high temperature, creating a hard, impermeable surface that does not need a glaze in order to hold liquids. (Usually, craftsmen add a glaze for decorative reasons.) Hard paste has a smooth look, a high resistance to heat, and doesn't craze (form accidental splits in the glaze, which make fine cracks) or stain easily. Some pieces, especially tableware, are translucent when held up to a strong light.

English craftsmen created soft paste in their quest to imitate the coveted Chinese hard paste porcelain. *Soft paste* is more granular looking, more easily scratched, and not as resistant to heat. The color can be creamier. By 1800, Spode (you can read more about this ceramics manufacturer later in the chapter) perfected a formula that became the standard body for making British china. Its extra ingredient is bone ash, so this type of porcelain is called *English bone china.* Bone china is the middleweight: less hardy than hard paste and more durable than soft paste porcelain. Bone china remains the standard for English porcelain.

You won't see much soft paste porcelain: After people knew the secret of hard paste, most factories stopped making soft paste.

Here are some defining characteristics of porcelain:

- Porcelain has a white body that's white all the way through.
- When held up to the light, a porcelain plate often has a translucency.
- Fine porcelain can have a ring to it, assuming that it has no cracks or old repaired cracks. Of course, the shape and size of the piece are factors as to how grand the ring will be. Before you tap, ask permission. Put the piece on your open palm and give the rim a light tap with your fingernail. Don't clutch the piece, or you muffle the sound.

  If you hear a dead sound with no resonance, the piece may be pottery or have a repaired crack.
- Porcelain is lightweight, hard, and strong.
- Porcelain is resistant to staining and crazing.
- Glazed porcelain is shiny.
- Porcelain chips and shatters like glass.

In the beginning, *china* meant "porcelain made in China" (which at one time was the only source of porcelain). Then the china label extended to European wares that imitated Chinese porcelain. Now *china* is often used as a generic term.

Pottery: A Simple Recipe for Great Dishes

Some people think of pottery and porcelain as branches on the same tree. Many of the factories we discuss made both porcelain and pottery, because the production process is quite similar. Pottery has a simple recipe: clay and water. The results of this recipe depend on the type of clay and the firing temperature. *Earthenware* is fired at low heat and is more porous, requiring a tin or lead glaze before it can hold water. *Stoneware* is fired at a higher temperature and can remain unglazed, because, like porcelain, it's impermeable. Stoneware is generally salt glazed.

Here are some defining characteristics of pottery:

- Pottery is opaque.
- Pottery is generally warmer to the touch than porcelain.
- Pottery is softer and easier to break.
- Pottery breaks in large chunks, rather than shattering. Its shards are not as sharp as glass; they have a more powdery quality.
- Pottery is more porous and more prone to crazing and staining than porcelain.

Crazes and stains are especially prevalent when pottery is subjected to heat. The stains appear when stuff, such as food, liquids, or dust, gets into the crazes (cracks in the glaze). Over the decades, the pieces accumulate dirt to become darker still.

Avoid an ordinary piece that has crazing. Collectors are more tolerant of crazing on rare and more important pieces.

By the late 18th century, companies in Europe and America were producing different types of utilitarian pottery: redware, yellowware, and stoneware (a heavy gray ware). Potters often used earthenware, a more refined form of pottery, for better quality tableware. Ironstone earthenware, which features a variety of hand painted or transfer-printed decorations, became a standard for all kinds of decorated tableware. You can afford to buy high quality Ironstone, and you can enjoy using it.

Something Old, Something New, Something Repaired, Something Glued

Getting to know porcelain and pottery should be a touching experience: The more you handle the objects, the more you understand the differences between the old and new.

Here are some general pointers for telling whether pottery and porcelain are old:

- Look for wear marks, such as scratches, on the bottom of the piece. On plates, look for scratch marks on the cutting surface from knives. Crazing is another sign of age. Old crazing is sporadic. Fake crazing (yes, some people are so crazy they fake crazing to make a new piece appear old) is typically even and appears all over the piece.
- Look for quality. Does the quality of the piece compare favorably with other similar pieces of the same age? For example, are the colors appropriate and applied with comparable skill? Is the detail in the molding as good?
- Look for period styles. Artists made the decorative objects to fit the style of the period. Eighteenth-century porcelain reflects the furniture styles of that time. (See Chapter 3 if you want a quick style refresher.) Ask yourself, does this piece have the aura of Empire, Rococo, or Art Nouveau? After you've looked at a lot of pieces, you'll sense the things made in the 20th century, even if they are patterned after 18th century examples.
- Look for anachronisms. Look at the decoration. Look at the dress, the hairstyle, and the subject matter. Style was popular only for short periods of time. Does the decoration fit with the period?
- The things most often faked were relatively famous or at least valuable or expensive and highly collected. Ask yourself, would anyone have faked this subject matter?
- After you've looked everything over, decide whether the mark or the absence of the mark makes sense for the piece. The mark is a great thing to understand and recognize but should not be the only reason you declare a piece "authentic." You find many 19th-century European ceramics, often made by smaller factories, that do not have marks.

Before the early 1890s and the McKinley Tariff Act, ceramics imported into America did not have to be marked with a country of origin. Ceramics that were not exported didn't need marks even after 1890. Some companies marked their pieces with paper labels or *overglaze marks* (marks put on after the piece has been glazed), which could have since rubbed off or been removed.

A Survey of Porcelain

We've listed some great porcelain possibilities that you should be able to discover at antique shops, shows, estate sales, and auctions. We've left out a lot of great companies. If it turns out porcelain is your collecting cup of tea, you'll want to read up on it in more depth.

Here are some books that may help:

- Some ceramic collectors don't go anywhere without their copy of *Kovels' New Dictionary of Marks,* Ralph and Terry Kovel (published by Crown Trade Paperbacks). This book gives you information about the major marks you encounter on your ceramic quest.
- *Antique Trader Books Pottery and Porcelain Ceramics Price Guide,* by Kyle Husfloen (published by Antique Trader Books), is a well-illustrated price guide for American and foreign ceramics. This book covers the "breakfront."
- For more of the inside story on ceramics, including prices, check out *Warman's Pottery and Porcelain* illustrated price guides. (See Chapter 23 for more about these and other great price guides.)

The sword and the porcelain: Meissen (Germany)

In the second quarter of the 18th century, Meissen, located in Dresden, Germany, was unquestionably the "best in the West" porcelain-wise. Meissen was the first and, for a while, the only western company creating the sought-after hard paste porcelain.

By the third quarter of the 18th century, other porcelain makers in Dresden were getting into the act. They copied Meissen pieces and even "borrowed" the Meissen mark of the crossed swords, as did numerous European companies. You can see variations of these swords on all qualities of German porcelain.

Meissen is synonymous with quality. Meissen porcelain is often translucent and rings like a bell. The decoration is hand painted and has good symmetry. Meissen pieces are ordinarily flawless. Recognizing Meissen takes a great deal of looking and comparing. Go to museums, auctions, and shops to get familiar with the real thing. The Meissen factory still operates, and their modern work is also finely crafted.

If you like early Meissen but don't want to pay a king's ransom for it, saucers are a good way to ease into Meissen collecting. An early saucer, mid-18th century, might have a gently gilded edge, a sweet pastoral scene, and have crossed swords on the back and possibly an impressed number.

Colored grounds are grounds for spending extra money on a Meissen piece. This means the background, instead of being whitish, is colored, such as turquoise, yellow, dark blue, or claret.

The Meissen crossed swords mark inspired many copies. The Meissen Company itself used a large number of marks throughout its history. (See Figure 11-2 for a picture of a Meissen mark.) Slashes across the swords can indicate the piece is less than perfect. But if you see sloppy swords, the piece is almost certainly not Meissen. Many collectors have bought a fake late 19th century piece sold as Meissen, only to find out later that the piece is not even worth a third of what they paid for it. Get a book and learn your marks. Use the marks as only one clue in Meissen identification. Style and quality are the real clues to recognizing Meissen porcelain. For a test, ask yourself if the piece is Meissen before you look for the mark.

Go figure

Meissen made thousands of different porcelain figurines. When you look for Meissen figurines, look for exquisite detail, as shown in Figure 11-1. You can sometimes see nearly every hair on the figure's head. Look for detail and realism on the fingers and toes and for natural-looking skin tones. Meissen rarely let figurines on the market that had any kind of flaw.

Some of the best 18th and 19th century examples include allegorical and mythological figures. Cherubs and children are particularly collectible. The 18th century figures are the most desirable and rare; the 19th century figures are a little more available, and they are going up in value.

Meissen still makes figurines. In the 20th century, Meissen reproduced earlier works, but these newer pieces are not as subtle and detailed as the older ones. Sometimes the new pieces are more expensive than the old ones.

Figure 11-1: Cherubs are a popular Meissen subject.

Courtesy of Brookside Antiques, Kansas City, MO.

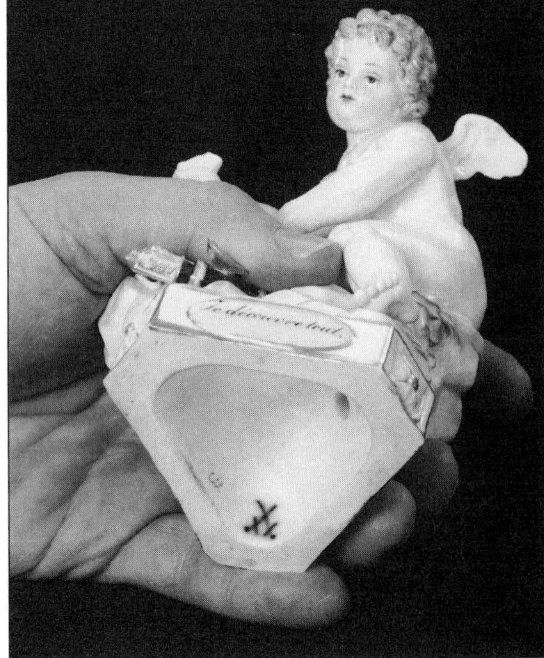

Figure 11-2: These blue crossed swords give you one clue that this wonderful cherub is Meissen made.

Appealing: Blue Onion Meissen

Although the Blue Onion pattern began in the 18th century, most of the patterns you find today were made after the mid-19th century. Meissen began this pattern, based on a Ming dynasty Aster pattern, and more than 60 companies created their own version. Some even created Blue Onion pottery. You often can find the crossed swords within the Meissen Blue Onion pattern, as well as on the back. These pieces are hand painted, with underglaze cobalt blue on a white background. Like other Meissen plates, they are high quality.

Every factory had its own recipe for colors, pastes, and glazes. Many tried to imitate Meissen, but the recipes remained a secret. If you see enough authentic pieces, you can get familiar with specific colors, glazes, and styles peculiar to Meissen. Of the many makers of the Blue Onion pattern, Meissen is the ultimate: the most desirable and the most valuable. (See Figure 11-3.)

Figure 11-3: Many companies have copied this popular Blue Onion Meissen pattern.

Dressed up porcelain: Dresden (Germany)

In the mid-19th century, the city of Dresden housed about 30 factories that produced Meissen-style works. Many of these companies simply faked Meissen wares. When you think of Dresden, look for dainty floral pieces and cherubs. Skirting the issue is a Dresden specialty on early 20th century pieces. On figures with women who had big skirts, the petticoats look like lace. These "porcelain dipped lace" skirts are fragile.

For years, the English and Americans labeled any porcelain that resembled Meissen as *Dresden china.* Dresden is often used as a generic term to describe ceramics made in Dresden.

Kings Porcelain Manufactory (Germany)

Eighteenth century Kings Porcelain Manufactory (KPM) competed with Meissen and made detailed figures and a large line of tableware and decorative pieces, replete with floral and pastoral decorations. The quality of KPM figurines can be extremely high. The earlier pieces have a tasteful amount of gilding; the later pieces really upped the gild level substantially (and we all know how overwhelming too much guilt can be). For a brief time in the 18th century, Meissen actually used the KPM mark. Most of these pieces are in museums, but you can always dream. KPM is known for its flat tile-like plaques, which feature portraits or scenes. Often, the frames cover the signature, which is an impressed mark or a cobalt blue underglaze mark, on the back of the piece. (Underglaze means the piece was signed before it was glazed.)

Before you buy, have the piece taken out of the frame and see whether the KPM mark is there. Even when you see a mark, you still need to judge the quality of the piece in its own right.

KPM produced blank tiles that were painted out of the factory. Even these pieces, which are sometimes crudely painted, can bring premium prices due to the prestige of the KPM mark.

On the mark and am I blue: Sevres (France)

Do not be deceived by de Sevres. The interlaced Ls factory mark of Sevres (which was originally in Vincennes before it moved to Sevres to be near an enthusiastic patroness, Madame de Pompadour) seems to be irresistible to forgers and fakers. Other French manufacturers often reproduce Sevres.

Sevres is known for its delicate color of sky blue. Learning the hue of Sevres true colors, such as the light sky blue, dark cobalt, and pompadour *pink,* is just one way to try to identify Sevres. Like Meissen, Sevres is one of the most copied porcelains in the world! Some forgers use a color that was originally created in one time period and slap on a mark from another time period.

The good news is that many copies of Sevres were made during the same time period as the originals and are sometimes of nearly equal quality. So those antique copies can be quite desirable in their own right. Judge by the workmanship. If a piece is of the right age and beautiful, it might be well worth purchasing. Good copies demand good prices. Sevres demands great prices.

Old ceramic stars: Chelsea, Worcester, Minton, Spode (England)

There is a wealth of wonderful English porcelain companies. We highlight just a few:

- **Chelsea** created soft paste porcelain and concentrated on the luxury market.
- **Worcester** made lots of teatime items and lots of dessert sets. They used soapstone in their formula, which let the soft paste porcelain be hardy in the face of boiling water. Worcester went through many phases, including transferware and the creation of a hard paste porcelain.
- **Minton's** hard paste had a smooth glaze and a look similar to Meissen or Sevres. Minton was also well known for its earthenware. Minton produced flow blue and was the maker of gorgeous majolica during the late 19th and early 20th centuries.
- **Spode** is often credited with being the creator of English bone china. Spode manufactured a range of items, including Japanese-Imari-type plates and their famous Blue Willow pattern.

Belleek (Ireland, America)

Belleek porcelain has a translucent, delicate look with a pearly luster reminiscent of seashells glistening upon a beach. Created in mid-19th century Ireland, Belleek is handcrafted and includes a line of intricate baskets. The earlier ones are woven with three strands. After the 1900s, the weave tightens with four strands. Belleek also made an unusually thin teaware in a variety of patterns.

The value of a damaged Belleek can be bleak. Because the porcelain is so thin, even hairline cracks can radically affect the value.

You can use marks to date pieces of Irish Belleek. Early production used three versions of black marks. With each period of production, the colors of the marks change, and you see other minor variations in the marks. Currently, Belleek is using brown marks, the green mark being its predecessor. Some of the earlier wares had the word *Belleek* impressed in the glaze.

The popularity of Irish Belleek inspired some American factories. American companies that produced a version of Belleek, which was quite different from the Irish, included Willets, Ott and Brewer, and the Ceramic Art Company, which became Lenox. These companies sold a lot of their blanks to amateur china painters, so the *ladies circle* (see the sidebar later in this chapter for even more news on this great group) decorated a lot of American Belleek. Because Belleek was one of the more expensive ceramics to purchase, you often find top-quality amateur painting on these blanks.

To have and Haviland (France)

Talk about do-it-yourself china: The Haviland brothers, china importers in New York City, set up their own factory in Limoges, France, so they could have fine quality china to export to America. By the 1860s, even the White House was using Haviland china.

This successful line was beautifully decorated with colored flowers and modified Rococo designs. Haviland made thousands of tableware patterns for the American market and also produced art objects, such as vases and sculptures. Some dealers specialize in matching up Haviland patterns.

Pickard (America)

Here's a company that literally "drew on a blank." Pickard was a decorating studio that began in Chicago in the late 19th century. They purchased blanks from other manufacturers and hired people to decorate them. The artists created and signed hand-painted scenic and floral pieces. Look for pieces signed by Challinor, a highly collected Pickard artist.

The bright gold that often trims Pickard china has a liquid look. Familiarize yourself with this gold, and you'll be able to notice a piece of Pickard across a crowded room.

Royal Copenhagen (Denmark)

Dining on Royal Copenhagen is a wonderful, wonderful experience. The Royal Copenhagen factory was established in the mid-18th century. They began making soft paste and soon graduated to hard paste. Royal Copenhagen created an intricate set of dinnerware for Catherine the Great in the late 18th century. (She died before this elaborate dinnerware was completed.) This pattern, called *Flora Danica,* features a different hand-drawn botanical picture on each piece. Royal Copenhagen still makes the pattern today, and artists still hand draw each piece. Many consider Flora Danica the "ultimate dinnerware pattern."

Royal Copenhagen dinnerware sets are popular with collectors, because they are high quality and their prices are compatible with contemporary china.

Antique dinnerware is one of the world's great bargains. Top-quality antique dinnerware in good condition typically costs far less than comparable contemporary china. Look for Royal Copenhagen patterns at estate sales, shows, and antique shops.

Beginning in the late 19th century, Royal Copenhagen developed a series of figurines that are quite collectible (see Figure 11-4). Many of the figures relate to Scandinavian mythology or nature. They created Swedish grandmas walking arm in arm, complete with traditional Swedish costume, as well as fauns (Pan-like creatures), animal figurines, charming children, and couples in love. Royal Copenhagen figurines are quite available and often reasonably priced.

Figure 11-4: Royal Copenhagen porcelain figurine of girl with goose.

Willow Ware (England)

From China to England to America: That is the way of the willow. In the 18th century, the English found a way to create pieces like the beautiful, hand-painted, blue and white porcelain imported from China.

Spode created the transfer-printed Willow pattern in the late 18th century. As the story goes, this pattern is based on an ancient Chinese legend. The willow story has at least 200 variations. This is one of them.

A gardener and a Mandarin's daughter fall deeply in love. The Mandarin has forbidden their love and arranged for his daughter to marry a fierce warlord. During the wedding festivities, the lovestruck gardener sneaks into the house to rescue his beloved. While everyone is intoxicated from the festivities, the gardener and the daughter make their escape. They flee, the wind rushing past them like the wings of large birds. But the Mandarin notices his daughter is gone and sets off after her at great speed. Breathless and full of fear, the lovers race across a bridge and hide in a little house. The next day they escape by boat, rowing until they reach a far away island. Here they live happily, supporting themselves by gardening.

Meanwhile, back home, the spurned warlord grows angrier and angrier. He vows to track down his bride and seize her back. And so, after several years, he does. He storms onto the island and kills the gardener. The Mandarin's daughter, rather than be pirated away by the evil warlord, takes her own life. The gods take pity on the two lovers and turn them into a pair of turtle doves so that they can forever share their love.

When you look at Willow Ware, you can see the lovers crossing the bridge, the father pursuing them, the house they hid in, the Mandarin's estate, the boat, the birds, and a willow tree (see Figure 11-5). Each manufacturer has a slightly different take on the scene, and you can learn to identify some companies by studying each willow pattern.

The English patterns used transfer printing instead of hand painting. By the 1830s, more than 200 English factories were creating variations of the blue willows. During the earlier years, the willow showed up in pale blues. The Victorians created a range of blues, and you can find some pieces in other colors, such as black, green, and yellow. Companies around the world still produce variations of the Willow pattern.

Willow is a desirable dinnerware pattern. You can mix and match between companies.

Willow is reproduced. Many of the marks are documented, so get a book with marks and take a careful look. The early willow does not have the country of origin; the later does.

Want to know more about Willow Ware and its legends? Visit the International Willow Collectors web site at www.willowcollectors.org.

Figure 11-5: We are showing just the essential elements of Willow Ware, usually pictured in the center of Blue Willow plates.

Lusterwares (England)

Thin metallic-like glazes on top of either pottery or porcelain create lusterware. Silver, copper, and pink-colored luster are all popular. The luster look can completely cover a piece or be specific to rims and decorative highlights. Splash luster is a mottled pink luster on a white body.

You can find jugs and tea and tablewares that have the glow of lusters. Some transfer-decorated pieces also feature luster. A great many English companies produced these wares.

You can add luster to your collection without spending a lot of money. Many lusterware pieces sell for less than $100. Lusterware is still rather easy to find; it has age and beauty and many pieces are in good condition. Early silver luster can be dull looking from years of exposure. Early 19th century lusterwares have been widely reproduced.

The ladies circles

From about 1885 to 1925, ladies circles painted porcelain blanks from many factories. Similar to those shops today where you choose a ceramic piece to decorate, *ladies circles* were often art classes where women learned the art of painting on ceramics. You can still find these plates, boxes, vases, and other pieces. Some of them look quite amateurish; some are very well-done. Some of the ladies signed their pieces; others will probably remain forever anonymous. The subject matter usually hovers around roses, violets, and poppies — the less complex flowers. Look for signs of these women's work at shows, auctions, and of course, in your own family's attic or basement. And note, china painting enjoyed a resurgence in the mid-20th century.

R. S. Prussia and related wares (Germany)

Members of the Schlegelmilch family created a variety of fine, thin porcelain and decorated the pieces with decals and airbrushing. Portrait pieces and pieces with animals and scenes are among the most desirable to collectors, as are pieces with iridized glazes. Unusual embossed borders featuring Art Nouveau style women's heads are also desirable. R.S. Prussia, the most popular of the Schlegelmilch porcelains, combines transfer decoration and airbrush painting, as opposed to painting with bristle brush.

Many patterns of R. S. Prussia have been reproduced, mark and all. The repros are often heavier; the real thing is made of thinner, finer porcelain. Sometimes just the Prussia mark itself is reproduced and simply applied to an unmarked piece of china.

Royal Bayreuth (Germany)

In addition to tableware, Royal Bayreuth produced novelty porcelain for the masses. They made serving pieces fashioned out of all sorts of animals and people, such as lobsters, tomatoes, coachmen, and Santa Claus. Some people collect in a certain subject matter, such as animals, florals, or tapestry wares. Their tapestry porcelain has a lightly embossed surface that looks like fabric.

If you are familiar with the forms Royal Bayreuth makes, you can sometimes find an unmarked piece, an unaware dealer, and thus, a good buy.

Pottery Potpourri

In the following sections, we focus primarily on English pottery, with spoonfuls of other Continental factories and a journey into America. You can categorize pottery in several ways: by its body (such as creamware or jasperware), its glaze or decoration (salt glaze, tin glaze), or its potter or factory (Wedgwood).

Here is one way to keep your eyes from getting glazed over: Knowing what kinds of glaze go with what kind of body helps you identify the ware.

- Tin glaze and lead glaze go with earthenware pottery. Earthenware really needs a glaze before it's functional.
- Stoneware, which can live without a glaze, nearly always carries a salt glaze.
- Some people throw salt out for good luck: Potters open the kiln and toss the salt in during the firing, to create the glaze. The salt glaze produces a granular surface, like the skin of an orange.

Reading *Miller's Collecting Pottery & Porcelain,* Janet Gleeson, editor (published by Reed International Books Limited), is a great way to increase your knowledge of different types and characteristics of ceramics. The book has great tips, succinct descriptions, and good illustrative photos.

The tin man's pottery: Majolica and friends

Minton (see the previous section) used the word *Majolica* in the mid-1850s for a line of sculptural, figural wares that are still popular today. Majolica features three-dimensional decoration, and its subject matters are mainly from nature. The glaze has a somewhat runny appearance and the pieces are fairly heavy and thick. Majolica, like all tin glaze ware, chips easily, so it's hard to find pieces in mint condition. Collectors typically are not too upset about minor imperfections. Lots of different companies have produced Majolica.

The 19th century Majolica was press-molded, with clay pressed by hand into the mold. It's heavy, and the inside may feel a little rough. The bottom of the 19th century Majolica typically has the same glaze as the rest of the piece. The repro stuff is typically poured into a mold and has hollow handles, which makes it lighter than the real thing. The inside is smoother and the bottom is not always glazed.

Transforming ceramics through transferware

Forget laboriously hand painting each plate. Transferware transformed ceramic production, using a transfer process that applied the design onto the piece. Especially in the Staffordshire pottery region of England, potters used this technique to produce less expensive wares. Transferware is typically smooth to the touch; you can feel the ridges of the hand painted piece.

Don't be fooled by transferware pieces that are enhanced by a few splashes of hand painting. At first glance, they offer the illusion of a full hand-done piece. Take out your magnifying glass and look for the dots that make up a transferware pattern.

Keep your books of marks handy when you look at transferware. Repros abound. Fakers use marks that look old, but size those marks up carefully. The "new" mark is sometimes much larger than the original. Look for other telltale signs of born yesterday, such as *dishwasher safe* or *oven proof* markings.

Rushing into the Flow Blue

Sometimes a little mess turns into a lot of beauty. Some say Flow Blue began as a mistake that almost immediately became a standard production technique. Early 19th century English china manufacturers were creating dinnerware with cobalt coloring. During the heating process, the cobalt flowed outside of its design. These flows of blue looked good to the American market — so good that a multitude of manufacturers began making the same collectible "mistake." Flow blue comes in different patterns. Oriental, Italian motifs, or scenes of ancient ruins are especially collectible. You can find a variety of Flow Blue dinner plates in floral patterns.

The leading Wedg (wood)

Josiah Wedgwood was a creative and marketing genius, using industrial production techniques to produce his innovative pottery. Wedgwood invited known artists to create designs for his pottery. We are including a few of Wedgwood's famous bodies of work.

Black basalt is an unglazed black stoneware created in the latter third of the 18th century. You'll find historical and mythological figures, vases, and busts.

Queensware is a popular type of creamware (a pottery refined enough to masquerade as a porcelain substitute). Wedgwood was one of the most successful manufacturers of creamware, dubbed *Queensware* in honor of Queen Charlotte. Queensware became popular and sold royally throughout the 19th century, often showing up as coffee and tea sets.

Jasperware, an unglazed stoneware, is one of Wedgwood's most famous creations. The bas relief look harkens back to the classical era, with white figures on a colored background, as shown in Figure 11-6. These figures are crisp and detailed, with a slight translucence in some areas. Blue, green, and black are key jasperware colors. The 20th century was colored by olive green. Turquoise was made only for a brief period of time in the late 19th century, so it's a rare find. Other companies made jasperware, including Spode and Adams.

Figure 11-6: This Wedgwood pitcher, creamer, and sugar feature white figures on a blue background.

Daisy Makieg-Jones created Fairyland Luster in the 1920s. The ware often starred birds, butterflies, pixies, and fairy subjects. *Fairyland Luster* brings you a bright world of fairies, all flying about on vases, urns, and bowls. A scarcer variation features dragons and is called Dragon Luster. These magical lusters are highly collectible and command high prices.

Wedgwood was one of the first Staffordshire potters to mark his wares. But one mark wasn't interesting enough: Wedgwood had more than 25 marks over its history. This firm never used an initial "J." with the name "Wedgwood."

It's never dull with Doulton

Doulton was another innovative and prolific factory in the 19th and 20th centuries. They began making utilitarian things and moved into the decorative items after they started producing items that nearby art students created. Doulton's work is usually impressed and often marked with the initials of the artist and the date. Doulton attracted a high quality of artists.

Doulton has produced many china figurines that are highly collectible now as well as whimsical Toby mugs, which were a spoof of a well-known Englishman dedicated to the drink. Doulton produced advertising items, such as bottles, ashtrays, soap dishes, dinner wares, and chamber wares.

When you buy Toby mugs, always follow your marks. Other factories created these mugs, as well, but Doulton's are especially desirable.

Staffordshire

The English Staffordshire district, rich with natural resources, is the home of many ceramic manufacturers. Some people use the term *Staffordshire* generically to refer to all sorts of 19th century English pottery. Staffordshire potters made everything from fine and decorative "groups" of animals, such as those shown in Figure 11-7, to dinner and tableware.

Figures that add up

Staffordshire figures were very inexpensive in their day, made to supply the middle class and lower middle class with ornaments for their homes. Itinerant peddlers often sold them. For the first time, the masses could buy inexpensive ceramic wares. The early figures were romantic shepherds and courting couples, modeled all the way around and brightly decorated. Then they created flatback figures. These press-molded figures have a wide subject range, from royal personalities to animals to famous theatrical figures.

Other interesting Staffordshire wares include pastille burners, which are like incense burners. Made in the mid- to late 19th century, pastilles are in the guise of English cottages or castles. The smoke from the incense goes up the chimney. Also collectible are stirrup cups in the shape of a dog or fox head, which were made for the foxhunt.

Figure 11-7: Staffordshire dogs are popular with collectors.

You find excellent Staffordshire repros on the market, so here's another area where you really need to know whom you are buying from. People have reproduced full figurines and flatbacks, complete with crazing and intentional wear to appear as though they are old. The new models are generally more perfect, and their bases are sometimes deliberately darkened.

Romance in dinnerware

Staffordshire transferwares included American historical scenes as well as English views. Between 1830 and 1860, the Staffordshire area created romantic wares with castle scenes, foreign lands, and nostalgic settings flowing onto the pieces. They featured Chinese and Japanese flowers, birds, and pagodas, and journeyed to India for the flavor of mosques and minarets. These wares show up in many colors, with lots of color variance.

In case you're tired of having plates "a round," try plates in octagonal or decagonal forms. You can find transferware in *iron red* (pinkish red), teal green, silvery gray, sepia, and several shades of blue as well as black. Some of the transferwares were enhanced with hand-painted polychrome enamel color or highlights.

Getting to the plate with history

In the early 19th century, American history took to the home plate. Staffordshire potters began creating scenes of Americana, including famous towns, people, events, and institutions. These pieces helped British potters regain their share of the American pottery market. Between 1820 and 1840, dark blue was the main color. Then more colors crept in. Americana is extremely collectible, and these historical scenes are quite popular.

Transferware from 1890 on marked with the country of origin is less collectible. Many potters made these wares. When the pieces are unmarked, you can often still identify the company, as many potters created a distinctive border.

The English potters frequently made mistakes in depicting American heritage. Historical figures are sometimes misidentified, which makes the pieces especially desirable.

Art Pottery in America

Inspired by the European and Asian ceramics at the Philadelphia 1876 Centennial, two groups emerged to begin the American art pottery movement: Hugh Robertson in Boston with the Chelsea Keramic Art Works, and two Cincinnati women, Mary Louise McLaughlin and Maria Longworth Nichols, with the Cincinnati Pottery Club, from which Rookwood Pottery evolved.

Social reform was creeping forward, and some were concerned about gainful employment for women. China and pottery painting was seen as a suitable occupation for the "frailer gender." Now women could put their biscuits in the oven and their clay in the kiln. An interest in home decorating and the excitement generated by the Centennial further fueled this movement.

Although art pottery's original purpose was aesthetic, the art form expanded and came to include assembly-line artware that is attractive, functional, and collectible.

For more information on types of art pottery, you may enjoy *Kovels' American Art Pottery: The Collector's Guide,* by Ralph and Terry Kovel (published by Crown Press). You'll get the inside stories on the major companies as well as product description, artists' signatures and marks, and wonderful color photos.

Even though this book is out of print, it's worth getting from the library: *Art Pottery of The United States,* by Paul Evans (published by Feingold and Louis Publishing Co.).

Watch your antique periodicals for art pottery shows in your area. This is a great way to meet knowledgeable dealers and see a range of pottery and really learn about the different manufacturers of art pottery.

To be a part of the American Art Pottery Association, write to

AAPA
P.O. Box 1226
Westport, Massachusetts 02790

Spotting a pot: How to look at Art Pottery

Some Art Pottery is handmade, and some is made in molds. One way to determine the difference is to look for mold lines or to look for concentric rings inside, which indicate hand throwing.

Look also at:

- **Shape.** Know the types of shapes your manufacturer created.
- **Glaze.** Glaze is a melted mineral mixture that can produce a glass-like substance or can be opaque or textured. If the glaze doesn't melt, the piece can feel sandy or rough to the touch. You might see places where oil or grease on the pot caused the glaze to miss a spot. Many companies marked these glaze goofs as seconds.
- **Mold.** When you assess a piece of production-line pottery, remember that they made hundreds of pots from one mold. There is a marked difference between the first pot and the hundredth pot from the mold. Sometimes, on the later pots from the mold, the detail is soft around the edges. Crisp detail is more desirable.
- **Authenticity.** At some Art Pottery shows, you see a display of fakes versus the real thing. Study the real and the fake. With Art Pottery, the differences are sometimes subtle. A mark or signature is no guarantee of authenticity because these too can be copied.
- **Condition.** Look for signs of repair. Watch for hairline cracks. If the dealer says he has found no signs of repair, ask for a written guarantee stating he is selling the piece as perfect. If he says, "There is no guarantee," use your best judgment. Flaking or chipping also reduces the value.

Accepting a good piece with a properly done restoration is a good way of getting a better quality piece for a lower price. Years ago, people refused to buy damaged pieces. But now, the pieces are rarer, and there is a growing market for pieces that are well restored, if they are priced accordingly. The rarer the piece, the more it's worth considering, imperfections and all.

For art's sake: Art Pottery studios

How do you collect Art Pottery? Let us count the companies. There were dozens of Art Pottery studios. Some of them had limited productions and were only in business for a short time period. Some of them produced thousands of designs and span long years of production. Some are still in business. We include only a small portion of the Art Pottery available, enough to get you familiar with the art form so that you can go searching for more information. Some types of Art Pottery even have their own collectors' club. We're listing three of the "big quantity producers" first: Rookwood, Roseville, and Weller. These companies created an amazing array and are quite collected. We follow with other important studios that were typically smaller in scope.

Lost in the Rookwood: Rookwood (Cincinnati, OH)

During the reign of Rookwood, more than 100 artists decorated and signed wares. Maria Longworth Nichols named her pottery after her girlhood home. The company began in an old schoolhouse in Cincinnati in 1880. The early decoration was dark brown, reds, and oranges, with a yellow-tinted, high-gloss glaze. By the late 1800s, they had created Iris and Sea Green glazes, and in the early 20th century, they developed a Matte glaze as well. Rookwood kept evolving, not only in what they produced, but in designs and finishes. They sent artists to Europe to study. Initially, all the pieces were made by hand. Then Rookwood added production pieces that featured molded decoration and varied glaze effects. Rookwood continued to do artist-signed hand-painted pieces as well. (See Figure 11-8.)

Rookwood's designs were cutting edge and included a varied line of items, such as decorated vases, tiles, plaques, and novelty items, such as book ends and lamps. Rookwood developed thousands of glaze formulas.

Rookwood is typically well-marked. From 1880 to 1887, the mark is a block mark. In 1887, they copyrighted an "RP" (the letters are back to back) mark with a flame over it and continued adding a flame per year until 1900, when a Roman numeral appeared under the RP, indicating the year. Artist-signed pieces are particularly desirable. Look for the artist signature incised or painted on the bottom.

Figure 11-8: Rare Standard glaze Rookwood portrait vase done by Grace Young in 1900, titled "High Hawk Sioux."

Photo courtesy of Cincinnati Art Galleries, Cincinnati, Oh.

The signed pieces by the more important artists can run in the tens of thousands. You can find beautiful signed pieces by lesser-known artists that are still priced starting in the mid-hundreds. Many collectors begin with production pieces, which are priced in the low hundreds. The early Standard glazed pieces are often bargains. The very earliest work is also often a bargain; this was before the peak of Rookwood artistry. (Van Briggle worked there during this early period.)

Almost all's Weller that says Weller: Weller (Zanesville, OH)

Few kiss the Coppertone frogs Weller created: They don't want to risk those adorable frogs turning into just another handsome prince. Frogs are just one of the wonderful collectible things that Weller created.

Weller created Louwelsa, originally in a rich brown glossy glazed line. The Louwelsa line was an imitation of Rookwood's Standard glazed wares. Weller continued to copy Rookwood's latest developments in order to expand their lines. Like Rookwood, Weller had fine artists working for them. One of the original lines Weller created was called Sicard, a hand-painted, iridescent-glazed ware named for Jacques Sicard, a French artist Weller employed.

The Hudson line, an extensive slip-decorated line was a significant part of Weller's early output. The line included florals, animals, and scenics.

Later, Weller introduced a wide range of molded lines depicting flowers and plants similar to Roseville. Over the years, Weller created an enormous range of styles, glazes, and forms.

Weller created some wonderful original figural animal and garden ornaments, including pop-eyed dogs, pelicans, and gnomes. Do your research if you're going to buy Weller animals: Some are reproduced, and it's hard to tell the difference.

A Roseville by any other name: Roseville (Zanesville, OH)

Roseville made a tremendous variety of wares. Like many other companies, their early work was handmade and decorated. Della Robbia was one of Roseville's most important art pottery lines and featured hand-carved relief decoration. Roseville's molded, assembly-painted vases, which appear in a variety of patterns, are highly collectible. Designer Frank Ferrell introduced a new line each year. Most of these lines bloomed with flower names, such as Cosmos, Water Lily, Jonquil, Iris, and Bleeding Heart.

The most collectible pieces were made during the Depression and had a more restricted output because of reduced sales. Some of the more rare and desirable lines include Futura, Falline, Ferella, Sunflower, Wisteria, and Baneda. (See Figure 11-9 for a glimpse of the Futura.) The Pine Cone line had the greatest number of different shapes, was made for a greater number of years, and was one of the most popular lines ever. As with many Roseville lines, it came in different colors.

The raised Roseville mark has appeared on Roseville repros, which are now rampant.

Color is key in pricing and collecting most Roseville lines. With Pine Cone, for example, a blue background is the most collectible and one of the more expensive, followed by brown, and then green. A pink background is a rare variation. Watch the market for subtle shifts in color popularity.

Losing your marbles and finding your pottery: Marblehead (Marblehead, MA)

You've seen the scene in the movies: patients in various types of recovery programs sitting around doing arts and crafts. Marblehead Pottery was born at one of those therapeutic institutions. Patients were to decorate pottery as part of their rehabilitation and healing. Although this was the initial inspiration, early on, the potter Arthur Baggs took over the studio and turned it into a professional plant.

Figure 11-9: A sampling of the Roseville Futura line.

Courtesy of Cincinnati Art Galleries, Cincinnati, Oh.

Marblehead focused on making simple shapes, such as vases and jardinieres with gray, brown, blue, green, pink, and yellow glazes. Marblehead products are hand thrown except for tiles and some pitchers, which were molded. Incised geometric, floral, or marine motifs decorate about five percent of Marblehead's ware. A deep blue is the most common color, and prices go up for unusual colors. You can find small and simple Marblehead pieces in the low hundreds of dollars.

The midnight ride: Paul Revere (Boston/Brighton, MA)

Born from a girl's club called the Saturday Evening Girls, girls and women played a big role in the Paul Revere pottery's ride to fame. Instead of brushing against the bad influences of "the street," these daughters of immigrant families brushed paints onto pottery. They worked in pleasant conditions, and someone read aloud to the girls while they painted. Paul Revere produced a large amount of plain glazed ware. Decorated pieces are the most collectible, including scenes of Paul Revere's real ride, as well as floral and animal motifs and sometimes mottoes.

Most of what they created was intended for use by children and includes cereal sets, pitchers, and bowls.

A taste of Teco (Terra Cotta, IL)

Teco was an architectural terra cotta company. With the popularity of art pottery, they began producing vases and garden pottery. Teco pieces were cast in molds and sprayed with glaze. The matte green glaze, known as *Teco green,* is the most popular color, but they produced a wide variety of colors. Teco made and numbered nearly 1,200 different shapes, including window boxes, urns, lamp bases, and mantel pieces. Teco's architectural styling set it apart.

When you're assessing a piece of Teco, look for shape. The architectural, buttressed forms are generally the most desirable. Some of the pieces look like little buildings.

Feelin' Grueby: Grueby (Boston, MA)

Decorative Grueby pottery was hand-thrown. The decoration was mostly leaves and flowers, hand-tooled on the side of the vase. In the late 1890s, Grueby introduced a revolutionary matte green glaze, which won gold medals at the 1900 Paris Expo. Like Stickley's new Mission furniture (described in Chapter 3), this glaze inspired a host of imitators. Rookwood, Weller, Roseville, Hampshire, Teco, and Marblehead later developed matte green glazes.

Stickley so admired this glaze that he used Grueby tiles in some of his plant stands and tables. Grueby made matte glazes in many colors, but green was the most popular then, as it is today. Some Tiffany lampshades have Grueby bases.

Teco, Fulper, and Grueby are all being reproduced by hand with the mark impressed in the clay. If you don't know who you're buying from and you don't have confidence in your ability to tell, you can really get stung.

The Newcomb on the block: Newcomb College (New Orleans, LA)

The dean of Sophie Newcomb College was thinking about "suitable employment for Southern women." Because nuclear medicine and strategic planning were not options in those days, china painting and pottery design naturally came to mind. Women drew the designs, and men made the pots, which women then decorated. The art department at Sophie Newcomb College joined with a struggling pottery company and formed Newcomb Pottery.

About 15 women graduates worked each year on the pottery, which won many awards. Artists drew native flora and fauna in the wet clay, carved the designs in relief, and then painted them with glazes after they'd been fired. Newcomb was known for a range of cobalt blues and sage greens. A tree hung with Spanish moss against a moon appears on many pieces. The pieces bore the initials of the college, the designer, and the potter. Each woman got half the sale price of her piece. Today, even a small piece can cost more than $1,000.

The world's greatest: George Ohr (Biloxi, MS)

George was the self-proclaimed "world's greatest potter." He worked for various Southern potters and then established his own studio in Biloxi, Mississippi. George was eccentric and creative, making miniature objects and creating man-size objects. He liked to twist his pieces and created puzzle jugs, log cabins, serpent handles, and a variety of glazes. He was proud of his work and felt people didn't appreciate it, so he didn't sell much during his lifetime. Years after he died, his heirs found a garage crammed with wonderful art pottery.

Ohr's ceramics are often exceptionally thin and are typically signed.

Van Briggle (Colorado Springs, CO)

Van Briggle worked for Rookwood and then opened his own studio in Colorado Springs in 1901. Van Briggle used molds for the pottery, and the studio still produces work. The cost of the new is significantly less than the cost of the older. Van Briggle has produced the Lorelei vase since 1901.

New pieces have different glazes than the old. To buy old Van Briggle, get familiar with the clay, glazes, and marks and look for the obvious signs of age and wear. The molds can look the same.

Going with the flow: Fulper (Flemington, NJ)

Fulper began with drainpipes and flowed into producing a line of art ware. The heavy New Jersey clay was molded into a huge variety of vases, bowls and decorative wares, including candlesticks, book ends, and lighting devices. (See Figure 11-10.) Fulper used matte, crystalline, luster, and high gloss glazes. The most rare and desirable pieces are lamps with both pottery shades and bases.

When you assess Fulper, glaze and shape are the key criteria. Glaze is the primary consideration — look for exotic color combinations; thick, lumpy, drippy glazes; and crystalline effects. As with any molded pottery, some shapes are rarer than others, and Fulper has some unusual handled shapes. With Fulper, size is also an important consideration. Often, bigger is better.

Figure 11-10: Fulper Pottery Co bowl, circa 1912.

Photo courtesy of The Chrysler Museum, Norfolk, VA.

Top percent tile: Collecting art tiles

Many of the art pottery companies also produced tiles. Some tile companies, such as Grueby and Teco, shifted into art pottery, and some art pottery companies, such as Rookwood, added tiles. Art tiles are a huge collecting area.

For definitive reading on tiles, get *American Art Tiles,* by Norman Karlson (published by Rizzoli). The author has collected tile for years. He breaks tile companies into regions and includes a history of each company, biographical profiles on important figures in tile creation, and a glossary of terms. The book also features good color photos and a price guide.

Chapter 12

The Metal Winner: Silver

In This Chapter

- Giving silver the twice over
- Knowing the score on English sterling and plate
- "Revering" American silver
- Minding your manners with Victorian silver plate

Silver is a multi-faceted metal that serves as currencies, eating utensils, food and beverage storage containers, and objects of decorative art.

Antique and early 20th century silver flatware is one of life's great bargains. You can frequently find older patterns at a lower price than you would pay for the same pattern brand new. The older silver is heavier and has finer workmanship, and a beautiful patina (which is a natural darkening you get as silver ages). The supply-side antique silver strategy says this turn of the century silver is still plentiful, and the demand is still relatively low.

You can buy silver to use or to collect or both. Some people collect by makers, such as Gorham or Reed & Barton. Some people collect by piece, such as cheese scoops, salt dishes, or match safes. Some collect flatware by style and mix in different patterns. Gorham has several styles, such as *Mythologique,* that feature mythological motifs on certain patterns. Some people like to mingle the patterns, so that each person at their table eats with a different character. Some people collect hollowware (silver you can put something in) such as teapots, creamers, or vases. Others stick to decorative objects.

Antique hollowware can often cost less than its modern counterpart.

Getting serious about silver

When you feel the urge to buy, get books that help you ID the various makers and markers of silver. *The Encyclopedia of American Silver*, by Dorothy Rainwater and Judy Redfield (published by Schiffer Books) and *Kovels' American Silver Marks: 1650 to the Present*, by Ralph and Terry Kovel (Crown Trade Paperbacks), are two great books for identifying and understanding American silver, its marks, and its makers.

For English silver, try the wonderful pocketsize book *English Silver Hallmarks*, by Judith Banister (published by Associated Publishers Group, Ltd.). If you get really serious about silver, you might also look at the pocket edition of *Jackson's Silver & Gold Marks of England, Scotland and Ireland*, edited by Ian Pickford (published by Antique Collector's Club). This book features many of the maker's marks of Britain.

For your bimonthly silver fix, you need *Silver Magazine*, which gives you interesting silver information, discusses fakes, describes new research and discoveries, and includes classified ads. Call (800) 756-1054 to subscribe.

The Silver Looking Glass: How to Look at Silver

Long before Ralph Nader, English hallmarks offered an early form of consumer protection. The hallmark guarantees that the product was tested at an assay office (government testing agency) and conforms to a legal standard of purity, 92.5 percent pure silver. (The extra 7.5 percent is other metals.)

The hallmarks consist of a stamped letter and other emblems, which give you a lot of information about the piece. This is where your magnifying glass comes in handy. On older handmade pieces, the marking sometimes doesn't leave a clear impression. The marks may be too small to totally fit into the space (such as the back of a spoon handle). Or the marks may be worn down and not as easy to read.

By looking up the hallmarks, you can pinpoint when and where the piece is made. Different marks were used during different time periods.

You may also run across small pieces of Britannia Standard, which has its own set of hallmarks, and has a silver content of 95.8 percent. Britannia is softer than sterling, with the silver having a faint trace of blue. You can spot this blue tint only after you've looked at lots of silver. (When you really know silver, you can taste and smell the difference between sterling and Britannia.)

While British and Continental silver have their hallmarks, after the middle of the 19th century, Americans stamped the word *sterling* into silver or sometimes 925, and indicating 925 parts silver out of a thousand.

Before you buy, study up on silver and look at lots of silver so that you know the look of older silver. You can distinguish sterling from silver plate by the marks (imprints) on the bottom.

Here are some questions to ask yourself when you're thinking about purchasing a piece of silver:

- **Has it been repaired?** Look at handles to make sure that they are not damaged or broken. Look at places that can easily break off, such as finials (a *finial* is the ornamental knob on top of a lid). Look at the feet. Sometimes people plunk down a piece too hard and that presses the feet in.
- **Is it dented or pitted?** With sterling, a silversmith can usually polish out and repair dents and pits. Silver plate is harder to repair, and sometimes requires resilvering. Resilvering can be costly. Avoid silver plate with deep cuts. Watch out for plated pieces with *pits,* which are small holes that look like black dots and feel rough to the touch. The cost of replating can be greater than the value of the piece. If silver is black, or the tarnish is very deep, sometimes discoloration has "eaten into" the silver. Avoid these pieces unless an expert says you can totally remove the tarnish.
- **Is it genuine?** Fakers can transfer an important hallmark from a broken silver piece and put it on a less valuable piece that's in good condition. Or they replace a mark on a great piece whose mark is degraded. Fakers can cut a hallmarked bottom out of one object and apply it to another piece, to make that piece seem more important. The genuine mark makes the piece more valuable. On pairs, such as candlesticks, make sure that both marks are the same.

  Breathe hard on the hallmarks if you're having doubts that they are original to the piece. If someone has added hallmarks to make the piece seem more valuable, you should see the hallmarks' outline.
- **Is it monogrammed?** If so, are the initials the same as yours? If not, do you like them? Many collectors prefer their silver in its original condition and keep the monogram. Depending on the depth and location of the monogram, its removal can really downgrade the piece because the silversmith has to buff away some of the silver. If you want to remove the monogram and don't know whether that will cause problems, ask if you can take the piece on approval to a silversmith to analyze it.

  Monograms can be works of art in their own right. Some are so ornamental you can't even read them. You can hunt for monogrammed sterling that fits into your family history in some way. Or you can choose a monogram just because you like it. Dealers are often pleased to sell monogrammed pieces for less because of their more limited market.

- **Does the type of decoration make sense with the purported age of the piece?** You can often place the piece in a general time period by analyzing the types of decoration. Sometimes a plain piece of silver is decorated at a much later date.

Tally Ho Silver: English

It is a jolly cold 19th century English winter. The windows are shut, and you are in a room with many unwashed people. Naturally, there are some strong and not entirely pleasant odors afoot. What to do? Why, merely draw out your silver vinaigrette and take a delicate sniff. This hinged little box, with pierced holes, the great aunt of the smelling bottle, was small and held a sponge that soaked up vinegar mixed in with other oils, such as lavender, lemon, or cinnamon. Vinaigrettes were often engraved; later they sported a ring so that they could be worn on a chain.

You can find English silver that dates from the 17th century onwards. The metal was abundant, the craftsmanship was skilled, and the wealthy were eager to own and use the elegant status symbol of silver.

From early times, English sterling silver has had official "marks" guaranteeing its purity. The lion passant hallmark signifies that the piece is sterling and also English. Some form of the lion passant (a walking lion who is looking at you) is on every piece of English sterling. You can find three to five hallmarks on a piece of English silver. They used one mark to indicate sterling, another mark for the town, and a letter of the alphabet for the date. Sometimes you'll see a king or queen's head, which means that the taxes have been paid. Also, you may find a maker's or factory mark on the piece. See Figure 12-1 for an example of English hallmarks.

Figure 12-1: One example of English sterling hallmarks.

A rare old silver spoon in good condition with a proven lineage can be worth far more than its weight in gold. In 1994, a pair of spoons that dated back to 1501 sold at a London Christie's auction for $50,230.

Even if you weren't born with a silver spoon, you can enjoy a rich variety of English sterling pieces. Here are a few examples of what you might find:

- **Sugar tongs:** Some tongs have beautiful engraving or wonderful monograms. Some feature pierced work. You can find nice sterling and plate tongs. Look at the arch of the tongs and make sure it's not cracked (or repaired).
- **Tea caddy spoons:** These small pretty spoons vary in their shapes. Look for cracks where the stem joins the bowl.
- **Fish knives and forks:** Fish servers are ornamental knives and forks that come in boxes of 6 to12 pairs. Having the original box is a plus. Check to see that the utensil is properly fitted into the handle.

Here are some items that are hard to find but worth looking for:

- **Silver rattle:** Shake it up, baby, with these 19th century toys made in the style of the day. Some were quite wonderfully decorated. If they're silver, they should be hallmarked. Sometimes each little part bears the lion passant.
- **Etui:** The *etui* (meaning "essentials") is the equivalent of a Swiss Army Knife. Everything fits precisely into this little box of necessaries, such as tweezers, little scissors, files, even a tiny tool to remove the wax from your ears. The military types had cutlery and corkscrews in theirs.
- **Fruit sets:** Fruit sets rest in a fitted case lined with velvet. Often graced with mother-of-pearl handles, a sterling ferrule and a silver plated blade, these sets consisted of small knives and forks to cut, peel, and eat fruit with.

Sheffield Plate (English)

In the 1740s, Thomas Boulsover found he could cover a thick piece of copper with a thinner sheet of silver. The exterior looked like sterling and gave less-affluent people a chance to own lovely silvered pieces, called *Sheffield Plate*.

When you look carefully into the areas where Sheffield Plate has been pierced, you can see the copper. (You have to look at it sideways.) True Sheffield Plate is made in England. Look for copper showing through on the old plate. Look for delicate handwork, such as silver-wired borders. Study the style of Sheffield Plate and know your dealer. Sheffield Plate items can range from the low hundreds up through the thousands.

On Sheffield Plate, the monogram or coat of arms is often engraved within a circular or rectangular piece of pure silver, which has been inset into the plating. When you breathe on it, you can see the outline of the silver. That helps you know the piece is almost certainly old Sheffield Plate. If it says "Sheffield Plate," you can assume it isn't genuine old Sheffield Plate.

Among popular Sheffield Plate items you might find are tea and coffee services, vegetable dishes, candlesticks and salt cellars, which are often lined with clear or colored glass.

Miller's Silver & Plate Antiques Checklist, by consultant John Wilson (published by Reed Consumer Books, Ltd), has good and practical information on plate and silver, including marks and characteristics of different pieces.

Marks on Sheffield Plate can be confusing. Some marks look a lot like sterling silver marks. Check your silver book if you are in doubt. In natural light, Sheffield Plate has a slightly bluish glow, which is different from the color of electroplate. Sheffield Plate has seams, while electroplate does not. Watch out for cheap imitations, including plate that has a reddish glow and is not as well made. Run your fingernail underneath the edge of the piece. If there is a rim, that indicates the piece is probably Sheffield Plate.

By the mid-19th century, electroplating became popular and Sheffield Plate waned.

Electroplate (English)

Electroplate, which was patented in 1838, let people imitate silver designs. The craftsman forms the pieces and then by using electrical currents, covers the object with a fine deposit of silver. You can date the pieces by knowing the style and decoration related to the periods. Nineteenth century electroplate looks different from modern, which has a harsher color.

In time, electroplating wears off. Choose pieces that are in good condition, because it is usually not financially sound to have a piece replated. If you replate, the piece can lose some of its antique value.

English silver plate is marked, sometimes with an EPNS (Electroplated nickel silver) or sometimes with an English stamp mark.

Hi Ho Silver: American

In Colonial America, the silver represented the family's life savings. Silver started with spoons, forks, mugs, and tankards, and then moved from being functional and valuable into being art. During the 1920s, flatware was a status symbol.

For many families, the family furniture, clothing, and glass are long gone. Silver is the only heirloom left. Silver has an intrinsic value. Plus silver was one of the few things passed down to the woman. Most silver was monogrammed, usually with the woman's initials, sometimes maiden initials. Specialists can use that monogram to trace the family history.

Early silver: To coin a phrase

The midnight silversmithing of Paul Revere is indeed revered. Revere is the most famous American silversmith before and after the American Revolution. He created coffeepots, teapots, and sugar bowls.

People often refer to 18th and early 19th century American silver as *coin silver,* which is approximately 900 parts silver. Much coin silver tableware was engraved with a monogram. Some is marked *coin* or *pure coin.* In the first half of the 19th century, American makers used pseudo "hallmarks," such as a star, anchor, or bust of a man. Coin silver is usually thinner and therefore fragile.

Before the mid 19th century, America had little silver "manufacturing." People went to the silversmith and ordered what they wanted. In the larger eastern cities, there were also silver retailers.

Sterling (American)

America did not adopt the sterling standard until 1868, when Gorham and Tiffany, two leading producers and designers of sterling, adopted the standards. That began the use of the word *sterling* on American silver.

Gorham had a "drop press" created in England, which allowed the mass production of silver. Gorham designed hundreds of flatware patterns as well as imaginative decorative objects. They created handcrafted silver that the middle class, hungry for status and elegance, could afford. The Gorham marks, which simulate the British silver hallmarks, appear on each piece: a lion, the traditional British silver symbol; an anchor, the symbol of Rhode Island; and a Gothic G. Figure 12-2 lists some samples of Gorham silver.

Don't assume that when you see a group of English-looking hallmarks you have a piece of sterling in your hands. Many early 19th century American companies used a variety of "pseudo" hallmarks, which are not the same as the English ones. When you look at English hallmarks, it is essential that you look in a book and be sure that every mark is present and accounted for in an exact and precise manner.

Courtesy of Gorham Inc.

Figure 12-2: A listing of Gorham Sterling Silver pieces, from the Gorham Sterling Flatware catalogue, 1888.

Home plate: Victorian silver plate (America)

Rule number one at the Victorian table: Never touch the food with your hands.

Rule number two: Never serve food without the proper implements.

In some quarters, if you did have not an asparagus server, you did not serve asparagus. If you did not have a berry server, it was apples for you.

Americans were trying to outdo England and form their own brand of aristocracy. During an elaborate ten-course meal, every food had its own utensil. There were literally dozens of special serving pieces and place setting pieces, such as oyster forks, macaroni servers, and ice cream knives. (See some wonderful examples in Figure 12-3.) Some patterns had up to a variety of soup-spoons to choose from. Need to pull out the delicious marrow from those bones? Of course, you reach for a marrow scoop. Dare to eat a peach? You need a fruit set. People's ability to use these pieces spoke volumes about their breeding and upbringing. During this period, Americans produced fine silver in both sterling and plate.

Much of American Victorian silver plate is quite affordable. Americans produced a volume of ornate plated material from 1860 to 1890. You can find attractive silver-plate spoons for under ten dollars for some patterns, and into the low double digits for lots of others. You can dish up soup, Victorian style, with a lovely ladle for less than $100. You can find butter dishes, cream, and sugar sets on trays and smaller plated trays in the low hundreds. After 1890, some silver plate took on a more colonial appearance, while other silver plate followed the current fashion. If you like ornate, you'll adore Victorian silver plate. Some dealers specialize in matching flatware and occasionally hollowware patterns for people who are collecting and need to fill in their sets.

For the inside story on American silver plate, Dorothy T. and H. Ivan Rainwater's book of the same title (published by Schiffer) is a wonderful treat. This richly illustrated book shows you the history of silver plating and how it was made. It includes detailed descriptions of various pieces, photographs, illustrations, and wonderful reprints from old silver catalogues.

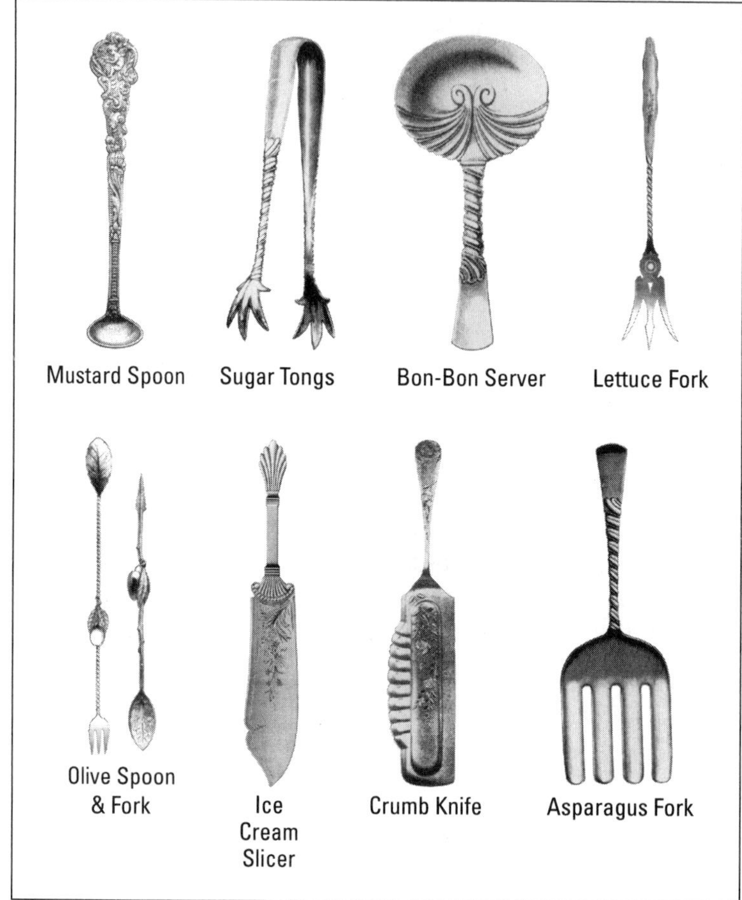

Figure 12-3: In 1888, these were some of your flatware choices from the Gorham Sterling Flatware Catalogue.

Courtesy of Gorham Inc.

Here are some of the Victorian treasures you might find:

- For a stirring collection, try **teaspoons, demitasses, ladles, serving spoons,** and other utensils. If you want to search out the more exotic, look for **macaroni servers, sugar shells,** or **mote skimmers** (used to scoop bugs and twigs out of afternoon tea — the barbed end was used to remove tea dregs from the spout).

To make sure that your pattern and the spoons you are buying mesh, carry a piece of your pattern with you. Or put your spoon on a copy machine and carry a copy of your pattern with you!

- Rings around the collar were not such a big a deal in the late 19th century, but rings around the napkin were. **Napkin rings** came in silver plate, sterling, pewter, porcelain, and wood. These were made post Civil War and are English and American. Napkin rings are a great way to introduce interesting antiques into your everyday life. Silver and silver plated figural rings are unique and elaborate. You might see angels, birds, animals, or trees, all poised to circle the napkin.

- In English and American silver, the **tray** was often as expensive as the tea set. So most people did without the tray or used a plated tray. Many manufacturers offered their popular patterns in plate or sterling, so you could have a sterling tea set and a plated tray in a harmonizing pattern.

The level of craftsmanship can be excellent in both sterling and plate. If you are looking at a tea set, check the marks of each piece carefully. Do not assume that because the teapot is sterling, the other pieces are. Examine the tray extra carefully.

- In the 19th century, the business card of the day was the "visiting card." One couldn't just let these cards rumble around loose: One needed a silver **card case.** Some are quite elaborate; others are quieter, with a swirl of initials.
- **Calling card trays** were popular as wedding gifts and many are available today in the low hundreds.

Some of the more valuable Victorian pieces have been reproduced. The casting on the newer pieces is less detailed and cruder. The silver-plating process for the repros is far less refined than the work of the great silver makers, such as Reed & Barton. Much of the new plate has a chrome look. Look for signs of wear on silver plate: After a hundred years or so, things start to wear thin.

Caring for silver

Some people put their silver in the dishwasher; other people find that makes their silver cloudy. If you do use the dishwasher, keep the sterling in a separate basket from your stainless steel. Also, handwash knives that are made in two parts. (The heat from the dishwasher can melt the glue that keeps these knives on the cutting edge.)

Don't use a dip cleaner or baking soda as they can take away the old patina. You want the *patina,* the naturally darkened area in the crevices of the design. Polish the highlights and the body of the piece. A really ornate design stands out better with a rich patina intact.

Condition is important with silver plate. You want the original silver plate as intact as possible. Some pieces may look horribly tarnished. Be careful that you don't remove the plate in the cleaning process. Using a regular silver polish, such as Goddards or Haggerty's is great. Don't use Simichrome or other highly abrasive silver cleaners for silver-plated pieces. (Although Simichrome is great for heavily tarnished sterling pieces.)

"Pacific Cloth" is sold for hollowware and flatware. You can buy this cloth by the yard, so you can wrap your bigger pieces. The cloth has a special chemical that prevents tarnish. You can also find large zippered bags made for storing flatware. Or you can wrap your flatware in tarnish resistant paper.

Part IV
Integrating Antiques into Your Home

"Look at that craftsmanship. Notice the patina. It's already three years old. In the computer industry, that makes it a genuine antique."

In this part . . .

"So now, what do I do with all this stuff?" a friend asked. We wrote this section to try to help.

Now we bring the antiques right into your house and even out into your yard. Suddenly you are sitting on them, playing cards on them, drinking from them, and eating mocha ice cream with them. And we get you "oriented" to the elegant world of the East, including Japanese woodblock prints, Chinese furniture and ceramics, ivory, and jade.

Chapter 13

Basic Decorating: Bringing the Past into Your Present

In This Chapter

- Discovering what you like
- Choosing your design style
- Marrying old and new
- Cross-training your antiques
- Understanding how designers work

You walk into the home, and you instantly feel at ease. Maybe it's the glow of the old copper pitcher on the mantel. Maybe it's the antique quilt resting on a well-worn steamer trunk. Like the screw-top wine you drank in college, the sofa is vintage yesterday, yet that wooden table behind it looks like it might have hosted a Victorian era card game. The chairs just barely escaped from the 1950s. The room is an eclectic blend of old and new, and it works.

The first rule of decorating with antiques is to buy what you like. You need to create a mixture that makes you feel comfortable and at home.

Shelter for the Spirit by Victoria Moran (published by HarperCollins) is a great way to get in touch with your inner decorating self. *Antiques at Home,* by Barbara Milo Ohrbach (published by Clarkson Potter), is a rich and fascinating guide to creating your own marvelous milieu.

One Size and Color Does Not Fit All: Discovering Your Decorating Niche

Eclectic, *je ne sais quois,* rag tag, comfortable, fascinating, warm, elegant, formal, welcoming. . . . How do you want your home to look and feel?

Mixing old and new is a way to create an individualized look, where things blend together without formally matching. Mixing old and new creates an eclectic style that adds interest, spice, and mystery and creates a room where the visitor is continually delighted by "surprises."

The first part of incorporating antiques into your home is figuring out what look and feel you like. Here are some quick ways to find out:

- **Notice how you feel when you walk into a room filled with old things.** Do you prefer being surrounded by history, or do you like just a splash of the past? What kinds of antiques make you feel comfortable and at home?
- **Look through some home decorating magazines and mark or tear out the rooms you like.** Keep a folder with pictures you like. Or keep them in a photo album (the sticky kind). Collecting these pictures lets you spot common themes in your likes and dislikes, and helps you hone your own style.
- **Focus on colors you like.** If you despise green and look terrible in it, chances are you won't be happy in that green upholstered Victorian love seat you're thinking about. Of course, if you must have it, just add in the price of re-upholstering.
- **Size up the situation.** If your rooms are small, you might gravitate toward smaller scale pieces. However, a piece that's grand in size, color, or scale can always make a statement.
- **Think about your living style.** Do you want comfort? Do you want elegance? Do you want antiques that are safe around curious children and frisky pets?

When you have an empty space you want to fill, experiment before you go shopping. Try furniture or accessories of different sizes, shapes, and colors in that space. Then, when you go shopping, you have a clearer idea of the impact you want to make and the space you are trying to fill. If you're still not sure how the antiques will look in your room, get the advice of an interior designer or an antique dealer you know and trust. Some dealers will look at your home and tell you where the piece best fits.

Design Elements: Noticing the Good Lines

With antiques, sometimes you need to look beyond the condition and the surface flaws. Here are some ways to put a creative spin on your antique search and to expand your decorating talents:

- **Consider the size and scale of the piece, the size of the room, and the scale of the other pieces in the room.** When it's a valued piece you want to work with the surroundings to show the piece off to its best advantage.
- **Look for shape and lines.** When you are considering buying a piece, ask yourself if the outline of the piece is beautiful or graceful? Is the carving on a piece of furniture compelling or noteworthy? After a while, you'll recognize the lines associated with different periods of design, such as the curves of Rococo, the classical lines of Neoclassical, the simple clean lines of Arts and Crafts. You can mirror these lines with other objects so you have a pleasing blend and flow of lines.
- **Appreciate the surface.** As copper, bronze, silver, wood, and various other antiques age, the surface shades can darken and mellow. This *patina* adds to the value and warmth of the piece.
- **Look for the visual weight of items that complement one another.** For example, one sofa could equal the *visual weight* (or space) of two chairs, which is why people often have a sofa and two wing chairs together. Those two chairs take up the same weight as the sofa.
- **Notice the space each piece requires.** Does every piece have the amount of space it needs? A campaign chest with simple lines can be right next to another piece of furniture. A more intricate bureau with gilding and inlay needs some space around it.
- **Consider the lighting.** Light can instantly highlight a piece or drain the color from it. Incandescent light adds richness to red, orange, and yellow hues, and drains the color from blue hues. Many fluorescent lights bring blues and purples to life.

Designing between the lines

There's an art to "designing between the lines."

- *Horizontal lines* are restful and inviting.
- *Vertical lines* give a feeling of majesty or dignity (such as a tall case or grandfather clock).
- *Curved lines* give you a feeling of growth and gracefulness.

If a piece has been crudely painted, but it has great lines, it may still be a worthy piece of decor and a good buy even after you factor in the costs of stripping and refinishing.

Starring Roles or Chorus Line: Auditioning Your Antiques

Start your journey into antique interior design with one or two items. Decide whether you want them to be a focal point or whether you want them to blend in with the rest of the room.

Some antiques do better in a group; others do better if you display them alone. You can decide whether to single out stars or have a series of great chorus numbers, depending on your tastes, the breadth of your collections, the types of antiques you have, and the space available.

For example, suppose that you just bought a lovely small tea table. If you put it in an entry hall, it can be a star. You can put a new mirror on the wall behind it, a Japanese Imari vase on top of it, and the table will be an eye-catching focus of that area. Shine a light on it, and it's a superstar.

If the tea table has scratches and scars and you love it despite the hard life it's led, you can let it blend. Nestled next to the sofa, topped with a lamp, the table can add to the warmth of your living room without attracting undue attention.

How do you know if you have a focal point?

When you walk into a room, notice where you look first. That can be a *focal point.*

A single decorative piece can add a lot of quality to a room. A beautiful old commode (chest) with marquetry and special veneers or a cameo glass vase can bring tremendous beauty to an interior. It's also fine to have several fascinating pieces as secondary points of interest.

Just remember, you can't emphasize one thing without de-emphasizing something else.

If you fall in love with a piece that's too big for the room, use mirrors to make the room look larger.

Something to look up to: The pedestal principle

You add instant importance to an antique when you display it on a pedestal. The pedestal lets you focus attention on a piece by raising it to greater prominence and singling it out.

Since few people are still on pedestals, where do you find them (the pedestals, that is)?

For a traditional look, seek out turn-of-the-century Italian marble and alabaster pedestals, which are great for displaying a large vase, a bronze piece, or a figural marble piece. Oriental pedestals (or stands) come in a variety of styles, shapes, and sizes. Some are extraordinarily ornate. Others are simple enough to accommodate pieces that are totally different in period and country of origin. Modern pedestals often work well with antiques. You can purchase them or you can create a stand, from wood or Lucite that meets the eclectic standards for your room. You can even turn a large ceramic planter upside down and use it as a pedestal.

Instant enlightenment

When you shine light on an antique, you bring the piece into glorious focus. Here are a few ways you can shed light on your favorite pieces:

- Position a floor or table lamp to highlight a bronze or porcelain figurine.
- Shine a ceiling spotlight that lands in the center of a vase or glass piece.
- Create a lighted display cabinet that illuminates your collection of French enamels and ivory miniatures. (This is especially powerful when the display cabinet is the only light you have on in the room.)
- Shoot a beam from a lighted base into your Gallé cameo glass vase so that it brings out the intricacy of the vase's five-layered landscape.

The over vocal focal

"Huh?" you say, when your hostess asks if you want something to drink. You simply can't take your eyes off the large vase that's spotlighted in the center of her living room.

You can take away the home-like feeling when you let one antique overpower a room. You want to design the setting so people notice and appreciate your things, but you don't want the antiques to overwhelm or distract people.

Your design attitude: The tuxedo or the khaki

Symmetry gives you a formal look, and asymmetry makes things more casual. The way you place things affects the feel of your room.

Suppose that you want to display an antique clock and a couple of candlesticks. For a formal look, use symmetrical balance: the clock in the middle and a candlestick on each side. For a more casual look, create an uneven balance. Push the clock to the left and put both candlesticks on the right. Raise one of them a few inches with a block of marble or wood to carry that casualness one step further.

Togetherness That Works: Creating Scintillating Groups

Look at the items that give you pleasure and think about the best way to display them. All you need is permission to play and a little imagination, and you can put together great groupings out of many different types of objects. Here are some ideas:

- Turn your family pictures into art when you display them in a grouping of antique silver or wooden frames.
- Make a grouping of different size boxes, from large to small.
- Group three square boxes and one vase, for a nice contrast.
- Group things by color. This works particularly well with antique glassware.
- Heap antique baskets under a large table.
- Display mismatched teacups (and their saucers) on a sideboard.
- Small cloisonné pieces of different sizes and shapes make a fascinating grouping.
- Create a wall display of various size English transfer ware platters.

The almost invisible display case

Lucite display cases offer a great way to display things without calling attention to the case itself. With clear Lucite and glass shelves, the case almost disappears, and the objects get all the attention they deserve.

Perhaps Great Grandma started a needlepoint that never got finished. Mount it on a neutral ground and put it in a shadow box or Lucite box, to create a personal record of family art and history.

When the refrigerator gets too crowded for all the incredible children's art, simply capture the pages behind plexi glass. You can display old family photos, letters, and papers the same way, matted with museum board (acid-free matting). This protects your precious papers. You can even purchase a type of plexiglass that blocks ultraviolet rays.

Developing Your Foreign Accents: Combining Period Antiques

You can play it safe and buy a dining room set where everything matches. Or you can be daring and mix a straight-legged rectangular Oriental table with 18th century Chippendale chairs and use a bombé chest for a server. These different worlds can complement each other and add a sense of interest, warmth, and excitement to the dining room.

When you add antiques to your home, you have many choices. You can jazz up your regular old furniture with a well-chosen antique. You can blend antiques from different periods. Or you can include antiques and reproductions in the same room.

Making the flow

What makes one room flow together and another room get on your nerves? Here are some tips to develop your own unique accents:

- **Pay attention to ornamentation.** For example, if you have an ornate Victorian sideboard, heavy with intricate carvings, your other dining room pieces may be carved, but less ornately. Combining pieces this way gives you similar ornamentation, but still lets you play off and highlight the sideboard.

- **Use antiques to set the tone for the room or to dress up the room.** An English antique chest and a well-placed piece of Meissen or Dresden porcelain can dress up a comfortable living room.
- **Think about the purpose of the room.** For rooms where you want calm and relaxation, choose neutral colors and furniture with simple, clean lines. For lively rooms, choose brighter and diverse colors and objects that invite conversation.

Cross-training your antiques

How do you take advantage of the best of both worlds: the charm and uniqueness of antiques and the functionality of the modern?

Give your antiques a new purpose in life. Become adept at *adaptive reuse,* an architectural term that means you modify an item for modern use. Don't throw away that old iron-legged sewing machine that no longer works. Keep it "bobbin" along by using it as a table in an entryway.

Foot baths and pitchers of all kinds are great for flowers. Float a rose in a *waste,* the part of the tea service that held the grounds. Dented silver vases, vintage flea market, make wonderful bouquet holders.

Antique armoires can provide you with both a focal point and a storage system.

Watch for older pieces that can do modern work. Hutches and pie safes also make a decorative statement while providing needed storage space.

- If you're antiquing on a shoestring, take an old door that has lost its home and use it as a conversation "opener." Hang it horizontally on a wall to emphasize its beauty. Or put that door to work as a table.
- Cut the wires off old brass-mounted wall lights and use them as sconces.

Mixing repro and real antiques is an art form. Repros work next to genuine antiques when they are not of similar style or finish. You can't put the Queen Anne antique piece and Queen Anne repro next to each other: The repro will scream out fake! But away from the reign of the real Queen, the repro can exert its own charm.

In Case You've Always Secretly Wanted to Work with a Designer

People frequently hire designers to help them make their homes better looking and more livable.

Don't worry whether your furniture is nice enough to warrant a designer. Don't worry that you're not rich enough or your home isn't large enough. Many designers use the best of what you have. Their job is to guide you to what you really like and keep you from making mistakes.

Choosing a designer

Choosing a designer is personal: You are looking for the combination of education, experience, creativity, and personality that's right for you.

When you see a room you love, ask how it got that way. Some people want to buy a look, and so they find a designer who produces that look. Familiarize yourself with the styles of different designers.

Ask around for referrals. Call the local or national professional organizations such as the ASID (American Society of Interior Designers). Call the national office of the ASID at (202) 546-3480 for a list of accredited designers near you.

Invite the designer over to see your house. Notice the designer's attitude. Is this someone who's going to take over or someone who's going to listen to you?

A well-informed designer gives you additional security in knowing the antique you selected is genuine. But learning about antiques takes training. Some designers love and appreciate antiques and enjoy using them in designing their rooms. Others focus exclusively on modern furniture and accessories. Find out how much they know about antiques. Ideally, the designer continues antiques training every year, through either formal education or experience.

Designers have different ways of charging. Make sure that you work through all the monetary issues and questions before you start. Some designers charge a percentage of the purchase price of the antiques they acquire for you; others charge by the hour. Some charge a design fee for a specific project. Some designers get paid a commission by the seller of the merchandise. Talk out the unexpected issues, such as what if you find an antique for the room. Do you still have to pay the designer a commission?

Ask whom they've worked with and find out their background and accreditation.

You've got a friend

If you want help and you're not designer-inclined, find a friend whose style you like and ask him or her to help you. You can have fun ferreting out great stuff together.

While you're searching, you are educating yourself in decorative arts and honing your own personal style. And hopefully your more knowledgeable friend is helping you to avoid some pitfalls in purchasing, while offering you thoughts about design possibilities.

Expecting the best

Many designers use the best of what you have. According to what you want done, they look at your existing furniture and work around it. Others may have a tendency to scrap everything you've got and start all over again. Interview the designer in your home and see if he or she feels good about your keeping the things that you like. If you aren't seeing eye to eye on this, look for a new designer.

Decorating Tips

One design principle is to create diversity and welcome surprises. This includes putting art objects in unexpected places. Silver-topped sugar shakers look great in a powder room filled with potpourri or in your own bathroom, holding your talcum powder.

Antique beaded purses make a wonderful wall display for a bedroom or bathroom. Simply pin the purses onto a board, put them directly on the wall with unobtrusive nails, or find a wonderful antique frame and mount them inside it.

Don't be afraid to decorate with antiques that are not "in style." In the early 1970s, mission furniture was not valued. Good antique shops wouldn't carry Mission furniture. Tiffany lamps were considered gaudy and could be purchased in the low hundreds of dollars. Both of these have since gone through a glorious revival. Be on the alert for antiques you like that are out of favor.

When you're looking for shape and lines, watch for country painted pine furniture. The paint jobs can be worn, even sloppy, and may have several coats of color. Look beyond the messy paint and see if this furniture — which includes armoires, kitchen cabinets, and wall cabinets — has good proportions.

Here are some more ideas:

- Victorians put their spoons in cut glass vases called *spooners*. Use a spooner for your own collection of antique silver spoons. Perhaps you have a random collection of souvenir spoons, or just different silver patterns. When guests come, let them choose their own spoon. Or you can create your own spoonerism: Put pens or flowers in your spooner.
- Use tumblers and taller antique drinking glasses as pencil containers or vases.
- Pre-owned silver is great for families who like to entertain. Give yourself an instant ancestry, with monogrammed silver.
- Use fabric to enhance a room's look. You can find great reproductions of traditional English upholstery patterns. Or if you want to lighten a too-heavy antique look use a more contemporary pattern or flowery chintz.
- Don't have time to repaint the windowsill? Put a miniature tea set on it. Or a perfume bottle with a blossom or two. Or a few pieces from your colored glass tumbler collection. The colors will be cheery throughout the day. Just be sure the heat or cold in the window is not so intense that it could break the glass.
- Toss antique lace pillowcases and sheets in a window seat for a quick and lovely look. These sheets and linens don't need to be perfect; you're mainly going for the lacey effect.
- Need an instant focal point? Fill a pretty silver bowl or crystal bowl with glass Christmas ornaments and let the reflections play off one another. (This works in the non-holiday time of the year, as well.)

Chapter 14

Remembrances of Repasts Past: The Kitchen and Dining Room

In This Chapter

- Sitting down for a meal: Tables and chairs
- Locking it up: The pie safe
- Drinking it in: Tea and chocolate sets and services
- Drinking it down: Steins, stemware, and liqueur sets
- Adding utensils that add fun and even utility to your kitchen

The microwave is humming; the espresso machine is gurgling; the food processor is whirring. The apple pie, fresh from — well all right, the grocery store — is tucked into the pie safe. Though your stove is hot off the press, your butcher block table is old and has the scars to prove it. Your antique Windsor dining room chairs remind you to stop and smell the coffee.

You can increase the charm and coziness of your kitchen and the elegance and style of your dining room when you add antiques. What better places to blend the efficiency of the present with the romance of the past, when eating was a time of nourishment and a time to show off civilized manners. You can find antique kitchen and dining room furniture and accessories as modestly priced as the new. This chapter gives you a sampling of some of the antiques that can help you savor and add flavor to your mealtimes.

Note that a lot of the things you might like for your kitchen are called primitive. Primitives often were used more in the country, have a nature-oriented subject matter, and are more crudely made.

Periodic Tables

An antique table provides a warm gathering spot for your kitchen or dining room. The mellow glow of older wood and the fineness of craftsmanship give you a unique centerpiece, something you will treasure and your guests will notice. We describe just a few of the many charming antique tables you can uncover in your antiquing journeys, (and cover again at your home, with a lovely lace tablecloth). These tables are an easy and functional way to add charm, history, and extra personality to your kitchen or dining room.

As you search out antiques for your dining area, you will meet unescorted tables, tables flanked by their own personal matching chairs, and tables in the company of an assorted adopted family of chairs. Unmatched sets are common, so don't be afraid to create your own antique dining set. Sets include tables, chairs, and sometimes a hutch and sideboard.

Generally speaking, most of the large complete "sets" available on the market are from the late 19th and on into the 20th centuries. If you want eight chairs and you can only find four, create your own set, choosing chairs that look compatible. Before you buy, sit in the chair at the table, to make sure your legs fit under the table.

Coming across sectional tables

Imagine your host asking you, "What section of the table would you like to be seated in?" During the late 18th century and into the Victorian period, some tables had separate sections that functioned as independent tables or fit together to make a larger table.

Instead of adding leaves to make the table larger, you add another table. For example, the French *demi-lune* ("half moon") table, typically made in pairs, comes together to make a circular table. The banquet table, usually made in three parts, each with its own pedestal or legs, gives you lots of seating options. The center section generally has two drop leaves; the end sections each had one drop leaf.

You can use demi lunes individually as side tables when they are not "serving" a larger purpose.

In autumn, she eats at the drop leaf table

Here's a table that can literally hang around, serving time in a cozy breakfast nook or as a serving table and then spring into action when two or more of you gather.

The drop leaf is ideal for apartments or small areas. With both leaves down, the table takes up a modest amount of space. Drop leaf tables are light and easy to carry, so you can even use them instead of card tables. You simply lift the leaf and then swing out the wooden support from underneath the table. (These supports come in various sizes and shapes.) When the meal is done and you want more space, simply hum "The Falling Leaves" and put the leaves back down.

Reflections on the refectory table

The earlier refectory tables are long and narrow, a mere one-person wide. In the monastery, these tables, often simply a board on a trestle, might be placed against the wall so that the monks had no distractions while they ate.

The refectory table moved from the sacred to the secular, got wider, and found itself hosting large parties of people, also crowded around, but with a decidedly different ambience. With a pedestal base and a thick, solid top made of either one or two boards, these tables are sturdy. The design is often primitive and can feature carving on the legs and apron.

The tavern table, bar none

"They barely touched a drop." These tables, which could be square, round, or rectangular, sometimes with a drawer, were made of pine or oak or other native wood and were frequently seen in taverns. The old tables often have worn and scrubbed-looking tops, although the scent of brew has long since "hopped" away. These tables are ideal for small areas that need a little personality.

Many early tables were a little lower than our tables. When you try to sit at the table, you sometimes can't cross your legs. If you have an antique table and you need to raise it a little, have someone create raised wood coasters for you.

Butcher Blocks

Before these tables showed up in the center of lush country kitchens, European and American butcher shops used them to slaughter the smaller animals and cut up the meat.

Lemon chicken, the hard way

Susan tenderly rubbed her "new" antique butcher block table with lemon oil and set about preparing a dinner for guests. She felt connected to the past as she tenderized chicken on the old block and created a sumptuous Chicken Kiev. But she was brought right into the present when her guests bit into a chicken that tasted strongly of lemon oil.

Craftsmen glued together many pieces of wood to form the solid top. Country butchers and farmers usually made their own butcher blocks. The blocks are made of hardwood so that they can endure the blows of the cleaver. (Hence the phrase, "Leave it to cleaver.")

Today, these butcher-block tables are reasonably easy to find. But don't try to get one home without at least three or four strong relatives or friends: They are heavy.

Truly old blocks are typically concave on top; the top is indented from years of use and has hundreds of chop, slice, and saw marks. These marks add character to the block, which adds character, as well as some utilitarian value, to the kitchen. Dance around this table and baby, you are "Rocking around the block."

If you're going to use the block, wipe it down with cooking oil every six months so that it doesn't split on the seams. If you're using it for decorative purposes, use lemon oil.

A Seat of Power: The Windsor Chair

Today, many antique chairs are available that will look great in your dining room. We introduced a number of distinguished chairs (such as Queen Anne, Chippendale, and Hepplewhite) in the furniture chapter. Any of them are great for wining and dining (or "whining and dining," as the case may be).

We are focusing here on a chair that spanned all classes: the Windsor. It comes in many forms and these are just a few.

Windsor chairs appealed to both the modest and the mighty. George Washington shelled out $1.78 for Windsor chairs, which sat on the porch of Mt. Vernon. Ben Franklin and Thomas Jefferson were won over by Windsor. And the Continental Congress deliberated while sitting in Windsor chairs.

The Windsor became popular in mid-18th century America because it was accessible and easily copied by the more "common" man. He could now make or buy what the wealthy had in their garden areas, and use it outside or inside. Plus, the cost of a Windsor chair was a fraction of what conventional seating cost.

Windsor chairs were often painted. Some say the chairs were painted to disguise the potpourri of woods; some say to see them better in the dimly lighted rooms; some say just for the aesthetics of it all.

Many Windsors were painted green and used as outdoor furniture in the garden areas of wealthier people's homes. Windsor's open construction helped keep them from blowing over in winds and provided ventilation on warmer days.

Windsors were mass-produced, with people often buying sets. The chairs took on their own personality, depending on the location of their manufacture. Sometimes Windsors were called *Philadelphia chairs,* because they were made in large numbers in Philadelphia. Windsor chairs make great additions to your kitchen and dining areas. They are easy to move around and fit in with a lot of different furniture styles. Figure 14-1 shows two of the many varieties of Windsor chair.

Figure 14-1: Two of the many varieties of the popular Windsor chair, the English wheelback and the comb back.

Safe As American Apple Pie: Pie Safes

Long before Mrs. Smith (or at least the Mrs. Smith who used a freezer) and long before screens and storm windows, pies cooled on window ledges where cats and birds and bugs could take a bite. Hence, the pie safe was created (see Figure 14-2). This way, pies — and other baked goods — could cool unharmed.

Figure 14-2: This pie safe still has its original finish, complete with hand-punched tins.

Photo courtesy of Amy L. Babb and Log Cabin Antiques, Danville, Arkansas

These utilitarian objects, which kept your ancestors in sweets, are quite collectible. The more intricate the panels, and the fancier the wood, the more valuable the safe. Today, most folks use the safe for storing sweets, other foods, or even special dishes.

Cool Collectibles: The Ice Box

Iceboxes were made of oak and were mostly American. They kept ice clean and insulated. They had shelves inside and porcelain, galvanized tin, or iron interiors. They had either one door or double doors. They opened from either the top or the front. The last ice boxes were made about the 1930 (that is, until the repros began to appear).

Today, use ice boxes to keep liquor bottles in and on, or for small tables. Ideally, they have all original hardware, an original interior, and an original top.

Tea Times and Chocolate Times

Prior to the late 18th century, having a "cuppa" was not a casual thing. You defined yourself by what you poured your brew into. In Europe, the porcelain tea service was a status symbol, a sign of wealth and power. (See Chapter 11 for more on the intriguing story of porcelain.)

During the Victorian era, the ritual of tea taking became more punctuated by accessories. You could find complete silver, silver plate, and porcelain tea sets. Those who preferred the comfort of warm cocoa could sip from a chocolate set.

It is still a glorious feeling to pour tea from a Victorian teapot or sip your jasmine from a Victorian teacup. Tea sets and chocolate sets add a spot of charm to your home. Some people use them for decoration; other collectors enjoy serving with their sets.

Be sure each cup matches its saucer. The pieces can look quite alike and still be a "marriage."

Tea for four or five

Tea sets can consist of a teapot, cups, saucers, sugar, creamer, and tray. Don't worry if you don't find a complete set. You may want to collect pieces from different sets. Many collectors buy just teapots or only cups and saucers, and many collectors specialize in creamers or lone sugar containers. Collecting this way is handy because finding old sets that are both complete and in mint condition is increasingly difficult.

In the late Victorian era, tea services were often made of silver plate, with the finer sets being made of sterling. Tea and coffee services from this era can include sugar tongs, tea caddy, tea strainer, a tea pot, a coffeepot, and a *waste* (a bowl so you could throw away the grounds).

Set on chocolate

The chocolate set is similar to the tea set, with the cups and saucers being smaller. These sets, popular during the late 19th and early 20th century, are usually made of porcelain and come with four to six cups and sometimes a serving tray. Chocolate sets are more unusual than tea sets and can be more expensive. The pot is taller, often cylindrical with a spout near or at the rim.

Finding quality tea and chocolate sets

When you buy a porcelain or pottery tea set or chocolate set, look for markings and condition. If you want to use the set, have the dealer guarantee that it will hold water. If you already own a cup that has glaze cracks, test the cup in the sink to be sure you haven't purchased the porcelain equivalent of an old "dribble glass," like the ones that were used for practical jokes.

Here are some tips for finding porcelain tea and chocolate services you can actually use:

- Check the spout and handles for sturdiness by looking for cracks and for signs of repair or regluing.

  If you gently tap the pot and hear a thudding sound, that could indicate a crack. Crazing (cracks in the glaze that do not go through the porcelain) are typically not a problem. Avoid a crack that you see on the inside and that you can trace to the outside of the cup. This type of damage seriously diminishes the value and usability of the piece.
- Check the finial (top peak) on the lid to see if it has been broken off. Lift the lid and look inside to see if there are any serious chips or cracks.

Sometimes you can smooth minor chipping with an emery board or cloth. But unless you collect for decoration and unless the set is reasonably priced, if a piece is not in excellent condition, keep on looking.

Getting Grounded: The Coffee Grinder

Before Starbucks, many people got their grounds in a general store. From the Victorian era until the 1930s, people learned how to create their own grounds, making coffee grinders more common.

They were wood and metal contraptions, with a utilitarian flair (see Figure 14-3). Talk about feeling your beans: You put the beans in the top and well, it was a good excuse to act out your "crankiness." The drawer below caught the ground coffee.

Counter grinder models, used in 19th century country and general stores, are desirable. Many of these are crude, with the cranks on top. Enterprise, Elgin, and Arcade were three of the big makers. Floor models often stood six feet tall. Tabletop models, for the home, were typically wood. By the late 19th century wall mounted versions became popular. These have an iron mechanism with tin fittings and a container that's ceramic or glass. Companies who made grinders in the 19th century used stenciling or stamps or wood burning to place the company name and the patent date.

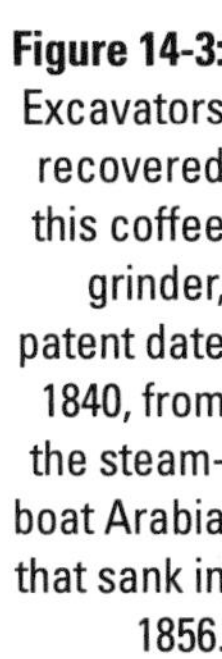

Figure 14-3: Excavators recovered this coffee grinder, patent date 1840, from the steamboat Arabia that sank in 1856.

Photo courtesy of the Museum of the Arabia Steamboat, Kansas City, Missouri.

Some of the most collectible coffee grinders include the company name, patent date, and the original wood finish. Watch out for grinders with a drawer missing. This can ruin the look and the functionality as well as much of the value of the grinder.

Many people use a coffee grinder to add a homey, country look to the kitchen. Some people use a good clean wall-mounted grinder to grind their own beans.

Drinking It In and Washing It Down

Antique wine and drinking glasses run the gamut, from the simple and inexpensive to the elaborate and pricey. Use the tips you learned in Chapter 10 to help you analyze glass steins and wines (stemware) and the clues in Chapter 11 to help you understand the ceramic steins. We include steins, Rhine wine glasses, and the Tantalus in this section: something for beer, something for wine, and something to hold your precious liquors and liqueurs.

Stein ways

Waiter, what is that fly doing in my beer?

Backstroke, sir.

Waiter, there's a moth in my beer.

Don't worry, it won't drink much.

Perhaps you're thinking, there should be a law against jokes like that. In Medieval Germany, there was a law that worked to stamp out such jokes. The law, also based on health principles, decreed that all steins needed lids, to keep out the unwanted flies. And so, those jokes stopped, in Germany that is, and the lids reigned.

A *stein* is a drinking vessel with a lid and a handle. Steins can be made of porcelain, stoneware, glass, pewter, and more rarely silver and other exotic materials such as ivory and agate. When collecting steins, some people focus on a specific type of stein, such as regimental; some focus on a company, such as Villeroy & Boch, makers of Mettlach steins; others prefer an eclectic mix. Display your steins in a china cabinet, a bookcase, or atop a sideboard. They add a jaunty flair to your dining room.

Now, here's a brief introduction to a few types of steins.

Meet Mettlach Steins

Some of the great steins were made in Germany by Jean Boch (and his father) and Nicholas Villeroy. In the 1840s, Villeroy and Boch merged and formed a stoneware factory in a monastery in Mettlach, Germany. They first produced relief designs on the stoneware. They began making their more famous etched steins about 1880 and continued until 1915. Mettlach steins are thought of as the Cadillac of mass-produced steins (see Figure 14-4).

Mettlach steins have different patterns and numbers on them. The lids were all pewter or pewter rims with ceramic inserts. A high quality Mettlach includes lids that are etched with detailed scenes. Scenes on the steins might feature drinking scenarios, courting couples, knights on horses, and other romantic and historic imagery.

Mettlach made steins through the Art Nouveau and early Art Deco periods. A fire burned down the factory in 1921.

The Mettlach wares were cataloged, using their own numbering system. Mettlach items, including steins, often came in a variety of sizes. When you really want to drink in the nuances of Mettlach, you'll need a Mettlach book to learn the markings and patterns.

Villeroy & Boch are again producing steins at Mettlach. These new steins look entirely different from the earlier etched steins.

Most Mettlach steins are marked with either the name Mettlach and an incised castle mark or the name Mettlach in a green stamp that has a winged Mercury on the top.

Question: What did the famous writer Mary Shelley drink from?

Answer: A Franken Stein.

Figure 14-4: Mettlach etched stein of a hunter with dog, mold number 2938.

Regimental Steins

Regimental steins are typically a commemorative, proving that the young man spent his time in the military. Before leaving his tour of duty, a soldier had the opportunity to buy a stein decorated with his name, unit information and scenes of military life, such as battles and soldiers marching. The stein might include some appropriate poetry such as "The artillery is the thunder of God for the fatherland," and the names of his fellow servicemen.

If you were a cavalryman, you served three years and got a stein that had a pewter man riding a horse atop it. Each branch of the service, the artillery, the cavalry, and the infantry had their own finial.

When you drank up, you were typically rewarded with a lithophane scene in the bottom. (A *lithophane* is a scene or picture created by varying the thickness of the porcelain, forming light areas and shadows.) Such a scene might be of a woman tearfully waving goodbye to her soldier while a train chugs in the background.

The new members of the regimental stein family may well reveal a naked woman as you drain your drink. The pewter lids look phony: Their only sign of aging stems from the moment someone spent dipping them into oxidizers to make them look older.

The original steins were hand-embellished with thick enamel paint. Typically, every button on the soldier's uniform is a dot of enamel. If you cannot feel the buttons on the uniform, it could be a copy. If you feel the buttons, look for other clues that the stein is old.

Look at the inside of the pewter lid. It should be shiny. If it's naturally oxidized, only the outside has the beautiful patina. If someone dipped the lid, the inside and the outside look the same.

Character steins

Some people like to look at figurines: Others like to drink out of them. A *character stein* is a figurine that opens up. Made primarily out of ceramics, these colorful and uniquely shaped steins depict everything from the letters of the alphabet to a jar of pretzels to famous Germans of the early 20th century. If you like variety, character steins could be for you. You can have a collection that includes cats, monkeys, vegetables, and more. Both the body and the lid are part of the figure. For example, on a face stein, a hat is the lid.

Working on occupational steins

In Germany, when you retired from your job, instead of a gold watch, you might receive your own personal *occupational stein.* This ceramic vessel had your occupation printed on it, your name, a scene depicting your work, and sometimes a saying that extolled your labor. If you were a farmer, your stein might say, "Hoch Lieb"(long life) and "Landsman, Hans, He that tills grows great things," and have a scene that showed wheat and work.

The personalized stein is more valuable. Later pottery steins that are marked "Made in Germany" or "Made in Japan" are of much less quality and are worth only a fraction of the finer steins.

Rhining and wining

Hand blown and cut Rhine *wines,* which are a type of stemmed glassware, come in a myriad of colors. In general, the bowl of the wine glass is a colored layer of glass blown over clear crystal and cut back to reveal a little of the base crystal (see Figure 14-5). The rarer Rhine wine bowls are layered with different colors and then cut to reveal all the underlying colors. The stem and foot are typically clear, leaded crystal, which also may have intricate cutting. Some Rhine wines have the extra embellishment of a decorative air bubble within the stem.

Figure 14-5: These cut Rhine wines are clear crystal with a color overlay.

When placed in china cabinets and lighted from behind, these wines add a striking presence. Some collectors search only for wines of a similar color, with cranberry, ruby, cobalt blue, and amethyst being the more collectible colors. Others choose to collect one of each of the colors, so that every place setting glows with a different color.

Rhine wines have been widely reproduced since their earliest days. The more modern ones tend to have less depth to the cutting on the bowls, less carving on their stems and feet, and will rarely include such "extras" as hollow-blown bubbles in the stem and additional overlaid colors.

The tantalizing "Tantalus"

Tantalus is a fancy liquor bottle holder and carrier with decanters inside. The frame is wood or metal. The cut or pressed decanters often have a sterling or silver-plated label on them, strung on a chain, inscribed with the likes of *Scotch, Rye,* and *Bourbon,* to identify the contents of the decanter. Some people collect these decanter necklaces. The bottles in the best Tantalus sets are made of leaded and deeply cut crystal; the less expensive ones are made of pressed glass. Some have highly elaborate cases and many are quite plain.

Tantalus sets lock, and many have their own unique ways of opening. Some have pullout or push-in pieces of wood or metal fittings that release so you can remove the bottles from their cases.

Here's one version of how the "Tantalus" got its name: Back in mythological times, Tantalus was a poor soul who displeased the gods and was hung from a tree over a pool of water. He couldn't reach high enough to pluck the fruit from the tree above, and he could not bend down low enough to quench his thirst from the water. He remained suspended in a constant state of hunger and thirst. That is, tantalized.

Needless to say, in the Victorian household, the patriarch was the keeper of the keys, and the poor unfortunates included the butler, all of the serving help, and most of the rest of the family.

The French version of the Tantalus set is a *cave a liqueur* (a liqueur cave) which includes four small bottles and a dozen liqueur glasses set into a holder, which was often gilded. An elegant wooden, brass, or inlaid box enclosed the set, so the bottles are typically hidden in their cave. The bottles are smaller and more bulbous than the Tantalus and more frequently etched than cut. Sometimes the wood was inlaid with rare woods or inlaid with "boulle" (inlay using brass and tortoiseshell, named after the famous French cabinetmaker Charles Andre Boulle).

For a special occasion, place your tantalus on the sideboard and use it for its original purpose.

Eating Up History: Table Topics

Even if you don't like to cook, you can still spice up your dining experience with antiques. We provide you with just a taste of some of the antiques that can add fun and function to your table.

Pick of the collectibles: Toothpick holders

Everyone knows it's gauche to floss at the table. That's why you need the elegant presence of the toothpick holder. Toothpick holders were created in the last half of the 19th century.

Why do people collect them?

- They are small and easy to display — you can have 50 of them and they don't take up much space.
- They have a great price range, starting very inexpensively.
- They are fun to look for — they can turn up in all sorts of places, including garage sales, auctions, flea markets, and antique shops.
- They are functional — you can pick your favorites and proudly set them on your table.
- They are made from a variety of interesting materials, such as glass (including Amberina, vaseline glass, cranberry glass, and Burmese) to bronze and silver plate to porcelain.

You can pick your teeth from souvenir holders that boast the names of states, fairs or expositions, or you can place your gold toothpick in a Favrile glass holder by Tiffany.

Caster set to the table

Caster sets include three to ten small condiment bottles inside a metal holder (see Figure 14-6). Salt, pepper, vinegar, mustard, and others were often included. The sets had many varieties and styles; bottles were made of cut crystal, Amberina, milk glass, and others.

Figure 14-6: This silver and crystal caster set gives you a great way to hold forth your condiments.

Here is another lovely and useful way to bring the romance of the past to the dining table of the present. Some stands are on a turntable. The glass often has etched designs and the silver plated or sterling tops are often engraved.

Even one damaged bottle decreases the value of the entire set. However, a good glass grinder can smooth away a small nick or chip.

Check each bottle to see if the glass and lid match the others. Sometimes the makers signed their name on the base of the frame holding the bottles.

Light weights: An illuminating topic

Today, you might use candles for a romantic dinner. In the 18th and 19th centuries, candles were one of the major ways to "see the light" while you were eating. Candlesticks come in a variety of sizes, shapes, and materials.

You can integrate antique candlesticks into your home in many ways. You can take the chamberstick by its handle and carry it from the dining room to your bedroom. You can keep a few silver candlesnuffers on the mantel so that you don't "blow it" when getting ready to extinguish the candles.

You may like to have a few brass push-up candlesticks — using a device in the candlestick's base, you can adjust the height of the candle as it burns. These sticks come in a variety of shapes and sizes, and often are found in pairs. The single stick is often less than half the price of a pair, and a group of singles placed together can create a delightful arrangement, especially for holidays.

Sometimes the push-up devices in these sticks are "frozen" due to decades of waxy build-ups, and no amount of cleaning or scraping can unfreeze them. Simply soak them for a few minutes in scalding water, and the wax will easily be "de-frosted."

For a long lasting light, try a candle jack. Usually made of brass, occasionally of silver, this "jack" holds a long coiled waxed "rope with a wick inside." The rope feeds out the top of the piece. As it burns down, you simply roll up more candle for more light! These are fairly rare, but if you know what you're looking for, they can also be a bargain at the right auction or in the right shop!

Courting candlesticks were like an alarm clock for beaus. It was said, a father set the candle height high or low, depending on how long he wanted his daughter to be with her "beau." Once the candle burned down, it was time for the guy to go home!

Stamping out butter

Some say there's an unwritten rule of butter stamping and molding in America: No two farms in the same area used the same stamp or mold patterns (just as no two ranches ever used the same branding iron on their cattle or horses). Frequently, local people made their own stamps. These stamps made the butter beautiful. Stamps featured designs such as flowers, pinwheels, animals (cows, of course), and the ever-popular pineapple. American stamps were often patriotic and boasted flags and eagles. The patriotic theme stamps are often highly prized by collectors and can be more valuable.

Odd designs are most valuable, such as eagles, cows, roosters, hearts, and stars. The more elaborate and higher quality the design and carving, and the better the condition, the more valuable. Some stamps or molds are even signed (usually with initials, but occasionally the lucky collector will find one with a full name signature).

Get your souvenirs

Souvenir spoons, made primarily of sterling silver or silver plate, were popular in the late 19th and early 20th century. Designed to commemorate events or places, the handles and bowls showed various people and buildings. State spoons spelled out the name of the state on the handle (see Figure 14-7). These spoons are still inexpensive to collect. Some dealers have large baskets of these spoons.

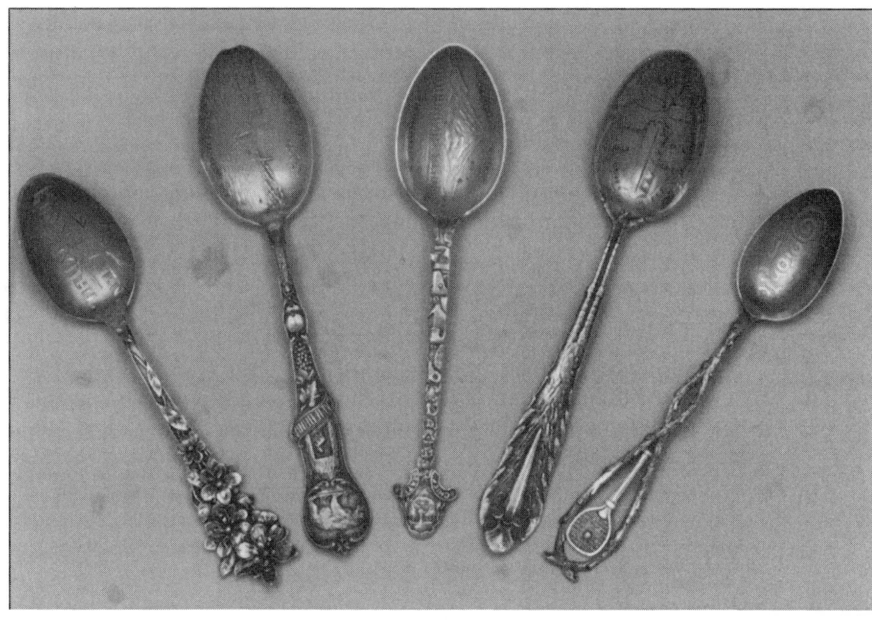

Figure 14-7: Souvenir spoons were popular in the late 19th and early 20th century.

Certain varieties of souvenir spoons are rare and can be considerably more expensive. These spoons might feature flowing designs of the Art Nouveau period, or Worlds' Fair or "Exposition" spoons. If you could be born with a silver spoon in your mouth, you would probably want it to be one of these.

Keep some souvenir spoons on your table, in a spooner or a ceramic bowl. Let your guests or your family choose the spoon of the day. These spoons add fun to a gathering, are nice conversation enhancers and add that extra delicious flavor to a dish of ice cream.

Get to know what was popular chitchat back in the 1890s through the turn of the century by looking through a basket of souvenir spoons. These spoons are like the local headlines today: reflecting some of what is on people's minds.

Salt and pepper shakers

Salt and pepper had to come out of the cellar and get a lid on it. Prior to the advent of the screw-top lid, these vital condiments lolled about in open dishes and were dispersed with small spoons.

But Mason's mid-19th century screw-top lid created an opportunity, if not for the movers, at least for the shakers. Early salt shakers are made of wood, glass, porcelain, and pottery. The screw-on tops are made of silver plate, sterling, glass, or tin.

Glass salt shakers in the 19th century usually feature a specially designed "agitator top" with a spike or prongs to loosen the often congealed salt. One of the most famous is Alden's Patent model, popularly called "the Christmas salt," since the design was patented on December 25, 1877.

Add seasoning to your table when you use your salt and pepper shakers. Some prefer collecting just open salts, while other collectors like the security of the lid. Either way, these make a pretty, interesting and functional collection.

Since many styles are reproduced, it's often confusing to tell old from new. Look for wear along the edges of the screw-top lid and the usual assortment of dings and bangs and wear marks on the bottom. Not all containers were marked, and getting "on the mark" is a whole study in itself.

Salt and pepper shakers are much less valuable when one is damaged or when only one is available.

Kitchenware before kitsch

You can cast your fate to the wind, or you can cast your iron to the stove. For the collector who wants a sense of history in the kitchen, cast-iron pots, cake molds, waffle irons, and muffin pans are heavy duty and still great to use. Look for the company name and town stamped on the bottom.

To bake the cake, the Victorian chef used wooden flour sifters complete with company name and date. They whisked through their eggs with the unbeatable handheld eggbeater, which varied from whisk-style to rotary crank. B.C. (Before Cholesterol) and A.C.W. (After the Civil War), hundreds of models of eggbeaters were available.

Tin nutmeg graters, looking like a mini cheese grater, were a common kitchen appliance. The old ones can be rusty and are still valued. Keep the dark nutty patina.

True, they didn't have gourmet stores back then, but they did have gourmets and gourmet appliances. Lemon squeezers, potato mashers, two bladed slaw choppers with blades that curve up (they would have been a hot item, had there been Infomercials in the 19th century), punched tin graters, strainers, and colanders are but a few of the wonderful antique kitchenwares you can collect.

For a wide menu of what's cooking in the antique kitchen, get Linda Campbell Franklin's *300 Years of Kitchen Collectibles* (published by Krause Publications). You can read up on a potpourri of kitchen utensils and paraphernalia, from pepper mills to cake molds to can openers. Franklin includes repro and look alike tips and wonderful line drawings and photos.

Chapter 15

Parlor Pieces: Living Room Antiques

In This Chapter

- Walking on art: the Oriental rug
- Sitting pretty on sofas and chairs
- Getting on and off your rocker
- Tabling your motions
- Finding miniatures

Imagine a 19th century parlor. People were sitting on the edges of their seats not because the conversation was so riveting, but because formality and furniture dictated that very exacting posture. The parlor was a place for showing off manners, not for relaxing.

You can now liberate parlor furniture by bringing it into your living room. You can create a living room that gives you present-day comfort and still keeps the elegance and charm of the past. We're showing you the living room from the ground up.

Putting Art on Your Floor: The Decorative Oriental Rug

There is something magical about walking on art every day. An old Oriental rug adds a rich warmth and flavor to your living room.

A wealth of mythology surrounds the rug — misinformation that has been handed down from generation to generation. This misinformation includes how rugs were made, the language used to describe the patterns of rugs, and the ways of valuing a rug.

We have information that grounds you in some rug basics and tips for how you can be comfortable buying an Oriental rug.

Why buy rugs?

The main reasons people buy rugs are for decorative and utilitarian functions, where design and color rule. This is a rug you are going to walk all over, so it needs to be functional, have plenty of wear left in it, and above all, appeal to you.

When you buy an old Oriental rug, make sure that you are spending your money wisely. First, find a rug dealer you feel comfortable with. Talk to a number of dealers, ask them questions, and get a sense of who knows what. Then, depending on your level of expertise and your comfort level with your dealer, you might consider getting a pre-purchase appraisal of your rug. In essence, you are getting a second opinion from a qualified and disinterested party.

To get a pre-purchase appraisal, you need a qualified appraiser with a specialty in Oriental rugs. Not every appraiser understands the intricate nuances of rugs! If you don't know someone reliable, see Chapter 20 to learn how to find appraisers.

This appraisal, plus a written description and guarantee from your dealer, gives you more assurance your money is wisely spent.

Sweep it under the carpet or under the rug?

In England, a "rug" is typically 8 feet by 5 feet or less. Anything more than 40 square feet is called a "carpet." (So if you get lucky enough to be invited on a magic carpet ride, invite some friends: There's plenty of room.)

In the United States, we tend to call any area rug a "rug," to distinguish it from wall-to-wall carpeting. Because we are talking about area rugs, we use the word "rug" throughout this section.

Oriental is the generic name for a variety of rugs that came from different countries, such as Iran (Persia), the Caucuses, Turkey, Afghanistan, India, and China. Rugs are typically named for the city or region they're made in or for the nomadic tribe who designed and wove them. Each geographical area or tribe had distinctive weaves, colors, and designs, and some had distinctive wool.

How the rug is made

If you decide to try rug-making at home, you may need a sabbatical from work. To be a rug maker, you not only need skill, you need a long-term strategic plan, patience, and good health. One rug can take from one to three years or more to create.

In some places, rug-making was a way to weave the family together: Women and children worked side by side at various tasks.

The nomadic peoples often wove from memory, with only a rough drawing to guide them. The more formal and elaborate "city" rugs were a knotty problem and required a special artist to create a design for the rug weaver. The design specified how many knots of each color were in each place.

Normally, big rugs or city rugs used cotton for a foundation. Tribal and village rugs often used wool for the foundation. The knots can be wool or a combination of silk and wool, or all silk. The foundation of the rug includes the *warp* (the yarn that is vertical) and the *weft* (the yarn that is horizontal).

First, the loom is strung with the warp. Then the weavers begin knotting. After they create a row of knots, they put in one or more weft and then pound the wefts down with an iron comb to hold the knots in place. When a rug is worn down to its knots, the "pile" is gone.

Not all rugs have knots. A *kelim* is a flat woven rug with no pile, consisting only of warp and weft and having no knots.

Rugs and their conditions

Condition is usually relative to the age of the rug and its construction. It's wonderful if a 100-year-old rug is in great shape. If it's worn, that is also acceptable and understandable.

In the decorative rug market, expect to find different types of rugs in different conditions. Some rugs are worn and threadbare and command high prices, because they are highly desirable in design and color. Rugs with less desirable designs and colors command lower prices even when their condition is very good.

For example, pre-1900 Heriz rugs, which are loosely woven and usually are found in worn condition but have great colors and designs according to the current decorative market, fetch higher prices than an old rug in very good condition that has burgundy colors and a densely floral design.

To get more information about rug types and conditions:

- Talk to your trusted rug dealer
- Attend seminars on Oriental rugs
- Look through price guides and Oriental rug auction catalogues

Preventing rug burn: How to really examine a rug

When you look at a rug, it's worth your while to get down and dirty. Here are some ways to examine a rug. Be sure you look at both the front and backside. Along with these tips, you might also need a trustworthy expert to help you.

- Get down on your hands and knees and look at the pile all over the rug. For the rug to have and maintain good value, it needs to be evenly worn. Look for moth damage, repairs, or any other problem. Turn the rug over and examine the backside. You can see a lot on the back that the front does not reveal. Moths tend to like the dark side and start feasting on the bottom. The backside of the rug is the best place to ferret out any patches, repairs, over-dying of worn areas, and any other color problems. When you see differences in color between the front and back of the rug, this might mean the rug has been painted on the surface to enhance the color and hence its desirability.
- Look for reductions, where the rug has been cut down to accommodate the size of the room and two of the pieces are reattached.
- If you think the rug might have dry rot or water damage, ask the dealer to do a crack test. The dealer will gently bend a small corner of the rug. The crack sounds like faint static electricity and indicates the rug has been damaged. The dealer is literally breaking the warp and or the weft of the rug's foundation.

  Do not do a crack test on someone else's rug. If the rug has a weak foundation, you could tear or split the rug open. If you own the rug, gently test a small corner of the rug.

Repairs shouldn't prevent you from buying a rug. You want to know about the repairs so that you can decide if the rug can handle the desired use and to be sure the price is adjusted accordingly. You want your dealer to point out the repairs. If the rug is for the floor, the repair should allow the rug to better withstand traffic.

Going for an unplanned carpet ride

People use many tricks to make rugs look old, such as having a team of people walk over and over the rug. Or they may use a chemical means to fade the colors and make the rug look older.

Watch out for stores that have continuous "going out of business" sales. And watch out for people who offer you huge discounts.

Maintenance tips: Sweeping it off the rug

Your rug has been around for decades. Here are some ways you can ensure that it survives a long, long time.

- The sooner you take care of any problems or repairs your rug needs, the better. Don't underestimate the power of the fringe element: When you see uneven fringe on your rug, have it repaired; otherwise, it can continue to unravel.
- Limit the rug's exposure to bright sunlight or room spotlights. Even older rugs with natural dyes will fade with too much light.
- Rotate the rug so that it wears evenly.
- Keep the rug clean. Every six months, or depending on use, turn the rug backside up, slowly vacuum it, then turn the rug pile up and vacuum it again. Keep the vacuum cleaner away from the fringe. The rug doesn't need too much suction, so use the vacuum sparingly. Use only the brush attachment and vacuum with the pile. Use a hand sweeper between times. If you do this, you may not need to wash the rug as often.

  Take your rug to a qualified Oriental rug cleaner. It's important to get the deepest part of the rug clean. If they wash the rug without first vacuuming it and getting the dirt out of the base of the rug, the remaining sand and dirt act like a saw, and over time cause a weakening of the foundation.
- Before storing your rug, have it cleaned and mothproofed.
- Do not store your rug in an uncarpeted basement or on concrete. Concrete can create moisture and rot the bottom part of the rug.
- Never put the rug in plastic; the moisture will cause damage. If you store your rug, open it up once or twice a year.
- Don't fold your rug: the fibers can break. Roll up the rug.

Believe it or not, people have used sauerkraut to brighten up rugs. Simply go to a barrel of sauerkraut (or a can) pick up a handful of kraut, squeeze out the excess juice, and then gently rub the sauerkraut on the rug, going with the pile. This gives the rug shine.

Sitting Suite and Pretty: Sofas, Chairs, and Parlor Sets

In the olden days, people settled around the one source of heat — the fireplace. They sat on the couch's precursor, a settle. The *settle* was BC (Before Cushions) and was a long wooden bench, properly armed at each end, with a high back. Some settles had a sturdy storage chest underneath them.

A settle was a multi-functional piece of furniture. You could use it as a chest; you could sit on it; sometimes you could even eat off it. Fling forward the attached top, open the supports on the bottom, and you have a *parson's table,* a place for the parson to sit and eat.

As houses got warmed, furniture became less austere. The settle evolved into the *settee,* which grew longer legs and a smaller back and more delicate arms. The settee cozied up into a love seat, which later stretched out into the sofa.

You can have a lot of fun adding vintage sofas and love seats to your living room. Choose a size that suits your space, from the demure love seat to the long sofas of the Victorian era. You can choose a piece of furniture that blends in, such as an elegant Queen Anne style chair or one that announces its presence, such as a 19th century Rococo piece. (See Chapter 3 for more about furniture styles and periods.) Here are some tips for buying the best seats in the house.

Sofa so good

You'll find many choices for sitting or reclining on elegant and interesting antiques.

People were lying about on couches (which were backless in those days) as far back as ancient Greece. At the end of the 17th century, the French used the word *sofa,* derived from the Arabic, and the English followed.

Here are some new ways to couch your language. Use these words to describe places where two or more can sit together:

- **Settee:** Evolving from the settle in the 18th century, the settee usually seats two to three. The chair backs are individualized, and any upholstery was usually just on the seat.
- **Canapé:** A French style sofa that often had more than four legs. Canapé is also a French word for *sofa.*
- **Confidante:** A large French sofa with a triangular seat extending from the arms (so that admirers could sit comfortably near you or friends could sit close to gossip).
- **Divan:** The word is of Persian origin. A divan is used as a place to sit, usually with cushions.
- **Couch:** In the late 18th century, the term *couch* was used to describe a day bed. With a back at one end and a "mattress" (a stitched hair cushion) and pillows, the couch was definitely a place for languorous lounging.
- **Sofa:** Fully upholstered furniture seating three or more, made from the 18th century onwards.
- **Love Seat:** A romantically inspired sofa for two, where three is definitely a crowd.

Couching the sofa in reality: How to examine a sofa

Of course, you want to see whether you and the sofa have love at first sight. Does the sofa speak to you? Is the form appealing? Are its proportions pleasing? Do you like its style? When you sit on it, does it feel like the beginning of a long-term relationship? If so, you might say, "Sofa so good." Then you want to look further.

When you buy a sofa, you are buying the frame. You want an authentic antique frame in good condition. Just because you see old feet doesn't mean you have an old sofa. The internal frame could be entirely rebuilt and just have the original legs tacked onto it. When you buy an upholstered piece, have someone show you the frame if possible. If not, ask to see pictures of the frame. Many dealers leave the underside of a sofa or wing chair open so that you can see the construction. (Check out Chapter 4 for tips on construction techniques.) Sometimes dealers leave the back fabric attached with Velcro so that you can see the back frame. If you can't see the frame, get a written description of what you are buying and a written guarantee of its authenticity.

The parts of the frame you need to examine include:

- **Back frame:** Look for signs of repair and replacement. Look for anything that doesn't feel right, such as a chunky floral carving added on that doesn't go with the original piece.
- **The legs:** Lots of stuff can happen to the legs. Look carefully to see whether the legs are all the same. Examine the feet. Look for signs of wood being added. The legs should mirror the furniture styles of the period, as they do in chairs. Look at the condition of the legs. Have any been replaced, spliced, or have they had carving or inlay added on that doesn't make sense with the period?
- **Stretchers:** If the piece has no stretchers, look for *stretcher marks* (signs on the legs that stretchers were once attached). If the piece has stretchers, look at how they are attached to the legs. Does it make sense for the era? Earlier sofas will have mortise and tenon joints. When you start getting into the machine age, they throw in the dowel. (The dowel rod goes into a hole that's in the stretcher and the leg; it's not as sturdy a joint.)
- **Arms:** Have the arms been replaced, repaired, or added to?

As far as the upholstery goes, don't expect to find the original. Antique sofas will typically have been reupholstered at least once. If the piece needs revitalizing, you need to factor in that cost.

Here's some trivia for you: Why did some Victorian folks have a fainting couch at the bottom and the top of the stairs? Some say it's because women were laced so tightly they were out of breath both coming and going. No wonder being around a handsome man kept your great-greats breathless: It's a cinch that they were laced up so tightly they couldn't breathe!

Chair and Chair Alike: Living Room Chairs

In the 18th century, the easy chair was usually intended for the bedroom. The chair was created for comfort and frequently concealed a potty seat.

During the 19th century, more people expected to sit in more comfort. Previously, the high cost of upholstery materials limited comfortable chairs to the wealthy. In Victorian times, mass production made parlor sets more accessible.

The parlor set might include a sofa, settee, love seat, side chairs, rocker, and a matching Mr. and Mrs. Armchair (the gentleman's chair being larger).

Adding antique chairs to your living room puts a new spin on "sitting pretty." There is no substitute for the mellow glow of an antique wood finish and the intricate craftsmanship of an antique chair. You can have comfort and elegance when you sink into an antique wing chair or well-deserved relaxation when you sit back (and forth) in a Boston rocker.

Victorian or revival furniture has lots of personality. You can find revival chairs with a distinctive look that are reasonably priced. Even one chair adds a wonderful accent to your living room. See Chapter 3 for more on furniture styles.

Sitting up straight in Victorian chairs

During the mid-19th century, French Rococo designs made a delicious comeback. You might see cabriole legs, curved backs, and a shapeliness to the Victorian era upholstered armchair. The chair backs were defined by *tufting* (an arrangement of buttons) and the elegantly carved woods were good quality rosewood, mahogany, or walnut.

Talk about the right stuffing: In the 19th century, the richer people used good quality horsehair and linen while the poorer stuffed their chairs with cotton batting, straw, hay, wood chips, and Spanish moss. The outer covering was haircloth, a slippery black fabric made with cotton or linen and the hair from horse's tails. By 1830, springs sprang into the marketplace, complementing the horsehair and making the seats more comfortable.

If the padding of an old settee is all lumpy, don't worry. This doesn't much hurt the value. But it will cost you to have it re-stuffed or upholstered, so keep that in mind if you're paying full price.

Almost anything older than Victorian will be reupholstered, unless perhaps it is in a museum or you are very lucky. Evidence of reupholstering includes scraps of fabric or threads trapped under tack heads and nail holes around the frame. It's fine for new upholstery to go over old. The original upholstery can heighten the value of antique furniture.

Check legs and arms for restoration. Common 19th century restoration includes legs being *ended out.* The chairs were made taller because the legs wore down, or because earlier chairs were shorter, like the people who sat in them. To notice ended-out chairs, look at all four legs and see whether there's a splice (a place near the bottom of the leg, where one wood meets another). Depending on how well it's done and how rare the piece is, ending out can reduce the value of the chair in varying amounts.

A "chairy" way to sleuth out the truth

A tip that will help you find wear on a chair
Is one that will work on a single or pair,
On chairs that you find in a shop here and there
Or even the home of your dear old grandmère
And help you call out with some French in a flair,
"Oh voilà!" At last it's become crystal "clair":
Beware of no wear when you look at a chair
'Cause when there's no wear nowhere on that chair,
That chair, if you care, may not be so rare,
For a chair that is rare should show wear and tear.
So here is a tip you can take, if you dare,
By putting your "you-know-what" square in that chair
And thinking things out while you're sitting right there!
Yes relax, take this tip sitting down, and I'll bet you're
Propping your feet right up on that old stretcher,
Like hundreds before you and many to follow,
You'll find that there forms in the center — a hollow!
Now lean your head back as though you were resting —
If you find there's wear there it would be just the best thing!
And now tap your finger on each old arm rest
And if there's wear there — your chair's passing the test!
Now look down and see where a zealous house maid
May have knocked feet with brooms and left dents, I'm afraid.
As you sit and inspect — and no clues neglect —
Perhaps, you'll reflect, it's a chair to collect!

When you're choosing antique furniture, sit on it. Just because your ancestors tortured themselves in ornate heavy and beastly uncomfortable chairs doesn't mean you have to. See whether you're comfortable, or whether you could get comfortable with a strategically placed pillow. Or perhaps you want something stern and no nonsense to discourage loitering.

Chairs to be lazy in

True, antique chairs have a dubious reputation among those who like their sit to be soft. Some of the early furniture seems to demand "Sit up straight and finish your vegetables." But other furniture is available that invites you to come daydream, read a mystery, and eat a bonbon. Easy chairs, often called *wing chairs,* arrived on the scene in the late 17th century and spread comfortably throughout Europe and America by the mid-18th century.

Bergère

It's not a folly to sit in a Bergère. These loose-cushioned armchairs have padded backs and arms and were made in France during the 18th and 19th centuries (see Figure 15-1). Furniture makers still reproduce this comfortable chair. The older chairs typically are made of mahogany or fruitwood; the newer chairs often have poorer quality wood, sometimes painted. This chair has a square, upholstered back, and a quiet no-nonsense style.

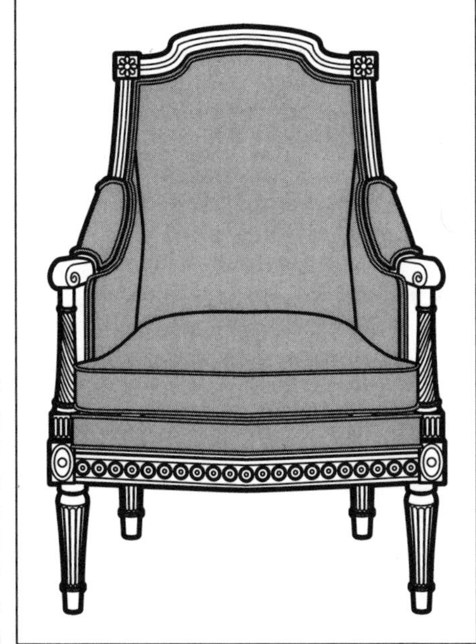

Figure 15-1: A Louis XVI bergère chair, with fluted tapered legs.

Some bergères feature caned backings (a backing woven from rattan). Even if the chair frame is old, the cane is likely to have been replaced.

Fauteuil

The *fauteuil* is like a tanktop chair: There's a space between the padded back of the chair and the padded seat of the chair, as you can see in Figure 15-2. These chairs were created in the mid-18th century during Louis XV's time and are often walnut or beech and are sometimes painted or gilded. *Fauteuil* is the literal French for "chair" and came in many variations.

Figure 15-2: A Louis XV fauteuil, with cabriole legs.

Morris and his chair

The Morris chair, created by Arts and Crafts guru William Morris, was one of the first practical reclining chairs. It's literally a "lay-back" chair, reclining the way a webbed patio chair does. By the turn of the century, many companies made them, and the better makers used an iron rod to adjust the chair. These are classy, streamlined-looking chairs.

Sociable: Chair or commitment

The sociable (or tête-à-tête) is two chairs linked together, either side by side or opposite each other, so that two can converse without anyone coming between them. These chairs bloomed in the mid-19th century, with button upholstery and cabriole legs created from walnut, mahogany, or rosewood.

Rock around the living room

Rocking chairs mirror other chair styles. You might find a Windsor or ladder-back style rocker.

Sometimes a chair began with a cane seat and when that broke, someone replaced it with a padded slip seat. If you pop out the slip seat (it slips onto a ledge along the inside frame of the chair), you can see the old holes where the rush or cane was woven through. When you see the holes, you know the chair seat was altered. This affects both value and authenticity.

Caned and rush rockers are hand-woven. They were more comfortable than the unforgiving wooden seat and more vulnerable to damage. Before you buy, examine the cane seating and find out how much repair work will cost.

Types of rockers

Here are some types of rockers you might see:

- **Boston rockers** evolved from the Windsor chair (see Chapter 14 for more words about Windsor). Noted for their comfort, Boston rockers feature a deeply S-scrolled seat to fit the human anatomy. These rockers have a high back with vertical spindles. The rockers can be painted or black with bronze and gold stenciled ornaments and trim (see Figure 15-3). The Boston rocker was the earliest mass-produced form of a rocking chair.
- Look for Boston rocker's bewitching cousin, the **Salem rocker,** which features a lower back and a flatter seat.

Figure 15-3: Boston rockers evolved from the Windsor chair.

- **Platform rockers** were attached to a platform with a spring mechanism. These rockers were popular from the last quarter of the 19th century until 1910 or so.
- **Rocking settees,** Windsor style, have spindle backs and can rock two to three people. These were originally used by women or children's nurses and often featured a lift off "gate" so that a baby could be on one end (protected by the gate) and the mom on the other end, with her hands free for handiwork.

You will find rockers in all woods. Early rockers are frequently country in style and feature painted decoration similar to their cousins the Windsor chairs.

What to look for in rocking chairs

If you sit in a rocking chair long enough, you can enter an altered state. Indeed, the rocking chair itself might be in an altered state. Take your basic comfortable and well-worn straight chair. Its legs got all scuffed and shortened from wear and from being dragged around on stone or wooden floors. So the craftsman in the family converted the straight chair into a rocker.

Keep on rocking! Ben Franklin designed his own rocking chair. As early as the mid-18th century, people were converting straight chairs to rockers. An early adaptation can in itself be valuable, so consider keeping the chair intact.

To see whether the original purpose of a chair has been changed, look for

- **Really short legs.** The legs will be shorter than normal and may interrupt a turned design on the legs, or have an awkward appearance. The height of the seat from the floor may be lessened.
- **Woods that don't match.** The rocker blades might be a different wood than the rest of the chair. The rocker blades also will look newer and have a different finish or patina (the natural buildup of wax and dirt that gives furniture a mellow look) than the wood of the chair itself.

On the Table

"Laying it all on the table" is more fun when the table has beautiful workmanship and a history. This is a great case of adaptive reuse: You don't have to use a needle, a deck of cards, or burn coal to appreciate sewing tables, game tables, coal hods (used as tables), or other antique tables.

Sew what? The sewing/work table

The proper young lady did not go to school just to learn to read and write; she also learned embroidery and needlework. When she had friends over, they brought needlework and sewed together. Even in well-to-do households with a seamstress, the lady of the house did the mending. The secretary-desk was an office for a man, and the sewing or worktable was an office for a woman.

The late 18th century sewing tables stood on four slender tapered or turned and reeded legs. Later tables featured a central pedestal support. Sewing tables had top storage for pens and paper, thread, needles, and other sewing tools, and a pouch for sewing material and sewing projects (see Figure 15-4). Some of the nicer tables are veneered with beautifully figured woods; some feature marquetry and parquetry, as well. Examine the legs carefully. It's hard to exist on slender legs for many decades without suffering the slings and arrows of outrageous foot-beating fortune.

Sewing tables make wonderful end tables. You can also use them to store "stuff," either actual sewing, or other lightweight projects.

Figure 15-4: Sheraton mahogany sewing table, with figured birch veneer, Massachusetts, circa 1800-1810.

Courtesy of Israel Sack Inc., New York City

Card tricks: Card and game tables

From as early as the mid-18th century to the middle of the 19th century, card and game tables were a popular parlor accessory. Some card or game tables were inlaid with chess or checker boards or have compartments for backgammon, chess and checker pieces, and dice. Many had swivel and *flip tops.*

The swivel top type often has a hollow interior for storage of cards, dice, and other game supplies. The top can rotate or one or two legs can swivel to support the top when the table is open. Many varieties of game tables are available; they're fun to look at and easy to recognize.

Sweet-as-piecrust tables

"Cuter than pie" is a one way to describe these delightful tables. Popular from the 18th into the early 19th century, these round tables usually have a top carved from one piece of wood, which features an intricate scalloped "piecrust." The table top is often attached to a tilting mechanism, sometimes in a form called the birdcage support. The table's pedestal shafts are supported by tripod legs. These tabletops tilt up to be out of the way when not in use (see Figure 15-5). You can find this style of top on tables ranging from small candle stands to large tea tables.

You can find lots of period tables with two or three board tops that do not have the carved pie crust edge.

Figure 15-5: Chippendale mahogany tripod tea table with a piecrust top, which tips and turns with bird-cage support. Made in Philadelphia, circa 1760–1780.

Courtesy of Israel Sack Inc., New York City

If you don't look carefully at a piecrust table, you may end up getting your just desserts. Check to see whether the tabletop is carved from one piece of wood. Repros can have the latticed "crust" attached to the round table. Remember, wood shrinks across the grain. To avoid buying a reproduction, also measure the table top along the grain and against to see whether there has been some shrinkage over 150 to 200 years. And while you're at it, make sure that the base and the top are meant to be together. (See Chapter 4 for the scoop about "arranged marriages" in the furniture department.) Many revivals of this style exist, from the 1920s to the 1950s.

The coal hod reborn as a table

In England, when old king "coal" still ruled, most rooms had small coal burning fireplaces or stoves. Close by stood a portable container or *hod* filled with coal. These coal hods, made of wood, tin, brass, or copper or a combination of these, range from the humble to the elaborate. Some coal hods have tops and work well as a low table next to a chair or sofa (see Figure 15-6). Hods, along with jardeniers, are great for catch-alls. Use them for magazines or newspapers.

Figure 15-6: English coal hod and coal scoop.

Getting the Little Picture: Miniatures

When you want to make a big impact in a small space, consider miniature paintings, delicate framed paintings with lovely portraits or scenes. The following sections offer a few tips for collecting miniatures on ivory, porcelain, and enamel.

Echoes of the past: Ivory

In the past, people were quite careless in their thirst for ivory, decimating the whale and walrus and later the elephant population. Some people shy away from ivory, but others find its rich beauty and history a living reminder to honor all species in the quest for beauty.

Ivory miniatures are usually painted in watercolor on top of a thin piece of ivory, and they need a glass coating to protect the miniature from moisture. Ivory miniatures generally have a slightly ridged texture and show a clear and consistent grain. If the grain is too consistent or too yellow, it might be plastic.

Repros rarely exhibit the same attention to detail that the fine old miniatures do. Watch out for prints rather than paintings: These can be tricky to spot if you're not looking for them. The handmade brush strokes on top of a print make it seem as if the entire piece is handmade. You may need to carefully examine the piece under a magnifying glass or a jeweler's loupe to prove otherwise.

Before you buy an ivory miniature, ask the dealer to remove the glass so that you can verify that it's ivory. Most frames have many small malleable brass triangles attached to their backside and the dealer can easily open them. When it's out of the glass frame, look at the reverse side so that you can see the grain of the ivory, or determine whether the piece is celluloid or paper.

If you want to wash the glass on an ivory miniature, remove the miniature first; otherwise, because these are usually watercolors, you could have a run for your money!

A little porcelain and enamel

You can find wonderful miniature paintings and boxes that are enamel or porcelain. *Enamels* consist of finely ground glass, re-melted at high temperatures and painted on brass or copper. Paintings on porcelain have been fired in the kiln and generally have a glaze over them.

Enamels have the shiniest and brightest of colors. Porcelain colors are also intense, but not as shiny as enamels. Paintings on ivory are typically more muted.

Enamel and porcelain don't need the protection of being framed under glass. Just make sure they don't get banged or scratched.

You can get ivory, porcelain, and enamels in larger sizes as well, and create interesting wall or table groupings with them.

Chapter 16

Welcome to My Boudoir: Bed and Bath Antiques

In This Chapter

- Analyzing antique beds
- Hoping for chests and trunks
- Creating your own closet cases with armoires
- Looking out for antique mirrors

Centuries ago, going to bed meant draping an animal skin over your pile of leaves and settling in. Then the leaf pile got thrown into a shallow chest. Sew what, they said and figured out how to stuff cloth with feathers and straw to make mattresses, which they threw on benches next to the wall.

The bed evolved into a status symbol. For the wealthy, the bedroom was also the living room. They lay in their opulent fabric-laden tester beds and entertained guests. Whether your bedroom is palatial or petite, a refuge or a mere resting-place, an antique or two or three adds to the bedroom's charm and ambience.

To Sleep, Perchance in an Antique Bed

To make an early bed, you had to know the ropes. Early beds had rope that ran across the underside of the bed frame to support the mattress and the persons. Mattresses were filled with horsehair, feathers, straw, or even cornhusks. Then wooden bed rails developed "lips" on the inside, which supported wooden slats. In the late 19th and early 20th centuries, the better beds used metal and wood mattress supports. Then someone raised sleeping to new heights by inventing box springs.

Beds also show the influence of the time period. Their legs, posts, and the carvings on the headboards often mirror chair legs or chair backs of the era.

Many wonderful antique beds are out in the world: The four-poster bed, with or without canopy, was the most expensive until the early 19th century. You can also find antique tester beds with a wooden frame that sits on top of the posts, and curtains tacked to the tester. And then there are the beds with a touch, or more, of brass.

The class of brass: Brass and metal beds

You'll see a hierarchy of brass beds as you cruise the shops, markets, and malls. The most elite is the all-brass bed, sometimes misnamed *the solid brass bed.* The brass posts on "solid brass" beds are almost invariably hollow. If they weren't, the bed would be extremely heavy, and a great deal of brass would be wasted. Still, even those hollow posts are pure brass.

The next tier down is the *brass-wrapped beds.* These bedposts have an iron core, with a layer of brass carefully wrapped around it. The brass-wrapped beds make up the majority of the late 19th and early 20th century brass beds you find on the market. Look for the seam, which, on the head of the bed, is usually placed so that it faces the wall. Because of its iron core, the brass wrapped bed is sturdier and less susceptible to denting than the all-brass bed.

Check for scratches on the surfaces of both solid and hollow beds. A professional can polish relatively shallow scratches out. On hollow beds, dents cannot be pounded out. Dents definitely detract from the value of the bed.

Another form of brass beds is the *brass and iron bed combo.* Some of the pieces are brass and some are iron. You can find many examples of these, ranging from the simplest of designs to the more decorative.

Finally, there is the *iron bed,* which was often painted. Repainting can require dipping, stripping, and sand blasting to prepare the bed's surface for a new coat of paint.

Many people have their old brass beds dipped to remove all tarnish, and then polished and lacquered so that the beds stay shiny. This is both a blessing and a curse. The lacquer eventually ages and turns a dingy yellowish-brown. If you see this yellowish-brown color on a brass bed, know that it will take a major stripping job to make your bed shiny again.

Before you go "beddy buy"

Here are some tips for selecting an antique bed:

- Use your sleuthing skills to check out age, construction, and condition. Beds are usually sold without the mattress, so you have everything framed out for you. Look for the usual signs of wear. (See Chapter 4 for a description of the usual signs of wear.)
- Measure the height of a canopy or tester bed to make sure that it is not too tall to fit into your home (be sure to measure your home's ceiling before you shop for beds). You can almost always remove the canopy, if you want.
- Measure the space for the mattress. If the bed won't take a modern size mattress, you can usually change the side rails to make the bed longer. Altering the rails can compromise the value of your antique, so consult a qualified restoration specialist. Keep the original side rails, in case you want to sell the bed.

If you don't want to alter your antique bed, use it as a sofa or in a guestroom.

Hoping for Chests of Drawers

Dualism is important when you have so little furniture that serves so many functions. Chests were important multi-functional furniture. You put things in them, such as clothes for a dowry, and you could put things on them. Chests of drawers became popular beginning in the 18th century. And they continue as a top-drawer part of the bedroom on into the present.

Chests or coffers were the earliest furniture. The earlier European coffers were simply hollowed out trees. In the 13th century, people nailed some planks together. Coffers frequently traveled and held the families' valuables and clothes. They were large, sturdy, and worked well. The only problem was that it was hard to get things out of the bottom. Hence the evolution of drawers, for the coffer's lower levels.

Hope chests spring eternal

Blanket and *hope chests,* or *dowry chests,* were popular in early bedrooms. They can have elaborate carving, be painted, or be totally plain. If the chests are large, they have strap hinges to support the weight of the lid. A hinged till box, on the far-left upper interior of the chest, held smaller items, such as jewelry and small personal or delicate items.

Hope chests are just as multi-functional and useful today, giving you a great place to both store and display your stuff.

Have trunk will travel

Domed trunks, including the popular "camel back" trunks, were made in the late 19th and early 20th century. These wooden trunks reinforced with metal were used for traveling on stagecoach, boat, or train. In the late 19th century, most trunks used for travel and storage were covered with canvas or decorated with sheet metal, which might be embossed or stamped with decorative designs. They might be lined with wall paper and have a patent date stamped on the hinge. The trunk could have been made several years after the patent date.

Here are some tips for picking a great old chest or trunk:

- Look for the till box. If it's missing, you can see the old screw holes or a lighter wood color where the box was attached. A missing till diminishes the value.
- Some old trunks had feet or legs, which can add to the value. But these feet have seen it all: Mice have chewed on them, and people have kicked and dragged them. These ancient feet should be dented, scratched, and worn. If there are no feet, the trunk's bottom should have many scratches.

Metal trunks were usually painted to prevent tarnishing. When you buy a metal-covered trunk, you often need to repaint or refinish it.

Top drawers: The bureau

Bureaus went from three to five drawers and followed the period style, in legs, feet, type of wood and type and style of hardware. The middle to late American Victorian period featured *handkerchief drawers,* small thin raised drawers on each side of the top.

In America and England, the bow and serpentine front style chests were popular in the 18th and early 19th century. The *bow* was an outward or convex curve, not as pronounced as the French bombé. The *serpentine* was an undulating (like a snake, hence the name) curve creating a convex and concave alternating effect when you look at the drawer fronts, especially from the side.

Remember days of the week underwear? The French had a special bureau for such, a *semanier,* meaning weekly storage chest, from the French word for week. This tall narrow chest featured seven narrow drawers, perfect for lingerie and other small delicate items. The English had a Wellington chest that was similar and often used for coins and collectibles.

Looking inside a bureau can offer clues to its country of origin. American bureaus most frequently do not have *dustboards,* boards that go between the drawers. English bureaus typically feature dustboards.

Coming out of the Closet: Armoires

In medieval times, *armoires* were created to store the implements of war. Armoires were revitalized and civilized in France when a "room" tax was levied. A closet was considered a room; the armoire was created as a beautiful and functional way to avoid paying that extra tax.

Armoires may feature one or two doors, with shelves and drawers inside. Usually the French version had paneled doors, which were more decorative and had a less heavy feel.

In England, the *clothes press,* or *wardrobe,* served the same function as the armoire. American wardrobes often had hooks and rods. Armoires are usually taller or bigger than wardrobes and may have mirrors on the doors.

Armoires are often tall, so measure carefully before you buy. You can take the top crest off when you move the piece. If the crest is missing, the value is diminished. Make sure that armoires are in good condition structurally. Do they wobble? Do the legs seem strong and stable? Armoires are quite heavy, and you want them to be solid, particularly if you want to put any weight in them.

You can use armoires in your bedroom to hold clothes, televisions, and stereos, hide computers or store your books.

A Look into Antique Mirrors

Look into an old mirror and you might feel like you're catching the waves. The glassmaking process was not quite refined, and distortion is common. (So what you see is not quite what you really get.)

Mirrors became popular in the mid-18th century and then only the wealthy could afford a large one.

How to examine an antique mirror

Before you fall into your antique looking glass, check out the tips in this section.

Look for original glass, which makes the mirror much more valuable.

- Old glass often has waves and clouded areas. Cloudiness creates an area where the mirror does not reflect or is mottled. Small clouds around the edges don't hurt the value; in fact, they help authenticate the age.
- Take a pencil and put the tip of the pencil against the mirror. If the tips appear to nearly touch, it's typically older glass (before the turn of the 20th century). With more modern glass, the tips are farther apart.
- Beveled glass has an angle on the edge closest to the frame and became common during the late Victorian period. For that period and beyond, you can find single, double, or triple bevel: The more levels of bevels (other things being equal), the more valuable the mirror.

After you see and handle a few mirrors 100 years or older, you'll be able to distinguish between antique mirrors and factory-made plate glass that is 10 to 75 years old.

Watch out for married mirrors — for example, an old mirror in a newer frame (Snow White's mirror in the Little Mermaid's frame) or an old frame around new glass (Alice's looking glass frame around Holden Caulfield's mirror). Good auction catalogues and dealers will always say "mirror replaced." Or "not original mirror."

Close shaves in shaving mirrors

Shaving mirrors were created in the 18th century. They sat on dresser tops through the Victorian period. The base had small drawers for cufflinks and shaving items. The man of fashion had a wash bowl set with his mirror. The mirror swivels on arms that come up from the base. The shape of the mirror frame, the legs, and hardware all help to date the mirror. Shaving mirrors had fancy wooden or metal screws that you could tighten to hold the mirror in place.

Horsing around with "chevals"

When you really want to see the full Monty, go for a cheval or horse mirror. This three-fourths or full-length mirror was in a frame that sat on the floor. The mirror is on a four-legged stand, like a miniature saw horse. The styles varied depending on the time period. Most chevals swiveled, with tall supports and fancy metal screws that you could tighten to adjust and change the mirror's angle. The jumbo version of the men's shaving mirror (without the drawers)!

Bathroom Baubles

You'll flush with pride when you add the best of the past into your modern bathroom. Victorian vanity sets include comb, brush, mirror, buttonhook, and sometimes much more, and are often made of sterling or silver plate. In the late 19th century, vanity sets also were made out of celluloid, a pseudo plastic.

Porcelain dresser sets give you a sense of early morning elegance. These sets often include a pair of cologne bottles, a ringtree to catch your many jewels, a hair receiver, a powder jar, a hatpin holder, and sometimes a candlestick. You may mix and match pieces, but generally, people prefer matched sets. Dresser sets were made into the early 20th century, and you can still find them at reasonable prices.

In Victorian times, women sometimes harvested their hair. They saved the hair from brushes and combs and created hair jewelry or weavings from it. When they cut their hair, they could often sell it. So the hair receiver served as a savings account for hair. Today, use hair receivers for cotton balls or bath salts.

Before little soaps and shampoos, you went into a hotel and found a wash set, called a chamber set, in your room. These include at least a pitcher and bowl, made of pottery or porcelain. The fancier, more expensive sets, had a pitcher, bowl, toothbrush holder, chamber pot, soap dish, a mug (used for shaving or drinking), a hot water pitcher (smaller than the big pitcher), and a matching waste jar (a slop jar that the maid emptied the chamber pot into). You can still find entire sets, and you can find pieces of sets, which you can use in your bathroom or cross-train them to do other designing things.

Chapter 17

Antiques from the East: Orientalia

In This Chapter

- Understanding Japanese woodblock prints
- Tapping into the ultimate hard rock, jade
- Recognizing the crosshatch and other signs of ivory
- Getting a taste for oriental ceramics
- Falling in love with Chinese furniture

Sometimes the chaos and demands of everyday life are overwhelming. You'd like to be sitting on an island somewhere, daydreaming. Oriental antiques let you create that island of beauty and calm right in your own home or office. The elegance and grace of the Japanese woodblock print, the intricately carved and magical jade figures, and the rich wood of the Chinese altar table, transport you to another way of thinking.

In this chapter, we just touch on the wonders of Oriental antiques. We chose antiques that you are likely to see. Many of these items, such as the Japanese woodblock prints, the jade, and the Chinese furniture, can be quite reasonably priced.

Someday Your Prints Will Come: The Art of the Japanese Woodblock

On days when the world is too full of technology and rationality, it's a delight to gaze upon art from "the floating world," or *Ukiyo-e,* as the Japanese woodblock prints are called.

The Japanese developed their own version of this art form in the mid-17th century. The intricate process is a collaboration of specialists that include the artist, carver, printer, and a publisher, who organizes and oversees the process.

Making a print requires precision and attunement: There's a carved block for every color. To create the harmonious and subtle details of the Japanese print, the paper is laid on successive blocks and printed one color at a time.

Japanese prints give you a lot of information you don't find on most antiques, including the artist's signature. Many also include the title of the print and if it's from a series, the name of the series as well. Often you find publisher's marks, and sometimes date and censor seals. All this information gives you a chance to research your artist and your print (see Figure 17-1).

When the blocks are new, the details of the print are often fine and crisp. As the blocks get worn from use, the details can suffer. This impacts the value of the print. The finer and crisper the detail, the more desirable the print.

You can still find wonderful woodblock prints at affordable prices. You can also find old reproductions of some of the more famous prints. Sometimes, only a true specialist can figure out that these are reproductions. If you have your heart set on original woodblock prints, find some knowledgeable dealers who can show you the real thing.

You can find quantities of lovely Japanese woodblock prints whose prices never reached the level that made them worth reproducing.

Seeing red and Prussian blue: Color

The harmonious blend of vivid and subtle colors initially draws many people to the Japanese print. Earlier prints used colors made from vegetable dyes, so the colors are typically subtler than the colors that emerged during the Meiji period (1868–1912).

As far back as the 1820s, the well-known artists Hokusai and Hiroshige popularized the exotic Prussian blue, using this rich color (imported from Europe) in their waters and skies.

Seeing red — when the shade is a bright crimson — is a sure sign you're looking at a print from the 1860s or later. In addition to the intense crimson, these newer artificial dyes also include a bright purple. These colors stand out in a print and are easy to recognize, after you've seen them once.

Many late 19th century printmakers use old and new dyes on the same print.

The prints of peace: Subject matter

In the early 1600s, the shogun gained control of all the warring states of Japan, and the country began a period of more than two and a half centuries of peace. Now the middle classes had time on their hands, and so the talents of Japanese artists and artisans flourished. They developed a new focus on the fleeting "floating world." *Ukiyo-e madness,* a live-for-today attitude, gripped many. They lived at the theater, they sang songs celebrating the ephemeral nature of life, and they immersed themselves in art and pleasure. The ukioy-e artists attempted almost every conceivable subject, from theater to nature to mythology to eroticism. Here are the details on several types of prints.

Noh was a no-no: Actors

The upper classes enjoyed *Noh drama,* a classical drama employing verse, prose, song, and dance, performed in a formal way. But there was no Noh for anyone else. Because the middle classes weren't privy to this form of theater (Noh way!), they created Kabuki Theater for their viewing pleasure. Kabuki was like those old Saturday morning movies that lasted all day: It began in the morning and acted its way through the day.

The actors became very popular. Long before *Modern Screen* and *People,* Japanese artists captured the actors in woodblock prints. The earlier prints had just the actors; later prints developed a background and then scenes.

Courting pleasure: Courtesans

Because women couldn't play a starring role (or any role for that matter) in the theater, they had to come to light in a different arena. The courtesans of the day were exceptionally talented, literary, smart, and beautiful. A day with some of these courtesans was said to cost the price of feeding rice to an entire town for one year. For those who had trouble feeding their own families rice for a year, woodblock prints captured these courtesans and also served as a historic record of the clothing styles of the day. Utamaro is one of the most famous and inventive artists of the "beautiful women" prints.

The Roads Taken: Landscapes

There was an edict against travel, so most people didn't even know what their country looked like. Hiroshige traveled throughout the land, sketching as he went. He traveled the Tokaido Trail from the old to the new capital and drew every one of the 53 way stations (stopping places). Several generations later, these landscapes are some of the most appealing to the western eye.

One of the ways the west learned about Japanese prints was by accident. The Dutch wrapped the Imari porcelain they brought from Japan in old prints. Some of the people opening the packages took a look at the wrappings and recognized a wonderful art form, every bit as powerful and exciting as the porcelain itself.

Figure 17-1: This 1855 print (dated the year of the rabbit, 9th month) by the artist Hiroshige is from the series "Illustrations of Famous Places in the 60 Odd Provinces."

Photo courtesy of Brookside Antiques, Kansas City, MO.

Some novel illustrations: Literature and mythology

Even though women couldn't act (on the stage, that is), they could write. In the 19th century, Japanese woodblock print artists loved creating prints to illustrate one of the world's earliest novels, *The Tale of Genji,* which was written by a woman in the 12th century. The artists also created prints about all kinds of mythological subjects.

The nature of things: The ordinary becomes extraordinary

Scenes of birds and flowers became a popular subject for Japanese prints. The earlier prints are often simpler, and the later prints get busier. Folks hanging around and enjoying themselves is another genre of Japanese printmaking. You can see picnickers by the banks of a river, revelers watching fireworks at a New Year's celebration, and pleasure-seekers whiling away the hours in the Yoshiwara, the pleasure quarters of Edo.

All other things being equal, such as condition, certain subject matters are often considered especially desirable. Some of these include snow scenes, rain scenes, and night scenes.

Sizing things up and special techniques

Prints come in a variety of sizes and shapes. The *oban* is the most typical print size, with a rectangular shape approximately 15 by 10 inches. The *chuban* is about half that size. When you need art for a larger space, look for two pictures that belong together, known as *diptychs.* A *triptych* is three pictures in a row that belong together and usually create one complete scene. Most of these pieces are designed so that they can stand alone: They are beautiful in their own right, even when separated from their mates.

Sometimes, the earlier prints off the block get the "special treatment." This can include *blind embossing,* which means they've created a texture or pattern on the paper simply by raising the surface of parts of the paper. Other special techniques include burnished lacquers in certain areas or the artist might also add metallic colorations, such as silver, gold, or copper.

Artists also created prints for special occasions. The celebrants at a New Year's Eve party might receive a *surimono,* a "specially printed" print. These limited edition, high quality prints could include extra flourishes, such as blind embossing and others mentioned previously. They are frequently smaller than the typical print and are often in a square format.

Made since the 18th century, surimonos were much reproduced during the Meiji period. The repros are often wonderful — you should expect to pay only a fraction of the cost of the originals.

The artists

Some of the great 19th century masters of the Japanese woodblock print include:

- Many people's first introduction to Japanese woodblock prints comes from a landscape by **Hiroshige.** Hiroshige created many series of landscapes that were as popular in his day as they are today. He was also one of the great masters of the bird and flower print.
- The artist **Hokusai** drew many everyday things. Some consider him the Rembrandt of Japanese art. He added a sense of whimsy and fun to the art form and produced the masterful series *36 Views of Fuji.* Some people think of Hokusai during every football game. He's the one who created The Wave.
- **Kuniyoshi** was the master of mythological subjects. He went "outside the box" by occasionally letting his art go beyond the border.
- **Kunisada** (who later changed his name to **Toyokuni III**) created thousands of images. His most famous prints can be quite expensive but you can find wonderful less famous prints by him starting in the low hundreds.
- **Yoshitoshi** captured the essence of the revolutionary Meiji Period (1868–1912). His series, "100 Views of the Moon," is particularly collectible.

When studying the art of printmaking, the student sometimes took the last two syllables of the teacher's name as the first two syllables of his name. So Kuniyoshi was Yoshitoshi's teacher. The artist Toyokuni was both Kunisada's and Kuniyoshi's teacher. This information can be useful if you want to know what lineage the printmaker came from.

Eighteenth century and early 19th century Japanese woodblock prints grow rarer and rarer. Still, you can find many prints from the third quarter of the 19th century on into the Meiji period in excellent condition and costing in the low hundreds. You also can find wonderful prints at reasonable prices by famous artists if you search out those prints that are not their most well-known.

Kawase Hasui and Hiroshi Yoshida are two of the great early 20th century woodblock print artists. Their works have become more expensive in the last decade, and late impressions and reproductions abound. But even these reproductions are quite beautiful and worth purchasing at lesser prices.

Condition

If the print you love is in a frame, you'll want to have it removed before you buy it. The following sections offer some "conditional" tips.

Factors that increase the value of a print

- The closer the print is to its **original condition,** the more valuable.
- The **earlier the impression,** the more valuable. That means, the first impressions printed from the woodblock are more valuable than the later impressions.
- The more **deluxe** the style of printing, on original prints created from the same blocks, the more valuable the print. Metallic decorations, rubbed lacquer, and blind embossing are indications of deluxe printing.

Factors that decrease the value of a print

- **Fading:** When the colors have been exposed to light, they can progressively fade and lose their vibrancy.
- **Centerfold:** Folding a print decreases its value. Sometimes you come across a print that has been folded in half. A light fold may not be terribly significant, but a deep crease, especially one that is discolored, can reduce the print's value considerably.
- **Trimming:** A print that is trimmed or cut down has a lesser value. Prints have different kinds of borders, so looking at several in the same series can help you determine whether a print has been trimmed. Some prints never had borders. Trimming is never good, but trimming that eats into the body of the print is the most serious. Prints usually get trimmed because the border was torn, stained, or glued onto a back mat.

  Master craftsmen can create new borders, which enhance the formerly borderless print. But this restored print will not have the value of the original.
- **Toning:** Look for browning or yellowing of the paper, where the print might have been exposed to the sun or smoke. You can see this type of damage quickly if the print has been in a frame. When you take the print out of the frame, the area under the mat will be brighter than the rest of the print. Depending on the amount of toning, the value of the print can be reduced minimally or significantly.
- **Stains and Smudges:** A smudge in the wrong place can affect the value of the print. A smudge or darkened area on the side of a print may not mean much, but a stain or smudge on a face can make a big difference. If the smudge draws your attention, you probably will spend your time looking at the smudge rather than the print.
- **Backing:** An acidic backing (an additional piece of paper permanently attached to the back of the print) can eat into the print. Check with a knowledgeable restoration person who knows the nature of the backing.

- **Wormage:** Yes, worms do have good taste, and they like to nibble on Japanese woodblock prints. If they create a hole in the edge or on the border, or in an area that features a highly brocaded fabric kimono, that hole can be nearly insignificant. If there's a hole in the face or in the middle of the print, that's more serious. Generally speaking, if the damage bothers you — if the imperfection draws your attention to it rather than the amazing beauty of the art — don't buy the print. Or buy it at a significantly reduced price.
- **Impression:** Notice how sharp the impression is. If the impression is not clear and sharp, the print is worth very little. Japanese print makers had excellent quality control, so a sharp impression is the rule rather than the exception.

All the news that's fit for handling prints

Before you touch a print, wash your hands. Don't touch the print itself. If you need to handle it, put it between your fingers so that your fingerprints are not on top of the print. Always be careful when you put a print back into its folder: You don't want to bend it.

Make sure that your print is framed in a 100 percent acid-free rag mat and acid-free backing. Acidic paper can eat into your print and destroy its value. Hang your print in a place that avoids direct sunlight. If you feel too much light is shining on your print, ask your framer to use special plexiglass that shields the paper from ultraviolet rays.

Images From the Floating World, by Richard Lane (published by Dorset Press) is a wonderful book for learning more about the Japanese Woodblock print. Also any books on Japanese prints by James Michener or Richard Lane are excellent.

Interesting note: The art of the Japanese woodblock print influenced many of the French impressionist artists. Several of them were collectors themselves.

Jade: A Hard Rock That's Really Cool

Jade is the stone of wisdom, the stone of heaven, the stone that possesses all virtues. It has long been a revered stone of China. You can still find many small and wonderful 19th century jade carvings. Carrying a jade carving is like taking along your altar, worry stone, or good luck charm.

The Chinese used jade toggles to counterbalance the weight of the medicine or money pouch they carried. Many carvings are human, animal, or vegetable subjects, such as holy men, bats, butterflies, cicadas, eggplants, and mushrooms. Each toggle figure carried its symbology, such as wisdom, longevity, happiness, or good fortune. Today, these small pieces make wonderful jewelry or pocket pieces.

The prices of small jade carvings can be very reasonable. Many are available in the low hundreds or even under one hundred dollars. Larger and earlier jade pieces can be quite costly, however.

People can get jaded trying to separate the genuine jade from its look-alikes. It's hard to tell some of the stones apart. Stones that resemble jade, such as serpentine, jasper, and soapstone, are softer and less valuable than the real thing.

True jade is two distinct stones: nephrite and jadeite. The older Chinese pieces are fashioned from nephrite, which in its pure form is white and shades to greens, yellow, brown, and black. Jadeite tends to be shinier and more varied in colors of white, green, lavender, red, and more. Much of the later Chinese-carved jade is from Burma. Most jewelry jade is jadeite, which is more translucent. This jade is often dyed in an attempt to enhance its value.

Here's a simple test to eliminate some of the imposters: Ask the dealer to take a piece of metal and try to scratch the stone in an inconspicuous place. If the metal leaves a white line, you've cut the material. If it leaves a black line, you've taken the metal off the knife. This test doesn't mean it's jade of course: Diamonds and some other stones are also hard. But the test helps eliminate soapstone, serpentine, and many of the pretenders.

The more genuine jade you handle, the more you learn to "sense" the real jade. Jade tends to maintain its coolness more than most stones.

Like all hard stones, jade is brittle. If you drop it on a hard surface, it can crack or shatter.

Tusk Tusk, Collecting Ivory

Collecting ivory begins with some basic questions: Is it ivory? How good is the carving?

You can easily fall into identity crisis if you don't understand what ivory really looks like. Oriental ivories are primarily from the tusks of elephants. Reproductions are everywhere, and often they are quite obvious. Other times they require careful examination. The repros are typically a plastic compound, stained to look old, or they are a composite of ground bone. You also see bone carvings that are not ivory and have their own value, although it's typically much less than ivory.

So, to start collecting ivory, you need to see the real thing. Real ivory has a natural beauty, sheen, and patina that is generally unmatched by the fakes.

Boning up on ivory

Ivory typically has a crosshatch pattern. Once you have seen ivory a few times, you'll be able to identify the crosshatch pattern. Of course, just to keep things interesting, you can find genuine ivory that doesn't show the crosshatch. So keep reading.

Bone is a natural material that bears some resemblance to ivory and is the most common ivory substitute. Bone is less dense than ivory. Use your magnifying glass and you can often see thin brown or black streaks. Also, bone has a duller sheen than ivory.

Here are some tips for ferreting out the real ivory:

- **Odorfree:** True ivory has no smell. Often a celluloid carving has a plastic smell.
- **Impenetrable:** If you heat the tip of a pin (ask permission) it will push into the ivory fakes (plastics or composites) but not into ivory or bone.
- **Color:** Certain fakes can look similar to the real thing. Sometimes composites are stained or darkened as if they were aged, to hide the fact they don't have grain. This kind of purposeful staining is more even and more extensive than the natural staining that can come from aging. The bulk of old ivory will not be purposefully stained. Natural staining on old ivory varies, according to how much it was handled and how much light the piece has seen. Old ivory tends to be darker on one side. The faked pieces are typically uniform in color.

Some of the less expensive composite reproductions have mold marks or casting marks. Look for these marks or for signs of polishing where the mold marks have been removed.

Carving out your ivory niche

The quality of the carving impacts the value of the ivory. You can find a hastily carved rather crude ivory elephant for much less than $100, and you can find breathtaking groupings that feature intricately carved people in extraordinarily life-like groups. Such treasures can sell for thousands and even tens of thousands of dollars.

When you look at the carving, look for detail. Fine detail work and wonderful facial expressions are a big plus in ivory carvings. Age cracks can be a natural part of old ivory, indicating the piece has been around for a while. A thin crack is acceptable, especially when it is in an unobtrusive place on a figure.

To prevent your ivory from cracking, keep it properly watered. Keep a cup of water in your ivory cabinet. (You do have an ivory cabinet, don't you?)

Uncloistering Cloisonné

Some people make an art form of putting their pedal to the metal. Others, such as artisans in China and Japan, make an art form of putting their enamel to the metal. Cloisonné involves a metal or ceramic body with applied glued or soldered wires that hold colored enamels in place. These enamels, which are finely ground glass, create a picture, which is fired onto the metal.

Cloisonné is still made today. You can find lots of inexpensive new pieces around. Although these pieces are common, they are often technically quite well done.

The Golden Age of Cloisonné

Though there are many varieties of cloisonné around, Japan produced much of the best of the best from 1890 to 1915 during the "Golden Age of Cloisonné." During this period, a German chemist introduced new enamels, which eliminated part of the constriction of the wires. This new technology invited creativity and experimentation.

Characteristics of the Golden Age include:

- Shiny and high gloss enamels, which are almost reflective.
- Thin fine wires.
- Expansive spaces of enamel without the wires. You might see a single iris against a dark blue background.

Some pieces have silver wirework. If the piece looks tarnished, rub it with your fingers and see if you glimpse silver. Other things being equal, the silver makes the piece more valuable. Many collectors appreciate the "patina" the silver develops over the years. If you wish to clean the piece, be sure to remove all traces of the cleaner to avoid future corrosion.

Distinguishing Japanese from Chinese

Chinese cloisonné typically never used silver wire, but the Japanese often used silver wire on some of their finer pieces. The Japanese also were innovators in their use of goldstone in their backgrounds, so you see glints of gold. Both frequently used brass for the base metal under the enamel. The Chinese also used copper for bases, and the Japanese sometimes used silver for bases. Pieces with wide open spaces are usually the Japanese variety of cloisonné. Also pieces of cloisonné with a final layer of clear gloss enamel are typically Japanese.

Innovations in cloisonné

Once artists got the whole cloisonné scene "wired," they experimented by removing the wires after pouring colors into those spaces between the wires. In wireless cloisonné, you may see a merging of colors, because the colors were not constricted by the wires.

Another form of cloisonné called *plique a jour* doesn't have the base casing of metal, so this variety of cloisonné is translucent rather than opaque. *Plique a jour* cloisonné is very fragile because it doesn't have a firm metal base supporting the enamel.

In *moriage* (pronounced *more-ee-ah-gay*) pieces, Japanese artisans built up the decoration in a raised relief.

The golden condition of cloisonné

Signed pieces of cloisonné are desirable and hard to come by. You can find small, unsigned pieces of late 19th century cloisonné in good condition that cost in the low hundreds of dollars or less. This is particularly true of the Chinese pieces, which are typically less expensive than Japanese pieces of comparable size and shape.

Cloisonné may look more substantial than glass, but it is just as fragile. Look the piece over carefully. Hairline cracks and chips greatly diminish its value.

Chrome rims mean pieces done from 1930 to 1950, usually from the 1950s. These pieces are desirable; just don't pay as much for them.

To learn more about cloisonné, get *Japanese Cloisonné: History, Technique and Appreciation,* by Lawrence Coben and Dorothy Furster (published by Weatherhill). This book shows the major artists' signatures, pictures the pieces on display at St Louis World's Fair in 1904, includes manufacturing techniques, and describes characteristics of the Golden Age.

That's Imari!

Imari, a hard paste porcelain, is named after the Japanese port of Imari, from which it was exported. Early Imari is blue and white; later they spiced it up with shades of reddish-orange, almost a paprika color; a little green; and sometimes a touch of other colors. Imari typically has underglaze blue, with other colors on top, and occasionally gilding. (An *underglaze* is applied directly onto the ceramic before the ceramic this glazed.) After you see a couple pieces, Imari is reasonably easy to recognize.

Analyzing Imari

Like many things, Imari varies in quality and in timeframe. People are still creating Imari. You need a group of indicators to guide you to the older Imari. Here are some tips for recognizing the true blue (and paprika) thing:

- **Flaws:** Look for signs that the piece is hand painted. A line around the rim of a large bowl may be slightly wavy. If the work looks too perfect, it's probably been printed. Some modern Imari is also hand painted.
- **The pits:** Older Imari was fired in small, wood-burning kilns (prior to the 20th century). Little specks of ash can fall into the glaze during firing, creating little dark pits. Most Imari from this period has some pits. These specks are assurances of age. Bumps also indicate age.
- **The Gilded Ones:** Newer gilding is shinier and more reflective than the old gilt. If you can see yourself in the gilt, you are probably looking into a newer piece.
- **Dirty Feet:** Old foot rims have some brownness; the newer foot rims are generally icy white.
- **Spur Marks:** Spurs held up the large pieces in the kiln; the smaller pieces may have one or none. Large plates always have some spur marks. A bowl may not. Around 1912, the end of the Meiji period, the spur marks stop, because the kilns modernized.
- **Undulating Glaze:** Look at the bottom of the piece in raking light (hold the piece at an angle so that the light reveals the imperfections). You'll see an undulation or unevenness in the glaze of older pieces.
- **Gray tint:** In the old days, they didn't try to cover up that gray. The older glazes have a blue gray tint; the newer tend to have pure white look.

Many English and Continental companies made things in the Imari colors. These companies typically made dinnerware sets, so the sizes and shapes are different from Imari. Check the bottom of a piece: Western pieces generally have their own mark and no spur marks.

Arita ware: Fewer colors and less costly

Arita wares, from the Arita province, are blue and white porcelain. This porcelain is often undervalued, typically selling for far less than the multi-colored Imari. You can examine Arita as you would Imari. They were both created in the same time period and decorated in many of the same kilns. The patterns are similar to Imari, but without the extra colors.

Choosing Imari

In the 18th century, the blue and white pieces were the most expensive. The overglaze pieces were less expensive because artists could take the pieces that didn't fire properly and paint over the flaws. (In an *overglaze* piece, the glaze goes on first and then the enamels are applied.)

You'll see lots of styles in Imari. Figure 17-2 shows one example. Some varieties may seem almost crude in their workmanship. Others are more constrained and detailed. Choose according to what you like. Imari is an expressive art form, and the less mannered pieces can often be just as valuable.

Figure 17-2: Late 19th century Imari plate.

The unusual shapes, such as fish shapes, boat shapes, and figural shapes are especially desirable.

As you shop around a little, you'll find quite a price range. Sometimes price is determined by condition and quality; other times, well, some dealers and some days at auction are simply more expensive. As a rule, you can find wonderful plates available in the low hundreds. You also will see vases, larger plates they call *chargers.* Pay for these with your charger card, of course.

When you get hooked on Imari, get *Imari, Satsuma,* by Nancy Schiffer (published by Schiffer Books).

Help You Need Somebody: Studying Satsuma

This is the down-to-earthenware export. Satsuma has an earthenware body with a crackled glaze (see Figure 17-3). If you see something that looks like Satsuma but it's on porcelain, it is not Satsuma. Satsuma colors are earthy: paprika, brown, and black, usually with gold trim, and sometimes with sprinklings of many other colors. The color scheme is about all some pieces of Satsuma have in common.

Satsuma quality varies from muddling to middling to amazing. The workmanship can be so finely detailed that only a single-hair brush could create it, or so loose it looks splotchy. The pieces range in size from immense palace vases to exquisite miniatures. Although the value of Satsuma is often in the details, the pricing of Satsuma is often inconsistent.

Reproductions can really get in your way when you're shopping for Satsuma. The repros can have crazing on them and often other signs of age. Only the level of detail isn't faked. You need to look at a number of real Satsuma pieces at a number of shops, so you can understand the real thing before you buy.

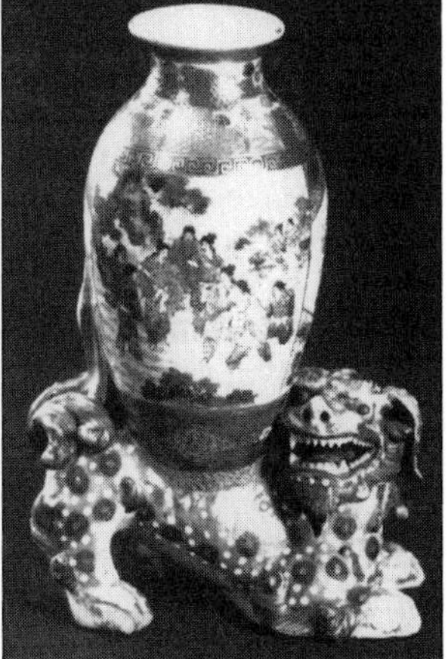

Figure 17-3: Satsuma has an earthenware body with a crackled glaze.

All in the Famille Rose

This Chinese porcelain features muted pink colors with green and sometimes sparks of blue and other colors. Although they created great pieces in the 18th century, the vast majority in the market today were made for export and are from the mid-19th century onward. Figure 17-4 shows a typical Rose Medallion plate.

Of course, you can find old famille rose and new famille rose. Look for signs of age, which include higher quality hand painting, impurities in the clay, pit marks, and foot rims that show signs of dirt and wear.

The later pieces are marked *China* and *Made in China.* People sometimes remove these marks to make a piece look older. If the marks weren't fired on, it's as easy as scraping them off with your fingernail. If you see a scar on the bottom of a piece, that could mean someone scraped off an underglazed mark.

Rose Medallion is the most popular of the rose family. You see alternating panels (medallions) of people and then floral scenes. The older roses generally are heavier than the newer roses. The glaze has a grayer color, and the pinks are subtler. Gold highlights in the hair are more indicators that the piece could be an old one. Detailed workmanship is often a good indication of an authentic piece rather than a mass-produced reproduction. If you see a green tint and a brown rim and lots of tiny pinholes, you may be looking at an 18th century piece.

Don't be fooled by signs of dirt. People dirty up Rose Medallion to create the allure of age.

Rose Canton, a less prevalent member of the rose family, is distinguished by decorated floral panels, which include birds but not people. *Rose Mandarin,* the lesser-known rose, features panels of people in the center, rather than alternating people with flowers. *Familles jaune*, *verte*, and *noir* also are part of this community of porcelains, but not as prevalent.

Look for unusual shapes and unusual pieces. In any dinner service, there were lots of plates and only one tureen. The survival rate on the plates is good. Finding a lidded piece with the lid intact is much more unusual. The tureens and larger pieces also are harder to find than the more common plates.

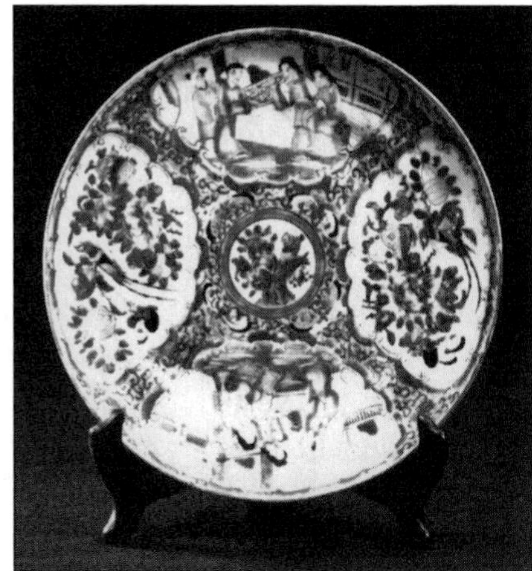

Figure 17-4: A typical rose medallion plate from the late 19th century.

A Moveable Feast from the East: Chinese Furniture

Chinese furniture embodies grace and elegance combined with function and strength.

Domestic antique Chinese furniture has a simplicity and quality of craftsmanship that lets it blend in with other types of furniture and décor. This classic Chinese furniture influenced European furniture styles, including Queen Anne and Louis XV.

For years, Chinese furniture has often been undervalued in the marketplace. Now, its stellar qualities are becoming more noticed. You can still buy some wonderful 19th and early 20th century pieces at reasonable prices.

The Chinese use a precise and complex interlocking joint structure to keep the furniture together. The joinery comes from the piece of wood itself, and it fits like a Chinese puzzle. This intricate joinery is one of the features that gives Chinese furniture its beauty and strength.

The chair man is off the floor

The various styles of classic domestic Chinese furniture date from the 14th century. The Imperial Court of China literally sat more comfortably and elegantly in their furniture 300 years before the courts of the West. The Chinese developed the "high chair" as a way to keep the sitter off the cold and wet stone floors. The stretchers were useful as foot rests. Footstools were popular, as well. A variety of Chinese chairs are available today, many of whose styles date back to the earliest days of Chinese chair-manship. These chairs make wonderful additions to your home. They are classically elegant, sturdy and comfortable.

Here are a few of the Chinese chairs you might see:

- **Horseshoe back chair:** The arms and crestrails are constructed in one continuous curving flow consisting of separate pieces (see Figure 17-5).
- **High Yoke back armchair:** The early chairs had extended crestrails and a high splat. (See Chapter 3 for more about crestrails and splats.) The variations grew with the family of Chinese furniture (see Figure 17-6).
- **Rectangular back side chair:** These come in varying heights and styles, with and without armrests.

Figure 17-5: This horseshoe back chair made of peach wood is light (less than five pounds), sturdy, and surprisingly comfortable.

Photo Courtesy of Brookside Antiques, Kansas City, MO.

Figure 17-6: One variation of a high yoke back chair.

Photo courtesy of Brookside Antiques, Kansas City, MO.

Most of the narrow benches you see were *gate benches.* That's where you sat after you were let in through the first gate and you were waiting in the entrance hall to be seen. In the south, the houses were smaller, and the benches were smaller. People often took them outside and used them with small tables for eating.

During the Victorian era, an ornately carved style of Chinese chair, crawling with dragons, phoenixes, and flowers, became popular. Much of this type of furniture was for export to the West.

Altared states and other Chinese tables

For centuries, most Chinese had ancestor worship as a major part of their life. They typically created a formal space for display and offerings in their homes. Many households used coffers for their altar worship; some households used a mere plank, and others used altar tables, as shown in Figure 17-7.

Figure 17-7: Carved Chinese altar table.

Photo courtesy of Brookside Antiques, Kansas City, Mo.

Besides the altar tables, you also find square tables that can seat from four to eight and small stands and pedestals, which held incense, flowers, and scholar's stones (which were strategically placed to inspire the artist or writer).

Tables similar to altar tables but on the wide side are called painter's tables. The true painter's table was a double square (twice as long as it was wide). The width lets the artist unroll a scroll to do painting and calligraphy. Artists typically painted standing up.

You bed your life

When it came to keeping comfy, even in bitter winter, the Chinese had it together. Before steam heat, the Chinese were king of kang furniture. A *kang* is a bed; *kang furniture* is specifically made for use on and with the bed.

During winter, the whole family huddled in bed to keep warm. These beds were often quite grand, with elaborate canopies. Some measure as large as ten by fifteen feet and can accommodate a variety of furniture created for use in bed. These kang pieces ranged from twelve to twenty four inches in height and were used for reading, writing, for tea and snacks for playing games and eating — while nestled in among the blankets, pillows, and bedwarmers.

If you were traveling across China and stopped at an inn, the whole travel party slept in one bed, from the camel driver to the ones they were taking across country.

A coffer you can't refuse

Coffer means limited access space. Any piece that has lockable drawers or doors is a coffer. *Butterfly coffers* have "wings" on each side.

In the earlier days of ancestor worship, portraits of deceased ancestors were stored in the coffer, along with the accoutrements necessary for worship. The early coffers had locking drawers across the top, no doors and storage cupboards underneath them. People accessed the space down below by removing the drawers. Craftsmen added doors to coffers at a later date.

Wood you believe

Jumu, which is similar to elm, is the wood you find most often in quality domestic Chinese furniture. Jumu is harder than pine and softer than the other true hardwoods. The grain, often called a *pagoda grain,* is beautiful and can look like a series of mountains, depending on how the wood is cut. Chinese furniture made from softer woods such as pine is more abundant. Local craftsmen in the outlying regions made many of these pieces of furniture, which have a country look and feel, although they are often based on classic lines.

The antique Chinese furniture composed of the hardwoods, such as zitan and huanghuali, is generally quite rare and expensive. A great many of the rosewoods and hardwoods that people consider classical Chinese woods are not indigenous to China and have been imported from Southeast Asia.

Of course, you want to buy Chinese furniture from a dealer you trust. Look for evidence of handwork. Having a spoke or stretcher replaced is not of extreme consequence. But pieces that are too "made up" lose a lot of their value. Watch for areas that have been recently cut into. If you see gunk around the joints, the seller may be trying to hide something.

Chapter 18

Antiques by the Yard: Outdoor Items

In This Chapter

- Finding garden antiques
- Ironing out the wrought from the cast
- Separating the carved from the cast
- Finding marble and bronze
- Using architectural salvage and old tools

Imagine a trans-seasonal perennial that always looks good, provides a focal point for your garden, and never needs watering or pruning.

Long after your mums have said their last word, your antique chimney pot will keep your garden interesting. One finial from an old building or one ancient watering trough or iron chair makes your yard so much more interesting. Garden antiques are a blossoming field with a diverse price range and lots of chances for creative expression.

Digging Up Garden Antiques: Where to Find Them

Two breeds of garden antiques are available: those pieces that were created and intended for the garden, and those pieces that you adapt to your garden.

If you look in the Yellow Pages and see nothing that hints of garden antiques, don't be discouraged. Not every city has a store specializing in garden antiques. Still, you don't have to go to a garden antique shop or garden auction to find great things for your yard. You can also visit architectural salvage stores and flea markets and transplant building parts into your garden area. You can go to country auctions and give rusting water troughs and aging wheelbarrows a new life of leisure in your garden.

Some auction houses and botanical gardens hold regular garden antique sales. You can also play on the Web, which has lots of listings. Doing so takes some weeding through the auction sites, individual shops, and reproduction antique sites. However, the Web can be a good place to view some high quality garden antiques and see what some of the prices run.

Reading *Garden Ornament: Two Centuries of American Taste,* by Barbara Israel (published by Harry Abrams, September 1999), is a good way to find out more about garden furniture. This well-researched book is beautiful and practical and includes a history of American outdoor ornaments; a makers' list with descriptions, addresses, and dates of operation; plus maintenance, security, and identification tips.

Irons in the Garden: The Cast of Thousands

Blacksmiths hand-forged wrought-iron furniture in the early to mid-19th century. This handcrafted furniture is light, feathery, and bolted or welded together. Then the Victorian version of plastic, cast iron, revolutionized outdoor furniture. Cast iron, which poured into the market during the 1840s through the 1890s, was molded into intricate shapes and curls, making lawn furniture inexpensive and available to those people with mere yards (rather than estates).

Today, you will see more 19th century cast iron than wrought iron. You will also see lots of reproductions of cast iron. Here are some ways to make sure that your purchase is the iron-clad real thing:

- Really inspect the objects, just as you would any other antique furniture. Garden furniture is a complex specialty, and many people simply do not know very much about it. Just as you inspect the drawers of a chest and the underside of a chair, you need to look under and inside garden furniture. Often you will find urns and planters filled with plants. Ask the dealer to remove the plants so that you can see inside. Don't worry that it's too much work or too messy. You need to look inside for rust, and you need to look at the bottom for signs of age. Old rust is brown and crusty; new rust is bright orange.
- Use a magnet to see whether the object is really cast iron. Try the magnet all over the piece. Much cast iron is made up of several parts. If a magnet sticks to the body of the urn and doesn't stick to the base or the handles, then you know something's been replaced. This "marriage" of unlike parts reduces the piece's value.
- Pick up the piece. Old cast iron is often heavier than new. Wrought iron is lighter than cast.

- Look for layers of paint. Without painting, iron simply rusts into oblivion. Layers of paint imply it's been around for many seasons.
- Look for true rust. An old urn is pock-marked with corrosion. True rust is less uniform and more brownish in color. Bright orange rust that is all over the surface is a warning that the piece is new.
- Look at the arms or back of a bench and feel for smooth, filed-down edges. After a piece of old cast iron is complete, the craftsmen "chase" the insides and file off all the rough edges. New urns typically have sharp and crispy edges where the casting was imperfect.
- Grinding marks can serve as a warning. Joints in new pieces often are not made as well as the joints in old pieces. Machinists have to grind the joints with a machine tool which leaves grinding marks. The marks could mean it's a new piece or they could mean it's an older piece that needed repair.
- Newer handles are often bolted on with shiny nuts and bolts.
- Study the design pattern of the cast iron. The old patterns are more uniform. New patterns are more hastily put together and show more unevenness of casting and construction.
- If everything else checks out, look for a mark. Marks on cast iron can add to the value of the piece. Some marks help you date the piece, because many companies moved frequently. J.W. Fiske and Robert Wood and Company are two marks you might see. As always, use the mark as just one clue in your quest to verify that the piece is authentic.

Familiarize yourselves with repros by looking at current catalogues featuring lawn and garden furniture. A horizontal seam running through the middle of an urn is a sign that the piece may be new. Just as you can find pre-washed jeans, you'll find pre-rusted cast iron. Urns can look crackly, rusty, and old but may have been born yesterday.

Some Victorian era molds are still being used. Watch for aluminum pieces, which are lighter and won't take a magnet.

All Wired Up

Wire was used to make furniture, such as planters and seating pieces. Impervious to weather and light enough to move it around, this furniture was always painted to protect it from rusting.

You should find multiple layers of paint or evidence of paint on wire furniture. Even if the wire is brushed off and repainted, you should still see some evidence of prior painting.

Carved or Cast Stone

Both carved stone and composition stone are desirable. Carved stone is more expensive.

Here is the way the costs range, from low to higher. Take a plain bench. New cast stone is the least expensive. Old cast stone is next. Old carved stone is more expensive, and marble is even more desirable and expensive.

How can you tell if it's carved or cast? This is a complex area; you need to understand the surface of the material and the style and quality of the carving. A carved stone piece should have carving marks. Also look for arms sticking out or other elements that couldn't be easily cast. Assume that the piece is cast until it's proven to be carved.

Here are some tips for analyzing stone pieces:

- Cast stone can be powdery to the touch. If you wipe your hand across it, you may come away with a residue of powder.
- If the detail is very regular, it's unlikely that the piece is hand carved.
- Look for wear on the feet or handles. Often, pieces of stone have been hauled around. Sometimes stone pieces have been damaged and put back together. If the piece is old and well repaired, it may still have good value.
- If someone tells you that you are looking at natural stone, ask to see a cast stone piece as well. When you see natural stone and cast stone side by side, you can tell the difference. But when you just see the cast alone, it's easy to make a mistake.
- In the cast piece, you can see the mold line. Look for little pits or holes where bubbles have popped. A cast piece is smooth on the inside, where it's been poured into the mold. A carved piece has chisel marks on the inside.
- Natural stone has veins and fissures and possibly fossils.

Of course, these pieces have already weathered a lot. You want them in one piece, with no serious chipping and not cracked all the way through. If a birdbath has cracks, for example, water can get in, freeze, and thaw, which can further crack and ruin the piece. If you want to buy such a piece, take it indoors during the winter.

Finding Your Marbles and Winning with Bronze

Marble pieces having a granular surface is a warning sign of deterioration. *Sugaring* means that acid deposits are deteriorating the material.

If the piece is a classical piece, you may wonder whether it's hundreds of years old based on the weathering and detail in the carving. Look at the most exposed parts and think logically. The top of the arm should be weathered, but not necessarily underneath. If the detail in the carving is crisp, ask yourself whether it could really be this crisp having been outdoors this many years.

Bronze statuary is everywhere, and much of it is new. Manufacturers add a uniform dark green "patination" with an artificial finish, and you have something that looks like it listened to King David. Make sure that you look at the base: Some of these "aged" pieces have polished new marble bases, complete with green felt underneath. Often, the detail on these pieces is lacking, and the finish work is less exacting than in the older pieces.

Salvaging Antiques by the Yard: Fun Ways to Display Antiques

With a little creative thought, architectural pieces can contribute to a unique garden area. Go to a reputable dealer who specializes in architectural salvage. They often get the contracts with the contractors who tear the buildings down. Here are a few possible garden-oriented adaptations:

- Turn a remnant of an iron fence sideways and use it as a trellis.
- Use pieces of buildings, such as gargoyles, corner pieces, and columns, as accent pieces.
- Old wheelbarrows and old rain barrels make fine places to set potted plants.
- Old farm implements can accent a rustic garden space.
- Watch for salvaged finials from old wrought iron or cast iron corner posts and mingle them with your plants and flowers.

Part V

The Care, Feeding, and Deleting of Antiques

The 5th Wave
By Rich Tennant
©RICHTENNANT
SOLD
"No, I don't know how fast I was going, but would you like to know what time it is?"

In this part . . .

"Uh oh." Sure, you are going to spill on them, bump into them, and tip them over. We've got a few hints on how to restore and conserve these precious pieces of history.

And if you decide you want to sell an antique, we have some tips so you can make the most out of that situation. We also tell you how to keep your antiques off the garage sales tables of the 21st century. (This is where appraisers come in.)

Chapter 19

Scratches, Spills, and Restoration Thrills

In This Chapter

- Knowing your material
- Helping your antiques make it through the years
- Dusting with the experts
- Getting to know your conservator

When you know how to take care of your antiques, you are nothing short of a historic preservationist. You are preserving your antiques as precious links to the past.

This chapter includes some general information on keeping your antiques safe and in good shape. In various chapters, you'll also find more specific tips on specific antiques.

The Material World

Taking care of antiques is a little like being a stand-up comic: You have to know your material.

Even strong and durable inorganic materials, such as stone, glass, ceramics, and metal, are vulnerable. Besides getting scratched, cracked, or broken, glass may grow cloudy, and metal may get too moist and begin to corrode.

Organic products, such as wood, paper, leather, and ivory, are even more vulnerable to the general forces of the universe. Many of the colorants or coatings on antiques are organic, so they fade easily. Even things you wouldn't think have a breath in them, such as plastics, can decompose.

Talk to a conservator or restoration expert before you try to repair something yourself. Many a person has stripped a valuable patina off wood or bronze trying to get it clean.

Weatherproofing Your Antiques

Even in the gentle environment of your home, a lot of weather is going on. Whether it's sun streaming through the white lace curtains, a desert-like dryness in the living room, or a discreet bug or two with a taste for the vintage, you can preserve your antiques by controlling the atmosphere.

Display's the thing

Keep your furniture and paintings and other organic pieces out of direct sunlight and other ultraviolet light sources. Light damage is cumulative and not reversible. Keep glass objects away from hot light bulbs. Make sure that breakables are safe, away from heavy curtains, not too close together, and on stable shelves.

Be a fair weather friend

Protect your objects from temperature extremes and too little or too much humidity. That means the basement, garage, and attic are not ideal storage places, unless they are temperature-controlled. An interior closet is generally a good storage place. The ideal setting for your antiques is between 40 and 60 percent relative humidity.

Before you display a piece, analyze the surroundings. It's great to have that ivory miniature on the mantel, but the heat from the fireplace may damage it.

Don't bug them

Examine your antiques occasionally for signs of bugs. If you notice little worm-like insects, small holes, or powdery deposits, put your antique in an airtight plastic bag (if possible) and call a conservator for advice.

There's a reason to get out all the dead wood. Firewood is a huge source of bugs. If you need to store firewood inside, bring it into the garage and cover it with plastic.

Dusting Your Antiques

Sure you know how to dust. But do you know how to dust antiques so that you are preserving them and enhancing not only their short-term good looks, but also their long-term outlook?

A little dust along the way won't hurt, but layers of dust (you know, the kind you can write your name in) can merge with smoke, moisture, and oil. This can deteriorate the finish and clog the pores.

The sensitive dust buster

Although you've probably dusted a lot of wood in your day, you may not have had sensitivity dusting training.

Here are some guidelines for dusting the venerable and the antique:

- Lightly mist a soft cotton cloth with distilled water and gently go over your furniture, in the direction of the grain, from top to bottom. You don't need to spray anything on the actual furniture. The dampness in the rag is enough to grab the dust.
- While dusting, check the furniture for loose areas of veneer or inlay that can be lifted by the cloth or duster.
- Be careful if you dust antique furniture with a dry cloth. Dry dusting can scratch the finish.
- Lift objects off the furniture to prevent dust from building-up underneath.
- Use a small soft brush to dust intricate carving.

Most finishes do not flourish under a feather duster. The feathers tend to break off and the rough ends may scratch delicate finishes and catch on carving or loose veneer.

Waxing poetic

Great news for the housekeeping impaired! Waxing once a year is probably plenty — and may be more than you need. A little wax can give furniture additional protection against heat, moisture, hard use, and other potential damage. When you wax, you are protecting the finish rather than wood. The finish protects the wood.

Getting a Handle on Antiques

Sure, they've been around for years, but antiques are often more delicate than they look. Before you pick up something, look at the condition and size of the piece. If you're not positive you can carry it alone, get help. Carry small pieces in a padded basket.

What if you luck into a museum quality piece? That's the time to tiptoe around and give your antique the "white glove treatment." Certain lacquers, metals, and porous ceramics are quite delicate, and the chemicals in your skin can damage them. If you move them from place to place, wear clean white gloves (for the official conservator look). Try the kind of gloves that have rubber dots on the palms; plain cotton can be slippery. (While you're at it, you can check the mantel for dust.)

Before you lift or carry an antique, remove jewelry and watches. Also watch out for belt buckles and over-exuberant buttons when you work with antiques.

Go for the soundest, widest, strongest part of the piece when you lift. Lift three-dimensional pieces by their body. Don't ever pull on an arm or a handle. Lifting furniture is no time to shake a leg. Lift chairs by the seat rails, and lift chest of drawers from the bottom. Lift tables by the apron.

Spills and Chills

Okay, so you left your sweaty glass of diet cola on your wonderful old table and now there's a white spot. True, you can cover it with a tablecloth. Or you can try to remove the spot.

Try your technique first in some out of the way place. That way you can guard against any unplanned reactions with the finish.

If the water spot is new, rush for a hair dryer. Set the dryer on the lowest setting and keep the dryer moving (so that you don't make a heat mark!). You're trying to evaporate the moisture trapped in the finish.

Do not attempt to remove white marks with furniture oil, wax, or polish. Polishes or waxes inhibit evaporation and seal in the watermark.

Do not use rubber mats or coasters unless they have felt beneath them. Some vinyl films and rubber compounds may stain or soften furniture finishes.

Storing History

You can't just store that antique in any old thing or in any old place. Keep your glass pieces away from erratic temperature variations and your furniture at a constant humidity. Store metals in dry conditions. Store silver wrapped in silver cloth, which you can find at jewelry and department stores.

Some plastic wraps contain chlorine. Wrapping silver in such plastic wrap can permanently mark the surface.

If you can't find archival quality tissues and boxes in your local art supply store or camera shop, call Light Impressions at 800-828-6216 or visit their Web site at `www.lightimpressionsdirect.com`. Another place you can contact is University Products, Inc. at 800-628-1912 or `www.universityproducts.com`.

Pad your objects and store them in labeled boxes that have enough room. You don't want things all squashed together, especially delicate objects made of glass or porcelain.

The Conservator: An Antique Hot-Line

Conservators are dedicated to prolonging the beauty and life of antique objects of art and to conserving our cultural heritage They work to repair an object's physical weaknesses, to stabilize any chemical instabilities, and to conserve the original appearance of the object.

Things you can consult a conservator about:

- How to display, store, and preserve your own objects of art.
- How to keep your antiques safe in case of natural disasters, such as tornadoes and earthquakes. (Many of the glass collectors in California are experts on this.)
- Changes you notice, such as fading or a flaking surface.
- Any bugs or mold threatening your antiques.

The AIC American Institute for Conservation of Historic and Artistic Works in Washington D.C. offers a Guide to Conservation Services. To learn more about preserving your treasures and about AIC services, visit their Web site at `aic.stanford.edu`.

Chapter 20

Getting Your Antiques Appraised

In This Chapter

- Finding a professional appraiser
- Understanding the appraisal process

People have their antiques appraised so that later they won't have to gnash their teeth and tear out their hair over the "it was just some old vase" syndrome.

Perhaps you've had this happen to you. Your sister sells "some old thing Mom gave me" in a garage sale for $7.50, and later you find out it was a genuine 18th century bronze statue. Or you give your daughter a sweet little piece of iridescent gold glass, which she then gives to her boyfriend, who later leaves her and takes the glass with him, and you find out it was Tiffany glass, the real thing.

An *appraisal* is a written valuation of your antiques, done, hopefully, by a qualified appraiser. Because in many states, anybody can label themselves a "personal property appraiser" or "antiques or fine art appraiser," we provide some recommended guidelines on appraising the appraiser.

When You Need an Appraiser

Appraising for insurance purposes is a common reason for appraisals. You and your insurance company need to agree on value before you run into any problems. Establishing values after something has been damaged, stolen, or lost is no fun.

Here are some other times you may need an appraisal:

- **Inherit the antiques:** If you inherit a house full of antiques, it's wise to get them appraised before you decide what to sell, what to keep, and how to divide the antiques. If the estate is above a certain amount, the courts or the IRS require an appraisal.

- **'Til divorce do you part:** In a divorce, you may need an appraisal so that you can figure out a fair way to divide jointly owned property.
- **Keeping it fair:** Some people have appraisals when they want to give antiques to their children and need to know the values so that they can keep things equitable.
- **Getting the right price:** An appraisal helps you sell your treasure for the right amount of money.
- **Preventing buyer's remorse:** If you're buying an expensive piece from a dealer you feel wary of, or a dealer who might not guarantee to reimburse you if the piece is found to be inauthentic, consider an appraisal before you buy.

We Have Come to Appraise the Appraiser

You want an appraiser who is qualified. You may want to select an appraiser who belongs to one or more of the appraisers' organizations. Some of the national appraisal organizations that certify their members are:

- ISA, International Society of Appraisers, (888) 472-4732, `www.isa-appraisers.org`. Ask for their free pamphlet: *Be Certain of Its Value: A Consumer's Guide to Hiring a Competent Personal Property Appraiser.*
- ASA, American Society of Appraisers, (800) ASA-VALUE, `www.appraisers.org`. Ask for their free brochure: *Questions and Answers about the Appraisal Profession.*
- AAA, Appraisers Association of America, (212) 889-5404. Ask for their free handout: *The Elements of a Correctly Prepared Appraisal.*

The purpose of several of these organizations is to certify and set standards of professionalism in a field that has been wide open for all levels of competence. Finding a certified or accredited appraiser is one way to qualify an appraiser. As in any field, you'll find people who are not certified or accredited and still are competent appraisers. Use your judgment when sizing up appraisers.

You want an appraiser with a love for and a background in antiques. If you don't learn of anyone through networking, or your antique dealer can't guide you, call one of the appraisal societies and ask for the names of qualified appraisers in your area. When you talk to an appraiser, here are some questions to ask:

- **What qualifies you to appraise my property?** It's a plus to have someone who has taken the courses from the appraisal societies and who knows the proper form and substance of the appraisal report. Bankers, bank trust officers, insurers, attorneys, and tax agencies often use the appraisal. They might feel more comfortable with an appraisal done by a qualified appraiser, although they may not require it. Ask to see the appraiser's résumé, which should include job history and professional accreditation. You might also want to see a sample appraisal report.
- **Have you been tested?** The test for certification should include ethics and the details of creating appraisal reports as well as testing on the appraiser's specialties. An additional certification requirement generally includes a certain number of years appraising antiques.
- **Do you take continuing education?** You want an appraiser who is up-to-date on appraisal standards and procedures, which are subject to change. Some appraisal organizations require a certain number of educational points each year to maintain certification levels, which the appraiser earns through educational seminars, teaching, and publishing.
- **How do you handle items outside of your specialty?** No matter how competent appraisers are, they won't have seen it all. They need to know how to describe, measure, photograph, and research antiques. They need to know other specialists in their field so that they can reach out for help when they have questions.

  Many appraisers have an area of expertise. Find out if your potential appraiser is knowledgeable in the categories you want appraised. If not, is the appraiser willing to get help from other appraisers or dealers in that specialty? For big appraisals, with many categories represented, appraisers may need to call in other appraisers on a consulting basis.
- **What is your fee? On what basis do you charge?** Major appraisal organizations feel that charging a percentage of the appraised price is unethical. Charging on a percentage basis disqualifies the appraisal for use by the IRS. Most appraisers charge either per item or by the hour or on a total fee for the entire job. Some appraisers charge for travel time within the city, and others only charge travel time if the appraisal is done outside of their city.

It is not unusual for an appraiser to do other work besides appraisals. Some are antique dealers, who also provide appraisal services. Others may offer estate liquidation services.

The Appraisal Process

Suppose that you have a highboy you need appraised. You've found a qualified appraiser. She comes in and examines your highboy. She might dictate a detailed description into a tape recorder. She estimates the age of the piece and describes the condition. She measures the piece and may take photographs.

Then she goes to do her research. She looks up other highboys and sees what they have sold for. She may use an auction database for antiques and arts. She consults auction catalogues and looks at other appraisals she's done, searching out similar pieces. She consults antique dealers. She tries to find at least three similar pieces so that she can select the price from a range of values.

She creates an appraisal report. The report:

- States the kind of value being determined, such as fair market, liquidation, and so on
- Describes the properties being valued
- Describes the procedures used to estimate the values, such as analysis of comparable sales
- Contains the signature and personal qualifications of the appraiser

Save the appraisal so that your heirs can ID your antiques and have some idea of their value. That way, your precious collection won't end up in a 21st century garage sale.

Chapter 21

Selling Your Antiques

In This Chapter

- Figuring out what you have and what it's worth
- Choosing the best place to sell your antiques: estate sales, auctions, malls, trade publications, garage sales, or antique shops
- Finding the right professionals

That old rocking chair passed down from your great Aunt Mara, or that set of Depression glass that's not really your style — antiques may come into your life unbidden. Sometimes you want to keep them, and sometimes you want to send them on to someone else.

You may want to sell antiques for other reasons, such as upgrading your collection, getting a little money, or for the pure fun of selling antiques.

Twenty Questions: What Do You Have?

Antique ID can be complex. If the antique is one you bought and understand, you're ahead of the game. If you inherited the antique and know nothing of its story, you need to do some research and ID the old thing.

Suppose that you have an antique you have expertly identified as an "old red glass vase." How can you figure out what kind of old red vase you have?

If you have a relationship with a dealer or knowledgeable friend, this is a great time to ask for assistance. You can look through glass books, particularly those with great photos, or you can look at the antique auctions on the Internet for similar things. After you identify your piece, including its age and condition, you can take the next step and try to figure out how much it's worth.

The Price is ???

Some pieces are much easier to research than others. The more unusual the piece, the harder it is to pinpoint a price. A common piece of pressed pattern glass, for example, is easier to price than a rare example of American Brilliant cut glass.

To determine the price, consult a knowledgeable friend or specialist. Price guides are a great tool, along with auction catalogues, trade publications, and Internet auction sites. You can also look in the marketplace by going to shops and antique shows.

Where Can You Sell It?

You have many options for selling antiques, from the hands-on approach of organizing your own garage sale to the recluse's path of selling via the Internet. If you have lots of antiques and they are of low value, a garage sale, flea market, or online auction might work for you. If you have a few antiques that are high quality, connecting with an antique dealer or a quality auction gallery might work. If you have lots of antiques that you think are of medium to high quality, you may want to contact an estate sale liquidator, an auctioneer, or an antique dealer who understands your merchandise and can purchase it from you or sell it for you on a consignment basis.

Sometimes, even with a fair price, it can take a while to sell antiques. If you're not in a hurry, it's fine to sit on that piece (particularly if it's a chair or a sofa!). Don't give something away just because someone doesn't instantly show up to buy it.

Newspaper chase and making the trades: Placing want ads

You can advertise your piece in your local newspaper. When you list the item, use its collectible name first, such as *Rookwood.* If you have several items, list the most exciting first. If you need to run the ad again, change it so that it will seem "fresh."

Read the regional and national antique trade magazines for listings of what people are looking for. You find people wanting glassware, ceramics, and all kinds of specific antiques. If you have a specialized item that you think won't appeal to your local market, put an ad in one of the national antique journals. (See Chapter 22 for a list of some great periodicals, as well as the Check It Out icons throughout the book.)

Collectors' clubs often have newsletters that list wanted items. The more you focus in on your market, the better chance you have of getting a good price for your antique. Some price guides list collectors' clubs. The *Antique Trader* lists clubs from time to time. Contact the club and ask how you can advertise in their magazine.

It's a beautiful day to sell in the neighborhood: Garage and yard sales

When you have a few antiques that aren't too high and mighty, you can use them to draw people to your garage sale.

Display your antique nicely. The nicer your presentation, the more likely you are to sell it for a good price. Use cloths or mirrors to heighten your display. Write up a card that tells the story of the antique. If it's real valuable, secure it in some way. Keep it close to you.

If you have friends and neighbors with antiques and stuff to sell, put together a neighborhood sale. This increases your traffic.

Selling and consigning with dealers

Antique dealers are an obvious outlet for selling your unwanted antiques. In addition to outright purchases, some dealers take antiques in on consignment. The dealer sells the piece for you and gives you an agreed upon price when the piece sells. This is not necessarily a quick way to sell, but you can often get a good price when you do sell. Consignment selling lets dealers work on a smaller profit margin, because they have no investment in the piece, other than space, overhead, and insurance costs.

With an antique shop, you also have a large audience for your antique and an unlimited time period versus the one-shot chance of estate and garage sales, want ads, shows, and auctions. Use a dealer you trust who understands your merchandise and has a clientele who appreciates it. Make sure that the shop has a good reputation. You get a better traffic flow in a shop that has posted business hours, rather than one that's open by appointment only.

Often the dealer who sold you the piece will take it back on consignment. If he sold it once, chances are, he can sell it again.

Selling through estate sales

If you're selling a significant percent of your household items, consider having an estate sale. If you have just a few antiques in the lot, you can use them for headliners, to draw people to your sale.

You can run the sale yourself or call in a professional liquidator. Word of mouth is a great way to find a reliable liquidator. You want someone who knows about antiques.

Whether you are having your own sale or hiring a liquidator, you'll benefit if you can attend a few sales in advance, to see how they are run.

Linking up with a liquidator

The Liquidator sounds like the bad guy in a grade B movie. But this person can be the good guy when it comes to getting a good price for the antiques in your estate. Here are some questions to ask the proposed liquidator:

- What percentage does he work on? What services does he offer? Is the liquidator setting everything up, advertising, cleaning up your pieces, and presenting them to their best advantage? Liquidators can charge a percentage of sales, generally ranging from 20 to 30 percent.
- How will he advertise the sale? Do you share in any of the advertising costs, and if so, what is the fixed fee or budget?
- What type of accounting does he provide? Does he provide you a line-by-line inventory of the major items sold and the prices realized?
- How much staff will he have on the sale day to take care of customers and protect your merchandise?
- Is he taking responsibility for all clerking, which includes handling of checks, and itemizing and tracking what each item sells for?
- Does he hold pre-sales, where he sells ahead of time to certain select customers? (See Chapter 9 for more about pre-sales.)
- Will he cover bad checks?
- Will he take care of the trash?
- Does he carry premises liability insurance or is it the responsibility of the seller?
- What about items that are unsold at the end? Does he sell it out? That is, will he let people bid on the end amount and take it all?
- Does he have an antique shop? If so, does that appear to be a conflict of interest? Will he buy anything from the sale? It's preferable the liquidator buys nothing from the sale. But if he does buy, make sure that he waits until the second day of the sale. That gives the public a fair chance and minimizes conflict of interest issues.

Ask for references from whomever you hire. Get a written contract that stipulates all of the charges, from the selling to advertising, setup, and any miscellaneous charges. People can get burned and lose much of their net proceeds from hidden costs.

Advantages of hiring someone

Take Grandma's kitchen chair, which is battered and has lost its paint and looks like several pieces of old wood loosely joined together. It could be just that or it could be a lovely Windsor, valuable just as it is. When you hire a liquidator, you are hiring expertise. The liquidator who knows antiques can sort the good from the bad and ugly. She ought to know a period piece of furniture from a repro, and if she doesn't, she needs to have staff or experts she uses to help her identify antique pieces.

You are also hiring efficiency. What might take you weeks to sort and categorize takes the estate sale crew days. They have a system. Plus, they don't need to stop and moon over every letter, examine every piece of art or ancient scrap of cloth. The ideal estate sale crew can efficiently put things in order, display them nicely, and price them fairly.

Doing their bidding: Auctions

If you have many antiques, an auction might bring you more money. Some people have expertise in both estate sales and auctions. They can help you figure out what venue would be the most financially rewarding.

You attract more out-of-town buyers at an auction. At auctions, buyers have an equal chance at getting the goods because they're selling to the highest bidder. At an estate sale, the first-come-first-serve theory makes a long drive much more risky.

Here are some questions to ask an auctioneer:

- What percentage does he charge?
- Does he set up? At an auction, part of setting up is creating boxed lots, numbers of items sold for one price. Often the family does not know how to do this to their best advantage. You might put something valuable into a box that deserves to be auctioned individually. (When you are on the buying side, this is what you hope for.)
- Does his commission include pickup charges and delivery if the auction is to be held in another place?
- What about insurance coverage for the items during any transit and before they are actually sold and paid for?

- Will the auctioneer allow you to set a reserve for a particular item? (That means you set a minimum price for that item; however, you may have to pay a "buy in" fee if the item doesn't sell.) If you feel that you cannot afford to stand a loss on a piece, you don't want to sell it at an "absolute" auction that allows no reserve.
- What kind of documentation do you get regarding the sale?
- How long does it take for you to receive your money?
- Does he clean up?
- Does he recommend having the auction at your home or elsewhere? With normal household things, auctioneers sometimes prefer to hold it at the house. With more extensive collections of antiques, it's worth it to hold the auction in a public place, such as a hotel and advertise nationally. If you have a lot of quality pieces, such as a great collection of American Brilliant cut glass, the auctioneer may be able to get the mailing list from that collector's club and send an auction notice to the members.

If you have a smaller number of antiques and you're going to be part of a larger auction, try to have your merchandise sold early in the sale. It's not good to be tacked on at the end of a sale: The big buyers might be gone or spent out. Things sold at the end often are sold more cheaply.

Net gains: Selling online

New online auctions are cropping up all the time. If you have some antiques you want to try to sell online, look in the antique trade periodicals for online auctions.

- **E-mail online auction houses and find out their rules.** What is their *listing price* and what is their percentage of commission? The listing price is a flat rate you pay to list the piece. For example, you may pay a mere 25 cents for items less than $10.00. Then you may pay a commission on top of that listing price, when you sell the piece.
- **Get clear pictures of the item you want to sell from every angle.** An ordinary camera will do. If you become a top sales person, you may want a digital camera, which takes ultra clear, crisp pictures.
- **Write a complete accurate description of the piece, including the way it looks and a full disclosure of its condition.**
- **Write out a return policy.** Some sellers allow a return only if they have inaccurately described the piece or if the piece arrives in a condition other than that described.
- **Check your e-mail daily in order to respond promptly to potential customers.**

- **Be prepared to change the item's category listing if you get few or no responses.** Many auction houses don't charge for changing categories. Or be prepared to reword the title of your piece. Sometimes a change of wording sparks new interest.
- **Make arrangements with a reliable packing and shipping company to wrap the item or learn how to pack fragile items.** If you get into larger pieces, you can have a packing place make boxes for you.

Start with small items. It's easier to take the pictures, and they are less trouble to ship.

The online auction business is booming, and new sites are constantly emerging. Ebay, `www.ebay.com`, is one of the more established auction sites.

A few other auctions sites that do include antiques and collectibles are:

- Ehammer (`www.ehammer.com`)
- Auction Universe (`www.auctionuniverse.com`)
- Yahoo! Auctions (`www.yahoo.com`)

See Chapter 9 for more about buying online.

Part VI
The Part of Tens

"I don't know what it is but it must be old. It was the only thing grandma didn't recognize."

In this part . . .

"Tell me more."

Once you get a taste of antiques, you'll want to add them to your daily menu. We have listed some of the great national periodicals, each fun and interesting in different ways. We also listed some price guides, to further your antique education and arm you with general price information.

Even when you're not buying, have fun reading about the wild world of antique deals and discoveries, fakes and frauds, genuine bargains and fabulous finds. You'll be armed with information and prices, so when that next "true love" crosses your path, you'll be ready.

Chapter 22

Ten Great Periodicals

In This Chapter

- Finding shows and flea markets
- Following reproduction news
- Increasing your knowledge of antiques
- Getting the inside story on auction results

Part of the fun of antique collecting is "reading the trades." The antique periodicals connect you with the larger world of antiques and give you news of prices, reproduction issues, and events such as shows and flea markets. Many periodicals give you educational information and offer a forum for asking obscure antique questions.

This chapter describes ten great periodicals focused on antiques. These are general periodicals. You'll find more general reading and more specific periodicals, such as *Glass Collector's Digest,* scattered throughout the book. We couldn't list all the great "rags and mags." When you go antiquing, look for regional and local periodicals.

Antique Trader

Antique Trader is a great weekly "fix" on the world of antiques. A variety of ads keeps you up-to-date on different pricing areas. A national list of shows, auctions, and flea markets keeps you in tune with what's going on near and far. We found area shows listed in the *Antique Trader* that were never advertised in our local paper!

You can send questions to a variety of columns, including "Glass Insights," by the *Trader* editor Kyle Husfloen; "Answers on Antiques," by Susan and Al Bagdade; "Reproduction News," by Mark Chervenka; and "Studying English Ceramics," by Bill Saks.

To get a 13-week trial subscription for a mere $8.00, call (800) 334-7165 or check the Web site at www.collect.com.

Maine Antique Digest

"You will never be lonely anymore" when you subscribe to the *Maine Antique Digest.* This tome is thick with great ads, auctions news, auction results (sometimes in the form of wonderful on-site reports), information, and international and Canadian antique news. You see wonderful full-page advertisements from leading auction houses, dealers, and shows, complete with well-labeled photographs. Just reading these ads is a great way to increase your antique IQ. Like so many of the antique periodicals, the *Maine Antique Digest* is fun. It has a folksy flavor that lets you feel part of the antiquing community.

Call (800) 752-8521 to subscribe for $43 for a year. Visit their Web site at www.maineantiquedigest.com.

Antiques and The Arts Weekly

Antiques and the Arts Weekly is another fat and fun publication. "The Bee," as its fans call it, reports on antique shows, auction prices, and museum exhibits, and lets you know what is going to happen in the world of antiques. They track many antique events and report on them afterwards. This is the next best thing to being there. We discovered a great antique furniture exhibit at the Met by reading "The Bee."

To subscribe, mail $56.00 for a year to Bee Publishing Co, 5 Church Hill Rd, P.O. Box 5503, Newtown, CT 06470-5503. Or visit www.thebee.com or phone (203) 426-3141.

Antique and Collectors Reproduction News

Even the most knowledgeable collectors make mistakes. If you know there is a reproduction alert on the objects you collect, you scrutinize your potential buys more fervently. This newsletter, devoted to exposing fakes and reproductions, keeps you up-to-date with what's being reproduced and gives you pointers on how to avoid fakes. Each issue features photos of the new and old, up close and side by side. The writing is clear and understandable. Spending money on this newsletter will save you in the long run.

Get 12 monthly issues for $32 by calling (515) 274-5886 (charge cards only) or mail payment to ACRN, P.O. Box 12130-Dept D, Des Moines, IA, 50312.

Warman's Today's Collector

Warman's Today's Collector is a monthly magazine that covers traditional antiques, such as furniture, glass, and pottery, and baby boomer and pop-culture collectibles, such as toys and advertising items. The typical issue includes color feature stories, auction highlights, book reviews, market trends, and collecting news and tips. You can find a bunch of interesting ads, as well. For those who are into antiques and also want to know what's up with collectibles, this publication covers both areas.

Call (800) 258-0929 for a year subscription at $23.98 or write to Krause Publications, 700 E. State St., Iola, WI 54990.

Antique Showcase

Antique Showcase gives you the inside story on the Canadian antique scene as well as interesting and educational articles. This is a great way to learn about the shows, shops, and malls of Canada. They also publish a directory of antique shops.

To subscribe send $28.99 for a year to *Antique Showcase,* 103 Lakeshore Road, Suite 202, St. Catharines, Ontario L2N 2T6. Or phone (905) 646-7744.

Antiques and Collecting

Antiques and Collecting has been around since 1931, offering advice on current trends and prices as well as informative articles on antiques and collectibles. It provides tips on acquiring, displaying, and selling antiques. The question and answer columns range from finding out if it's "antique or junque" to restoration issues.

To get a year's worth of issues at $32, call (800) 762-7576.

Antique Week

Antique Week describes itself as a weekly antique, auction, and collector's newspaper. It features a great deal of auction news and ads, as well as educational information. The magazine offers at least one feature highlighting a certain antique and often includes a question and answer column on refinishing and working with antique furniture. It's interesting to read the want ads.

To get a 13-week trial subscription for $3.95, call (800) 876-5133. Or write to *Antique Week,* P.O. Box 90, Knightstown, IN 46148.

New York-Pennsylvania Collector

Even if you don't live in the region, the *New York-Pennsylvania Collector,* a monthly newspaper, is worth considering. It's filled with educational information on various antique topics. It's fun to read the reviews of different shows and to read about record-breaking auction results. The periodical is one-third auctions, one-third antique shops and shows, and one-third stories and articles.

Call (800) 836-1868 and spend $21 for a year's subscription. Or e-mail them at `wolfepub@frontiernet.net`.

The Magazine ANTIQUES

When you're ready for luxurious reading, open *The Magazine ANTIQUES,* a lovely four-color glossy magazine. This publication ignores the clamoring world of collectibles and lures you into the elegance of art and antiques. Shouldn't everyone know about the latest in museum accessions? Between the sumptuous ads, you'll find educational articles and book reviews and editorials.

Send $39.95 for one elegant year to *The Magazine ANTIQUES,* P.O. Box 10547, Des Moines, IA 50340 (800) 925-9271.

Chapter 23

Ten Essential Price Guides for Antiques

In This Chapter

- Finding the prices that are right
- Widening your knowledge of antiques

Price guides are functional and fun. They're like a giant catalogue chock full of great antique information and prices. Looking through price guides is a great way to get introduced to antique categories. Often, specific subjects have their own price guide.

In this chapter, we first focus on some of the more general guides and then move to the more specific. Guides give you both pricing information and subject information. They might feature a picture for the subject, a blurb about the topic, and then describe individual pieces with prices. Most guides use a team of people across the country to help collect these prices. Guides often come out yearly, so make sure that you get the most up-to-date version.

Schroeder's Antiques Price Guide

Schroeder's Antiques Price Guide, by Sharon and Bob Huxford (published by Collector Books), is a big book, chock-full of great information. They include a list of their contributors, a list of clubs, newsletters, and catalogues. Schroeder's includes extra background material on the basic subjects and then uses one-line descriptions (with abbreviations, so a lot of information is packed in).

Kovels' Antiques & Collectibles Price List

Kovels' Antiques & Collectibles Price List, by Ralph and Terry Kovel (published by Three Rivers Press) is full of prices interspersed with both small drawings and photos. Kovels' includes a color insert of emerging markets. They also give some of the record breaking prices for the year. Throughout the book, they lace in tips on maintenance, security, and other antique issues.

Antique Trader's Antiques & Collectibles Price Guide

Antiques & Collectibles Price Guide, by Kyle Husfloen (published by Antique Trader Books), is a compact price guide that deals with well-established antiques and the newer categories of collectibles. Black-and-white pictures dotted through the book help you "picture" what you're reading about and the thorough descriptions get you into the details.

Warman's Antiques and Collectibles Price Guide

Warman's Antiques and Collectibles Price Guide, by Ellen Schroy (published by Krause Publications), gives you a list of periodicals and auction houses, including specialty auctions. This guide also contains reproduction alerts. For pricing purposes, they assume that the object is in very good condition, unless they otherwise note. They provide a nice synopsis for each major category of collecting.

Miller's International Antiques Price Guide

Miller's International Antiques Price Guide, by Judith and Martin Miller (published by Reed International Books, Ltd.), features a picture for each item, along with a description. This guide tells you where the item is sold and whether it has damage, and gives an estimation of value, which is expressed in a range. On some pieces, the guide describes why one piece is better than another. This guide comes in hard cover and includes color photos.

Lyle Official Antique Review

Like *Miller's, Lyle Official Antique Review,* by Anthony Curtis (published by Perigree Books), gives you a picture per description. Looking through this book is a great way to learn to identify lots of different antiques Lyle's also includes historical facts on each topic and tips and advice from auctioneers.

Specialized Price Guides

As you become more focused on the areas you want to collect, you need more targeted price guides. Here are some examples. You can find others sprinkled through the book and there are many more others we didn't have space to list. You find price guides for specific areas, such as Art Nouveau, Depression glass, and Carnival glass.

Warman's English and Continental Pottery & Porcelain

Warman's English and Continental Pottery & Porcelain, by Susan & Al Bagdade (published by Krause Publications), provides the company history, a listing of applicable reference books for each category, museums that carry such wares, and reproduction alerts. The book also has a nice representation of black-and-white photos, as well as detailed descriptions and prices.

Warman's American Pottery and Porcelain

Warman's American Pottery and Porcelain, by Susan and Al Bagdade (published by Krause Publications) features nearly 150 companies. They give the history of each company, complete with marks and general information. They provide a state of the market report and divide their book into four categories: art pottery, dinnerware, general manufacturers, and utilitarian ware.

American Pressed Glass & Bottles Price Guide

When you are interested in glass and want to delve further into prices, *American Pressed Glass & Bottles Price Guide,* by Kyle Husfloen (published by Antique Trader Books), is a great book. The book includes collecting guidelines, glass clubs and museums, plus a glossary of glass terms. More than 7,000 breakables have detailed description and pricing. The book has clear black-and-white photographs to help with ID.

American & European Decorative & Art Glass Price Guide

American & European Decorative & Art Glass Price Guide, by Kyle Husfloen, editor (published by Antique Trader Books), gives you a great guide to art glass and its prices. It includes sketches of common art glass shapes and company markings and books for further reading. Each category features a description, appropriate markings, and photographs that highlight the price list.

Metalwares Price Guide

From aluminum to zinc, *Metalwares Price Guide,* by Marilyn Dragowick (published by Antique Trader Books), pictures and prices 19 categories of metals. This is a great way to learn about the different metal collecting opportunities, such as silver, iron, pewter, copper, and tin. The book is competently illustrated with black-and-white photos. For some fun, read through the gold chapter and imagine sipping oolong tea out of a gold Tiffany demitasse cup — the set of twelve is a mere $27,600.

Collector's Value Guide to Oriental Decorative Arts

Collector's Value Guide to Oriental Decorative Arts, by Sandra Andacht (published by Antique Trader Books), provides basic information about each collectible category and then lists and describes specific objects and gives price ranges. The book also includes a chronological guide, a list of clubs and organizations, museums with permanent Oriental collections, marks and pronunciation guides. This book is a good way to learn a little about a lot of Oriental antiques at once.

Index

• A •

• C •

• F •

• I •

• J •

• M •

• T •

• V •

Discover Dummies™ Online!

The *Dummies* Web Site is your fun and friendly online resource for the latest information about *...For Dummies®* books on all your favorite topics. From cars to computers, wine to Windows, and investing to the Internet, we've got a shelf full of *...For Dummies* books waiting for you!

Ten Fun and Useful Things You Can Do at www.dummies.com

1. Register this book and win!
2. Find and buy the *...For Dummies* books you want online.
3. Get ten great *Dummies Tips™* every week.
4. Chat with your favorite *...For Dummies* authors.
5. Subscribe free to *The Dummies Dispatch™* newsletter.
6. Enter our sweepstakes and win cool stuff.
7. Send a free cartoon postcard to a friend.
8. Download free software.
9. Sample a book before you buy.
10. Talk to us. Make comments, ask questions, and get answers!

Jump online to these ten fun and useful things at **http://www.dummies.com/10useful**

For other technology titles from IDG Books Worldwide, go to **www.idgbooks.com**

Not online yet? It's easy to get started with *The Internet For Dummies®*, 5th Edition, or *Dummies 101®: The Internet For Windows® 98*, available at local retailers everywhere.

Find other *...For Dummies* books on these topics:
Business • Careers • Databases • Food & Beverages • Games • Gardening • Graphics • Hardware
Health & Fitness • Internet and the World Wide Web • Networking • Office Suites
Operating Systems • Personal Finance • Pets • Programming • Recreation • Sports
Spreadsheets • Teacher Resources • Test Prep • Word Processing

IDG BOOKS WORLDWIDE BOOK REGISTRATION

We want to hear from you!

Visit **http://my2cents.dummies.com** to register this book and tell us how you liked it!

- Get entered in our monthly prize giveaway.
- Give us feedback about this book — tell us what you like best, what you like least, or maybe what you'd like to ask the author and us to change!
- Let us know any other *...For Dummies*® topics that interest you.

Your feedback helps us determine what books to publish, tells us what coverage to add as we revise our books, and lets us know whether we're meeting your needs as a *...For Dummies* reader. You're our most valuable resource, and what you have to say is important to us!

Not on the Web yet? It's easy to get started with *Dummies 101*®*: The Internet For Windows*® *98* or *The Internet For Dummies*®, 5th Edition, at local retailers everywhere.

Or let us know what you think by sending us a letter at the following address:

...For Dummies Book Registration
Dummies Press
7260 Shadeland Station, Suite 100
Indianapolis, IN 46256-3917
Fax 317-596-5498